GENDERTRAPS

GENDERTRAPS

Conquering
Confrontophobia,
Toxic Bosses, and Other
Land Mines at Work

JUDITH BRILES

McGraw-Hill
New York   San Francisco   Washington, D.C.   Auckland   Bogotá
Caracas   Lisbon   London   Madrid   Mexico City   Milan
Montreal   New Delhi   San Juan   Singapore
Sydney   Tokyo   Toronto

Library of Congress Cataloging-in-Publication Data

Briles, Judith.
    Gendertraps : conquering confrontophobia, toxic bosses, and
other land mines at work / Judith Briles.
        p.   cm.
    Includes index.
    ISBN 0-07-007895-5
    1. Office politics—United States.   2. Sex role in the work envi-
ronment—United States.   3. Organizational behavior—United States.
I. Title.
   HF5386.5.B75   1995
   650.1'3'082—dc20   95-20745
                                                      CIP

McGraw-Hill

*A Division of The **McGraw·Hill** Companies*

1 2 3 4 5 6 7 8 9 0 BKP/BKP 9 0 0 9 8 7 6 5

ISBN 0-07-007895-5

*The sponsoring editor for this book was Betsy Brown, the editing
supervisor was Penny Linskey, and the production supervisor was
Suzanne Rapcavage. It was set in Fairfield by Priscilla Beer of McGraw-
Hill's Professional Book Group composition unit.*

Printed and bound by Quebecor/Book Press.

For the Renaissance Women:
Jaclyn Kostner, Carol Ann Wilson, Ellen Tryon,
Denise Fonesca, and Stephanie West-Allen

CONTENTS

CHAPTER 4. TRAP 2: COMMUNICATIONS BARRIERS 53

CHAPTER 5. TRAP 3: SABOTAGE—CAUTION, WOMEN AT WORK 77

CHAPTER 6. TRAP 4: MANAGEMENT CHAOS— TROUBLE ON TOP   101

CHAPTER 7. TRAP 5: PAY INEQUITIES— UNEQUAL PAY FOR EQUAL WORK   133

CHAPTER 8. TRAP 6: THE BALANCING ACT— FAMILY VERSUS WORK   153

CHAPTER 9. TRAP 7: CONQUERING CONFRONTOPHOBIA—ELIMINATING THE ROADBLOCK TO RESOLVING CONFLICT   173

CHAPTER 10. TRAP 8: APATHY, COMPLACENCY, AND CHANGEOPHOBIA—LAND MINES TO OBLIVION   197

PREFACE

Every woman knows that workplaces are not perfect. Nor are they ideal settings in which the majority of the "alert" awake hours are spent. No. What is perfect is usually a fantasy, a myth, a fairy tale, or a line in a romance novel or movie. You know the part—it's where everyone lives happyily ever after. Nice, but not real.

Women know what reality is. It's a far cry from perfect. Reality includes the flaws, hiccups, potholes, and land mines of life. In the workplace, millions of women (and men) sidestep, hop over, crawl under, and plow into the divots of their environments. Some are self-created, some are passed on by assumptions by both work and gender generations, and some are forced on individuals. I call them GenderTraps.

GenderTraps *are situations, conditions, or strategems that will inhibit, encumber, or catch women and men in their workplaces.* Sometimes, they are blatant and bold; other times, they are subtle and seductive. They range from miscommunications to sabotage, to management chaos, to being changeophobic. Identifying and exposing these toxic conditions and behaviors and offering realistic solutions in dealing with them is the purpose of this book.

For many years, I have been asking women and men to tell me about their experiences within the work place. Previous responses that encompassed national surveys and phone interviews have been published in my books *Woman to Woman, The Confidence Factor,* and *The Briles Report on Women in Health Care.* Those books, in turn, generated additional questions by the women and men who purchased them or heard me speak.

As a speaker, consultant, and researcher of women, I have been keenly aware of the problems that working women are dealing with—salary disparity, juggling family and job, miscommunication, sabotage, prejudices, and inept management. Since I began my quest as a professional speaker full time in 1986, my audiences have ranged anywhere from 50 to 5000. All I had to do was ask them what their concerns were—and they talked back. Verbally and in writing.

Many times, I have been ahead of the wave, spotting and identifying problems women face. The results from the GenderTraps survey deeply discount the media hassle around the glass ceiling and sexual harassment. Women say, "Pay us—pay us equally and fairly for the work we do. The hell with 60 percent, 70 percent, 80 percent, 90 percent of what men make! If we are qualified and do the work, pay us 100 percent—no more, no less."

If women were paid equitably, many of the biases and prejudices that they encounter would disappear. If women were paid equitably, the world would be a better place. At work, in relationships, and at home.

ORIGINS OF THE MODERN WORKPLACE

The workplace of the 1990s is different from that of the 1980s. Companies are still downsizing; technology is screaming ahead. Skills that are valid today are invalid next month. We are moving at such a fast pace, that many are gasping for air. Granted, research shows that we can mentally take in more information, learn more tasks and skills. But the emotional side of learning is almost totally ignored.

Physically and mentally, many can move faster. Emotionally, many aren't able to or can't jump ahead at the same pace. The end result is that we end up being out of synch—with ourselves, society, and the workplace. Our "sped up" environment fuels the growth of the GenderTraps.

My previous book, *The Briles Report on Women in Health Care*, focused on women undermining women in a female-dominated workplace. In the past few years, sweeping changes have hit the health-care industry. As I completed the study for the book, I began to wonder what the impact of downsizing and rampant change has had on other workplaces. Women in my audiences who don't work in health care routinely tell me that their workplaces are sick because management doesn't walk its talk. Dictums from the top state that discrimination, sexism, and harassment won't be tolerated, yet employees observe such behavior on a routine basis from "the boss." Rules charge employees with accountability and responsibility, yet there is a different set of rules in place for management. And management is rewarded with bonuses and pay raises while employees experience pay cuts, downsizing and increased workloads. A sick workplace!

In the past few years, the media have pursued the storyline that the biggest problems that women encountered in their workplaces are sexual harassment and the glass ceiling. Honorable mention went to child care. I began to ask questions of the 5000 women I spoke to between the dates of October 1993 through April 1994. Specifically, as part of my Workplace "Trap" Survey, I asked about the "Top 3" problems they encountered at work. Some of the responses, I expected; some surprised me; and some amazed me. Examples:

- Out of 1270 written survey responses, only 21 women identified sexual harassment as a "Top 3" problem.
- Only 26 women identified the glass ceiling as a "Top 3" problem.
- Only 11 percent of all working women are in midlevel management and higher.
- A majority of women are not interested in upper-level management positions. Instead, they want to get paid equitably.
- Women still try to do it all.
- It is not uncommon for women in management to pass over other women or to measure their value and production differently from the way they do a male employee.
- The animal feeder at a zoo makes more than the average day-care provider.
- The "F" word is one of the workplace's dirty secrets; a woman who is fat will be discriminated against more than a man who is fat in the same situation.
- Sabotage from women toward women has significantly increased over the past 8 years.
- Prejudice in the workplace is the number-one problem women face today.

In the fall of 1994, the Women's Bureau of the Department of Labor released the results of Working Women Count. Over 250,000 survey responses were received. In addition, 1200 phone calls were made to verify some of the results. The Working Women Count survey supports the results of the GenderTraps survey, which was conducted at the same time.

It's also important to note that the number one GenderTrap—The Prejudicial "Isms," is no surprise to the GenderTrap participants. Why the "surprise" reaction by the media via the OJ Simpson trial/circus throughout 1995 that prejudice is a problem amazes me. One does not need a PhD to determine that prejudice is indeed an issue for the nineties. Just open your eyes, your ears.

THE AUDIENCE FOR *GENDERTRAPS*

This book is written for several audiences, including men. Although the voices you read, and hear, are predominately women, it's not for them exclusively. By understanding what is bugging women, male CEOs, managers, coworkers, spouses, and family members can more readily support them in their quest to alter the workplace and themselves.

Readers will be able to recognize GenderTraps that they are in, as well as those in which their friends and coworkers are stuck. Viable solutions are offered along with tools to measure progress. It is my hope that readers of this work will be able to quickly identify their own GenderTrap(s) and understand that there are reasonable options and methods that can untangle them. The step from identifying a problem to creating a solution is in their hands.

Judith Briles

ACKNOWLEDGMENTS

No book ever gets into a reader's hands without a team behind it. From titles, to content, to those hidden heroes behind the publishing curtain, hundreds are involved in a book's production.

GenderTraps was birthed in a brainstorming meeting with McGraw-Hill's marketing guru Laura Friedman and ace editor, Betsy Brown. Rounding out the visible team was editing supervisor Penny Linskey. Each of these talented women carried my vision to press. I thank them.

A book's title is a critical feature. Most authors spend megahours fine tuning theirs. I was fortunate to have it from the beginning of the project. Combined with observations of my own, a dinner with friend Gary Truitt and a deposition with my attorney Randy Herrick-Stare regarding one of my GenderTraps, the title stuck. Each of us knew it was perfect.

The survey respondents came from all over the United States. Occupations ranged from being a jail house cook to a brain surgeon. Over one thousand women generously gave their time to complete our workplace survey. Over one-hundred went the next step and agreed to a personal interview to further explore their identified GenderTraps. Their voices are woven with different names throughout GenderTraps. A thousand plus thank yous for their time, energy, and enthusiasm for this work.

Professionals who are recognized as experts in gender differences: Stephanie West-Allen, Carolyn Zieger, Patricia Noonan, Deborah Flick, Nicole Schapiro, Barbara Fielder and Stephanie Allen were supportive, encouraging and made themselves available when I had questions. Thank you. And thank you to all the professionals who dedicate their careers to gender issues. Their work has opened doors that have allowed authors and researchers such as myself to continue the quest.

Finally, the transition from written survey to computereze to manuscript would have been impossible without my husband and partner, John Maling.

A special thank you for all those who read the manuscript and offered their endorsements:

Marjorie Hanson Schaevitz
Susan RoAne
Jaclyn Kostner
Marilyn Koss
Brian Tracy
Carole Hyatt
Terri Murphy
Judy Mann
Mark Victor Hansen

Betty Rendel
Susan RoAne
M.L. Hanson
Nicole Schapiro
Diana Booher
Linda Holland
Stephanie Allen
Daniel Burrus

WHAT WOMEN SAY ABOUT THEIR WORKPLACE

When I was a kid, my report cards were often accompanied by a note from my teacher for the year that I was just too "too." I spoke too much, I spoke too loud, I spoke too soon, and I was usually disruptive. Little did I know that those report cards of the 1950s would be the bellwether of what I'd find myself doing a few decades later.

As a speaker and a researcher, I find I sometimes have spoken out too soon and have been too loud for some. Being disruptive filled another niche.

My first paid speech was in 1974 to a group of approximately 40 women. The topic—investments. At that time, I was a stockbroker with E. F. Hutton. During that decade I did not have a clue that speaking, much less writing, would become my livelihood. Nor did I know I would write a book which in turn would lead to many other books.

As I moved through this thing called life, sometimes swimming quite well, and other times feeling as though I would drown, I would encounter various land mines along the way. When the land mines exploded, my little-kid voice/reaction surfaced with the classic question, "Why?" The most common adult response, "Because," didn't fit.

As my speaking career unfolded, I found myself in front of audiences of 20 to 5000, and discovered that many others were raising the very same questions I was about the land mines encountered in the workplace. I decided to study these issues further.

Workplace problems, "traps," are encountered every day. Traps like communications styles, sexism, discrimination, sexual harassment, salary inequities, the glass ceiling, and childcare. There are dozens, even hundreds of different traps. What are yours?

Please identify the three biggest "traps" that you have encountered. Describe how they have impacted you and how you have dealt with them.

1. ─────────────────────────────────

2. ─────────────────────────────────

3. ─────────────────────────────────

Figure 1-1.   *Workplace Trap Survey.* (Copyright © 1994 The Briles Group)

In order to get the pulse of working women today, I found a terrific technique in gathering data and information to the many questions I had and have—namely, to distribute surveys to audiences, which in turn distributed them among friends and coworkers. In 1993 and 1994, we distributed the Workplace "Trap" Survey shown in Fig. 1-1. A single, two-sided page, it was simple and straightforward, but telling. Respondents were asked to identify the top three problems they encountered in their workplace. Most responded with three problems—some with more, covering attaching pages—while others listed only one or two. These workplace problems that women encountered were identified as what I call *GenderTraps.* GenderTraps *are situations, conditions, or stratagems that inhibit, encumber, or catch women and men in the workplace.* They can range from prejudice, to miscommunications, to salary inequities, to management chaos, to resistance to change, to sabotage among coworkers, bosses, and self. As you read more in depth, in later chapters, the voices of over 1000 women and men who responded to the survey, you'll hear pain, fear, anger, and frustration.

GenderTraps is an answer to three questions:

• What are today's problems for women in the workplace?
• Why do these problems exist?
• What are the solutions to them?

THE SURVEY

Survey questionnaires were distributed at all of my speaking engagements for a 7-month period in 1993 and 1994 (see Appendix for details). Of the 5000 surveys distributed, 1270 individuals responded. My team also followed up with 130 personal in-depth interviews. Although several hundred men attended my workshops and lectures, only 31 of the 1270 surveys were returned by men. The survey was initially geared toward women and the low return by men reflects that premise.

It's also important to note that the men participating in the Workplace "Trap" Survey represent a small number. Since the objective of this book was to identify problems and solutions that women were encountering in today's workplace, the small number of men who participated in the survey did not alter the statistical truth and weight of women's responses.

While neither the study nor the survey was conducted by an independent polling group, its results are consistent with the results from the poll conducted by the Women's Bureau of the Department of Labor that was released in the fall of 1994. (In that poll, 250,000-plus surveys were completed by women and analyzed with an additional 1200 follow-up phone calls conducted by an independent polling company.)

Results of the survey are representative of all types of workplaces, some female-dominated—the so-called Velvet Ghettos: occupations in the fields of health care, teaching, banking, retail, child care, restaurant services, cosmetology, flight service, clerical-secretarial, public relations, and government, as well as positions in industry, finance, and manufacturing. The workplaces surveyed included both those that have an even mix of men and women— marketing, sales, finance, manufacturing—and those that are definitely male-dominated—engineering, science, architecture, construction and advertising. Homemakers were also among the respondents surveyed. All women work. Some get a paycheck; some don't.

Throughout *GenderTraps*, you'll hear the voices and personal stories as they unfold within each trap. You'll at times hear and understand their fears and pain. You may even experience outrage at some of their revelations. Even though the particular scenario described may have taken place in an operating room, in the midst of a political campaign or in a secretarial pool, you will be able to relate to the fact that this too could have happened (or may happen) to you in another time or at another place. In other words, these experiences can be easily transposed to other workplace environments.

Here are the 10 most common GenderTraps in the workplace:

1. Prejudicial "isms"
2. Communications barriers
3. Sabotage
4. Management chaos
5. Pay inequities
6. The balancing act: family versus work
7. Confrontophobia
8. Apathy/complacency/changeophobia
9. Self-sabotage
10. Misuse of power

THE PREJUDICE TRAP

The number-one trap identified by survey respondents was *prejudice*—63 percent said it was *the* key trap in their workplace. Within the prejudice umbrella are discrimination, racism, sexism, ageism, and lookism. Among the respondents who identified prejudice as the top trap, two-thirds said that the prejudice they encountered was discrimination and sexism, with the other one-third split between racism and ageism. Lookism surfaced from the 130 follow-up personal interviews. Several respondents also reported reverse discrimination as a factor.

Hundreds of surveys had comments about discrimination, sexism, racism, ageism, and lookism. No one wrote "lookism" specifically. This was identified when comments were probed about weight, height, dress, hair, and youth (as opposed to being terminated because of age). Whatever "ism" one could think of, the GenderTrap respondents had experienced them.

Prejudice is solely in our mind; it is an attitude, an idea or opinion that is often held despite facts to the contrary. Prejudices can be directed toward gender, race, culture, and age.

Everyone has prejudices. No one is born with them; they are

learned and developed as people grow up. Because someone is prejudiced does not mean he or she has to act on it and discriminate by being sexist, racist, and the like.

SEXUAL HARASSMENT AND THE GLASS CEILING TAKE A BACK SEAT

One of the actions that results from the prejudicial umbrella is sexual harassment. Ironically, few of the respondents placed sexual harassment or the glass ceiling among the top three problems they encountered in the workplace.

Surprisingly, only 2 percent of the respondents indicated that sexual harassment* was a problem. Likewise only 2 percent indicated the glass ceiling as a problem. I was intrigued by this incredibly low number.

In the 130 follow-up interviews, respondents were asked if they had encountered, observed, or were aware of situations that did involve sexual harassment or the glass ceiling. The majority said they were definitely aware of the problems surrounding these two issues, but in their workplace lives, neither sexual harassment nor the glass ceiling had priority over other areas that they felt were far more important.

Although sexual harassment and the glass ceiling are missing as specific traps in the top three, it is important to acknowledge that they are real and of concern to both women and men. Numerous studies and reports show that a significant number of women in the workforce have experienced some form of sexual harassment.†

I believe that the lack of significant responses on those two highly publicized areas indicates that today's women in the workplace view racism, sexism, discrimination, ageism, and lookism—as well the other traps identified from the survey—as more ongoing

---

*While several of these respondents didn't specifically use the words "sexual harassment" or "glass ceiling," their written responses were interpreted from observations such as the following:
- "Crude remarks were routinely made about women's body parts and functions."
- "The doctor told grossly descriptive jokes to deliberately embarrass staff."
- "I've been with the same company for 21 years—there has never been a female VP or officer."

†For example, in 1988, a survey by *Working Woman* magazine found that almost 90 percent of the Fortune 500 companies had had complaints of sexual harassment in the previous year. It also found that a typical large firm will lose $6.7 million per year from productivity losses, absenteeism, and turnover all related to sexual harassment.

and recurrent in their everyday work lives. The glass ceiling is an important issue, but to fewer women.

It is essential to recognize that not every woman is propelled to seek upper or senior management levels. This is particularly true of the Generation Xers, the under-30 group who at least at this point in their lives indicate that their druthers are not to work the 60 hours a week that their mothers did. What women in the workplace are saying is that they don't want to be discriminated against *and* they want to be paid fairly and with equality *now*—attaining jobs in upper and senior management can wait. It's significant to note that this viewpoint was voiced by educated women: over 50 percent of the respondents had a college degree, and 31 percent were taking additional courses to expand their skills in the workplace. In the postinterviews, many of the women at all levels stated that being in charge was not a primary objective for them at the present time. They left open the possibility that at a later date they would reevaluate their career options.

A common experience for many was the awareness of having been the object of some form of discrimination, but being hard-pressed to describe the exact action in words—whether it be racism, sexism, or discrimination or possibly a combination. *Discrimination* means to make a distinction in treatment or show partiality. Ageism is discrimination based on age. Sexism, then, is discrimination based on sex or gender, and racism is the practice of discriminating racially, as in segregation. Lookism is discrimination against an individual's appearance.

Lookism primarily takes the form of discrimination against overweight people. Many interviewed respondents referred to the "F" word—*fat*. Lookism is far more widespread for women. One woman wrote, "I gained 60 pounds after being put on steroids. When potential employers saw my résumé, interviews were set up immediately. However, when I arrived for the appointment, I would be told, 'I don't think you are right for us.'"

Complaints about ageism included that of a nurse who said that because of her age, she was no longer allowed to do private duty for infants—she was only 60! One can choose to seek legal recourse. The key issue then becomes who will pay for it. And this can turn into a real bind for many women when they are illegally and blatantly discriminated against. Certainly, if they have the funds, it is easier to proceed. Or if they can get an attorney to take a contingency case, they can proceed. Either way, however, a crucial question still surfaces: *Should* they? These suits take enormous time and energy—mentally and physically. It becomes a matter of which battle you want to take on.

Many of the survey respondents reported other forms of discrimination: between full-time versus part-time employees; employees with children (70 percent had children) versus employees without children; employees who had an educational degree versus those with no degree but years of experience; or employees of one ethnic group versus those of another ethnic group.

For example, several women reported jobs going to men because the men were the assumed "breadwinners" and supporting a family. Or in another case, a language instructor reported that she was discriminated against by the Hispanic population because she was not a "native" speaker of Spanish, although she had grown up in a bilingual family and had advanced degrees in Spanish.

Survey respondents who worked in health care stated that in the case of male nurses, managers tend to make excuses for them and not reprimand them even if valid complaints are made. They are often granted special favors and treatment. In addition, in a blatant example of sexism, male doctors are said to listen more to a male nurse than to a female nurse.

Or take the case of an insurance agent who wrote that while she was content and successful in her own business today, prior to that, she had been hounded for $3\frac{1}{2}$ years to leave her job at another insurance agency. Yet she had been among the top 10 percent of revenue producers. Her crime? She was the wrong color—she was black.

Many reported having their promotions blocked because they were the wrong gender, and a number felt the brunt of double discrimination against disabled women. Some noted that a backlash has surfaced since the Disabilities Act was put in place when President Bush was in office. Employers are finding excuses not to hire them, or even to keep them on payroll because of the added costs required to meet the workplace requirements dictated by the law.

Sexism flourishes in the workplace. Women reported that they experienced condescending attitudes and were treated as lower class by the usually male managers. Several women attested to being forced to work in an open, bullpen environment, while their male colleagues, even nonmanagers, got offices with doors that closed. Women from particular industries (i.e., defense, finance, and transportation) responded that not only were they perceived as less intelligent, but that bosses, female or male, would ask advice and input from the male staff, often ignoring the female staff.

THE COMMUNICATIONS TRAP

The number-two trap identified by the survey respondents was *communications,* both verbal and nonverbal. Thirty-six percent of the respondents included communications, or mis- or noncommunications, among their top three traps in the workplace. These communications problems might come from any source: from a boss, from coworkers, or from support staff.

One respondent reported that she felt like an "idiot" when pertinent information was not relayed because coworkers didn't have the skills to verbalize or prioritize what needed to be passed on. Another reported that coworkers and bosses delivered "zingers" in the form of their choice of communication style and/or constant put-downs.

Common complaints were that communications are poor to nil in the workplace, and that the lack of any reasonable communications leads only to a continuation of conflict. A major factor is that communication styles vary greatly, not only between males and females, but also between different cultures. Often each group is governed by an unexpressed set of dos and don'ts—unfortunately, all too often these dos and don'ts are only revealed after it's too late.

Some respondents reported that communications were so poor in their workplaces that task forces were formed to identify exactly what styles of communications were being used within their team. One respondent wrote that she resented the lack of communications between members of her team because it complicated her job and consumed precious time that could have been better spent doing other things. Many of the women said that not only men and women but also different races and cultures use the same set of words with totally different meanings.

Summing it up, all felt that it was difficult, if not impossible, to perform their jobs when communications are incomplete.

THE SABOTAGE TRAP

Previous studies, revealed in my books *Woman to Woman: From Sabotage to Support* (which focused on women in the general work force) and the *Briles Report on Women in Health Care,* examined sabotage and undermining behaviors among women in the workplace.

When the study was initially done for *Woman to Woman* in 1987, over 53 percent of the women responded that they had been undermined by a female coworker. In the subsequent *Briles Report* released in 1994, a study was completed on women who worked in the health-care field. Seventy-one percent of the respondents stated that they had been undermined and sabotaged by female coworkers; this represents a 34 percent increase over the 1987 women-in-the-general-workplace study.

In the written survey for *GenderTraps,* 33 percent of all respondents reported that *sabotage*—being undermined by another woman—was the third biggest trap encountered in the workplace today. Common complaints that were heard included taking credit for another's work; receiving an annual performance review that was substantially lower than what had been verbalized by the supervisor throughout the year; accessing another's computer and altering or destroying personal work; and taking another's work and submitting it in national competition without acknowledgment or credit of the originator. In one such case, an award was won, and no one, including the creator, spoke up about the injustice that had been done.

Other complaints include workplace sabotage resulting from sloppy and unprofessional practices, not taking responsibility for jobs, and letting one's team down. Complaints were aired about coworkers and bosses and the overall toxicity that many are experiencing in the workplace of the 1990s. Gossip continues to be headliner for destruction and old complaints of cliques; envy and jealousy continue to weigh heavy in the workplace.

THE MANAGEMENT TRAP

The fourth trap dealt with *management*—too much, too late, the wrong kind, the lack of, the wrong concepts, and the wrong people. Twenty-seven percent of the respondents said that management was one of the top traps in the workplace. In today's workplace, the Peter and Patty principles are alive and well.

Many of the respondents reported that they had experienced bosses and coworkers, both male (Peters) and female (Pattys), who had been promoted above their level of competencies. The women resented training and covering up for individuals who weren't qualified or skilled to handle the tasks required.

Too many men and women advance into management without the proper qualifications and credentials, and have, unfortunately, stayed there. Common complaints include the impression that upper management is nothing but the good-old-boy network; management lacks communication skills; management treats employees as if they were the children and management was the parent; management is done by intimidation; communications stop at the upper-management level, and employees are supposed to be telepathic in order to determine what is supposed to be done.

Total quality management—TQM—was in the thoughts of many of the respondents. They felt that while it is a nice concept, many of their managers never follow through with it. The result is that they don't feel they count, that they feel belittled, and that their sole purpose is to support upper management exclusively. A few of the respondents used the term "zinged." They felt zinged by their managers with either misconstrued information or communications.

Many reported that they had been given a title that conveyed some kind of management function but carried no authority. Just the same, they were expected to solve whatever problems were out there. After 18 months of terrorism on her job, one respondent finally "took it and shoved it," and found another job where put-downs and innuendoes weren't practiced.

A large number of respondents reported being interrupted and talked over in meetings. At times they were accused of not being team players because they would disagree with their boss or manager.

Several of the women in the survey reported that when they were promoted into management or were being considered for management, men in the organization raised loud voices in the form of heated statements and accusations or reverse discrimination (i.e., they were accused of being considered or promoted just because they were women). The response of the women was that they had the proper credentials, degrees, and experience that any manager would need to qualify for the position.

THE PAY INEQUITIES TRAP

> *Unfortunately,* pay inequities *are alive and well in today's workplace.*

Nineteen percent of the respondents said that *pay inequities* were a top problem for them. These inequities were reported from women with jobs that varied widely from jailhouse cook to director and senior manager.

A survey respondent who worked in a payroll department stated that male laborers with few qualifications earned more than the clerical females who were expected to handle much more complex duties.

Many of the women reported that the promotions they received had a dual edge. The good news was that they were promoted into management positions, positions that had previously been held by men. The bad news was that even with the same credentials and titles, they received several thousand dollars less than their predecessors.

One exception to this dismal picture is that in male-dominated environments, such as in the engineering profession, there was more likely to be equality in pay, at least initially.

THE FAMILY/BALANCE TRAP

Juggling family and work was a key problem for 17 percent of the respondents. The superwoman concept still haunts many of them, some stating they feel indispensable, both financially and emotionally, rarely finding time to take a breath. Women who are married and have children were criticized by single women for the health-care coverage and other benefits they received. Many singles felt that if their employers covered healthcare costs, families received a form of "cash" bonus monthly—regardless of the quality of care.

Women who had children late (i.e., after 40) felt they were particularly caught. Many had achieved high visibility, recognition, and success within their specific occupations. Yet, when they had children, both men and women assumed they would no longer be interested in, much less capable of, maintaining their career tracks. The end result was that they had to work doubly hard, taking on extra tasks. Many resented the fact that they had to prove themselves again, after they had gone through all that during their twenties.

Finally, day care was a concern expressed by a great number of respondents. Women addressed multiple issues relating to both the day-care provider and the day-care consumer: lack of centers, lack of quality of personnel, inconvenient site locations, high costs, and company politics when sites were assessable through the workplace.

THE CONFRONTOPHOBIA TRAP

According to numerous studies, most people would rather die than speak to a group of people. And most feel the same about *confronting* others. Twelve percent of the respondents cited entering into a conflict or confrontation as one of their top problems in the workplace. I believe that the percentage will be higher in future surveys, as more recognition and awareness surface of women's aversion to confronting and dealing with conflicts. Conflicts are normal, in the workplace as well as in one's personal life. The real problem occurs in how they are managed.

Women, as girls, are not taught to engage in conflicts.

Some respondents reported that when they were in a conflict or a confrontation was needed, they quit—gave up, walked away—instead of confronting the issue. Many described problems with women and men who had passive-aggressive personalities. They found it difficult to confront passive-aggressive people, because such people were more likely to be covert and manipulative in their actions and reactions.

Management and confrontation appear to be dual problems. Several of the women reported that their managers refused to talk about a problem when it surfaces, taking the position that tomorrow was another day, as if the problem would go away.

THE APATHY, COMPLACENCY, AND CHANGE TRAP

Apathy is indifference, lack of emotion or just plain listlessness. *Complacency* is contentment and smugness. *Change* is anything that makes a difference. Today's workplace exudes change. Where the buzzwords for the early 1990s were "downsizing" and "rightsizing"; the mid 1990s has embraced "delayering." Same thing, just sounds different.

Technology is moving so fast that it can be overwhelming just keeping up with the vocabulary, much less what it all does. When change is fast-moving, it is not uncommon to dig your heels in and say "enough."

Women who are caught in the apathy, complacency, and resistance-to-change trap feel lost. Eleven percent of the survey respondents stated that apathy, complacency, and change are among the top problems that they encounter in the workplace.

Several of the women wrote that apathy leads nowhere. Many indicated that they had become careless and lazy in their profession, not stretching and reaching and continuing to learn new things. Some said that because of the management chaos they had experienced, they had lost all respect for management and had given up on their aspirations.

With workplace downsizing and reorganization, there is next to no accountability or follow-through. The result is that many find themselves not working at the professional level that they had envisioned. Instead, employees turn into procrastinators, and develop a "woe is me" martyred complex, exemplified by helplessness and hopelessness.

The good news is that several of the respondents viewed the downsizing and the massive reorganization of the past few years as a wake-up call. They had to get reinvolved in their careers by taking more classes, expanding their credentials for whenever the inevitable happens.

Both women and men wrote that the rapid growth of the 1980s had trapped them into a false sense of security, leaving them to feel immune to any upheaval that could come their way.

THE SELF-SABOTAGE TRAP

When sabotage occurs, it is assumed to be done by another. Many of the respondents indicated that they were masters at *self-sabotage*. Ten percent stated it was a major problem for them in their workplace. Here is my definition:

> *Self-sabotage* is the undermining and destruction of personal and professional integrity, malicious supervision, and damage to personal and professional credibility—*caused by oneself*. Any of these can lead to the erosion and destruction of self-esteem and confidence.

Self-sabotage includes negativity, having low self-esteem and confidence, not being able to handle criticism, having an aversion to risk, having a bad attitude, being narrow-minded, being careless, carrying personal problems to work, blaming others for problems, being immature, not following through, passing the buck, being moody, avoiding negotiations as well as any conflict or confrontation, and being caught in the "should haves," "ought tos," and "if onlys." Self-sabotage also generates the *terrible toos:* too nice, too agreeable, too naive, too quiet, too overworked, too afraid, too dependent, and too guilty.

When women participate in self-sabotage, they stir up their own "sticky floor." The more they undermine themselves, the more likely they are to remain stuck—stuck in their careers and their relationships.

THE POWER TRAP

The final trap that surfaced was *power.* The percentage of respondents who counted power plays among their top problems was substantially lower than for the other traps. Only 3 percent of the respondents indicated that it was their number-one problem in the workplace.

Respondents wrote that women were not handling their newfound power very well. Women bosses put pressure on them just because they were women to support specific causes that were supposed to be for women. It didn't matter if they agreed or disagreed with the position.

Many women stated that if they appeared to be too assertive or competitive, the odds were that they would not get the promotion. They were just as likely to be passed over for promotion because of their gender, *even* if the decision maker for the promotion was a woman. A number of the respondents reported that women bosses had a different set of criteria for the women they managed than for the men. Women bosses were inclined to be less supportive and responsive to other women, because the supervisors did not want to appear to have gender favorites. The Queen Bees, the Princess Bees, and the Phantom Bees are active in today's workplace.

SUMMING UP

The survey and results represent today's working women. The surprising exclusion of sexual harassment and the glass ceiling from the top 10 traps is a wakeup call to the media, business, and women's groups.

Too much media hype has been directed toward the glass ceiling issue, when the majority of women are really stuck in the muddy bottom. There is no denying that sexual harassment exists. But when women view the other problems and traps of their workplaces, it dims in comparison for most.

CHAPTER

TWO

ALL IS NOT EQUAL IN THE WORKPLACE... STILL

When Astronaut Sally Ride stepped out of the cockpit of the space shuttle *Challenger*, a message was heard around the world. No job will be off limits to women. Today, according to the Women's Bureau of the Department of Labor, over 58 million adult women are employed. By 2000, there will be an estimated total female population of 141,000,000 with 72 million (51 percent) women working for pay. If women represent such a huge percentage of the working population—in many cases, they represent the majority of those employed in their specific occupation—why are there still concerns and complaints vocalized about racism, sexism, discrimination, pay inequities, management chaos, communication snafus, and the like? Sally Ride needs to reactivate her astronaut status.

WOMEN AND MEN *ARE* DIFFERENT

The reality is, today, no one knows exactly why or what the real breadth of difference is. Men and women *are* different in a variety of ways: their psychology, behavior, and physiology.

Gender differences often cause confusion and create conflicts. And just because everyone speaks the same language (whether English or Japanese or Spanish) doesn't guarantee understanding. Let's say your boss and coworkers all speak English. Depending upon interpretation, tone, even gestures, there are times when even the simplest of words and phrases will take on an aura of a foreign language.

Numerous books have surfaced in the last few years on the gender-speaking topics. Women and men have been placed on other planets, as in John Gray's *Men Are From Mars and Women Are From Venus*. Others have explained things such as why men don't ask directions when they get lost, as in Deborah Tannen's *You Just Don't Understand Talking* and *From 9 to 5*.

Are gender differences created from upbringing and societal influences, or are they physiological—determined by genes, hormones, and so on? The answer is yes—all of the above.

Some researchers believe that gender traits reflect biochemical and biological differences that occur during prenatal development. Another group believes it is how the brain is organized that explains the differences between men and women. Still others believe that it is how adults pass along their gender bias to children as the primary influence on behavior. In other words, children's (and later, adults') behavior is merely a reflection of how society expects the genders to behave.

Researchers are focusing on biology—genetics, hormones, and the brain. Weighing in at 3 pounds, the human brain for both men and women looks the same. For most, the left hemisphere is primarily devoted to verbal functions, and the right to nonverbal, cognitive functions.

Ongoing research indicates that there are similarities among all women, as well as similarities among all men in the organization of the brain. The bridge that connects the left and right hemispheres (the corpus callosum) and the location of the cognitive functions within each hemisphere (lateralization) are the key factors in the differences between men and women, according to the research. Men are more likely to have language skills in their nondominant hemisphere, which is usually the left. Women, on the other hand, have language functions in both hemispheres.

Some argue that the difference means that women are more balanced, and are able to expand their vocabularies and learn foreign languages far easier than men are. Research on children indicates that girls begin speaking at an earlier age than boys do.

In *BrainSex*, authors Anne Noir and David Jessel summarize research indicating that when the fetus is exposed to hormones, these hormones can alter brain structure and behavior. They find that the male hormone (testosterone), acting on the brain, is the root of a male's aggression.[1] In the workplace, this can translate to a more competitive work style, including men's ability (desire) to boast and expound on their accomplishments.

Most researchers are uncertain on how differences between right and left hemispheres relate to the differences between the genders. The bridge—the corpus callosum—is actually made of nerve fibers that connect the left and right brain. In females it is usually larger. Some researchers speculate that, because of the difference in size, females have a greater communication between the two hemispheres, and therefore, their brain is more bilaterally organized. It is speculated that one of the outcomes of this difference is that females have a greater breadth of interests.

For centuries, society has identified gender-appropriate roles. When women or men would step out of those roles, it was usually for a temporary and often emergency situation, such as Rosie the Riveter during World War II. When the men came back, Rosie was expected to give up her job and go back to the kitchen. When boys and girls, and later men and women, land in the slots that are deemed appropriate for either, parents and society affirm their positioning.

It's okay for girls to cry but, for boys, it's not. Because of the nonsupport for boys when tears surface, they learn to keep them down. Eventually, some even forget how to cry. I can clearly remember telling my three-year-old son that big boys don't cry. Today, I bite my tongue when my eight-year-old grandson sheds tears.

Learning theory proponents say that all communication and behavior is learned via a system of rewards and punishments. "That's a big boy," is the verbal reward from mom or dad when the tears stop.

Television has become a major influence for most children (and adults). The great majority of programs today carry the familiar stereotypes, although, there are some that portray both male and female action heroes. Children are very keen observers. They imitate the roles and moves of the adults in their lives. This type of learning, or social modeling, may be a significant factor in the division of gender roles.

WHAT THEORY HAS TO SAY

Ongoing research by Eleanor Macoby indicates that children under the age of 11 prefer being and playing with their own gender. Much has been written about team play, girls' and boys'—and sometimes lack of girls—involvement in playing in teams as kids. Because of the same-sex preference, according to Macoby, girls are unable and unfamiliar with how to influence little boys, and little boys are unable and unfamiliar with how to influence little girls. Girls' styles of persuasion seem to work best among themselves.

The rough-and-tumble play style of boys tends to put off girls. Because they are put off, they in turn don't play with boys.[2] In their early years, girls don't learn the rough-and-tumble techniques that sometimes get translated into the adult world. In the adult work world, when women do attain levels of senior management, their role models are usually men, and not other women—the same men who grew up in the rough-and-tumble model.

Granted, more women have moved into senior management in the last several years, but their numbers still remain small, which makes it tough. Overall, 6 million women are in middle to senior management—only 11 percent of all working women. It is lonely at the top, whether you are a man or a woman. And when women make it to the top, they rarely look, walk, talk, or dress like their predecessor. And if they do look, walk, talk, or dress quasi-like their predecessor, they are looked down upon as not feminine by their male colleagues, and too male by the females who work for them in subordinate positions. Definitely, a workplace Catch-22.

THE GREAT DIVIDE

When Professor Higgins spoke the words, "Why can't a woman be like a man?" men around the world collectively sighed, "Amen." The reality is that women are not men, nor men, women. At times there are great walls and canyons between their observations, their feeling, and their experiences with one another. Over the years, I have collected my observations, as well as those of colleagues, friends, and other reporters on what men and women think and feel. Examples:

- Women want to be fair, to hear all sides.
- Men want justice now.
- Women say that men are too insensitive; they don't feel enough.
- Men say that women are overemotional and too sensitive; they feel too much.

- Women protest that men don't share an equal division of child care and housework.
- Men feel they don't have to share equally in child care or housework, since they produce more than half the household income.
- Women feel that men don't know how to listen.
- Men feel that women talk too much.
- Women feel that men are too boastful and competitive.
- Men feel that women don't know how to win.
- Women think that men are crude.
- Men think that women are too prudish.
- Women feel they are sexually harassed.
- Men feel that their behavior is misinterpreted.
- Women fear men's physical power.
- Men fear women's emotional power.
- Women feel anger when men don't take no for an answer.
- Men believe that no means yes.
- Women feel they are more moral than men.
- Men feel they are more logical and financially oriented.
- Women believe that men are the cause of divorce.
- Men believe that feminism and the women's movement are the cause of divorce.
- Women say that men cause war.
- Men feel that they are the disposable sex in war.
- Women believe that men (and business) are largely responsible for destroying the environment because of their greed and insensitivity to environmental needs.
- Men feel that women working has led to the destruction of the family.
- Women feel that they aren't taken seriously in their careers.
- Men believe that women will have babies and quit their jobs.
- Women believe that they don't get paid equally.
- Men believe that women are paid fairly.
- Women believe that men take advantage of them.
- Men believe that women take advantage of them.

- Women feel that they aren't heard.
- Men feel that women complain too much.
- Women deny their capacity for abuse and retaliation.
- Men deny being the victim.
- Women believe that men don't "get it."
- Men don't know what "it" is to get.
- Women believe that men are in control in the workplace.
- Men believe that women are taking over the workplace.
- Women deny their own power.
- Men fear exposing their vulnerability.
- Women believe it is still a man's world.
- Men feel women are manipulative.

As you went through the above list, you may have thought, "This is a crock! How can men feel this way, or women, that way?" In reality, if you will step back and look in the mirror, whatever your gender, you've most likely felt, or even said, a majority or all of the above statements at one time or another. And, in probing further the statements regarding the opposite sex, you have felt they are true. There are always exceptions, but as a rule those generalizations fit a great majority of the population. And there are often two, maybe more, sides to any particular issue or belief.

ATTITUDES DO COUNT

Each of the GenderTraps identified from the survey is real. Some are fairly new, and are compounded as more women enter today's workplace. Others were seeded millions of years ago, when the roles of males as hunters and females as gatherers and nurturers were practiced with no questions asked. It is difficult, and some say impossible to unravel millions of years of imprinting.

Social, biological, and psychological factors contribute to the differences between men and women as well as to each of the GenderTraps identified. Biologically, the connector (corpus callosum) between the two hemispheres of a woman's brain gives women an edge on verbal abilities. For men the greater separation between the two hemispheres, or lateralization, appears to contribute a greater weight toward abstract reasoning, which could be a factor in why more men are in science than women.

Authors such as Deborah Tannen as well as Carol Gilligan (*In a Different Voice*), Virginia Satir (*People Making*), Suzette Elgin (*GenderSpeak*), and Warren Farrell (*Why Men Are the Way They Are*) have said that psychologically men tend to want more space and women tend to identify who they are and gain a sense of self through their relationship with others. Socially, women are more inclined toward what's fair, where men focus on what is perceived as justice.

Attitudes that come from our biological differences, psychological differences, and social differences impact the gender culture of today. The end result is that girls and boys, men and women receive different behavioral training. Those differences resurface in prejudices, communication, undermining and sabotage, power plays, salary inequities, management techniques, family issues and values, conflicts and negotiations, and the attitudes and reactions of apathy and complacency and aversion to change.

In evaluating these differences, many believe that much of the conditioning that girls receive is sexist. Sexism leads to stereotypical positioning and reactions. On the flip side of the coin, it is important to know that boys receive their own form of sexist training. Boys are taught logic, denial of pain, how to be focused on goals and winning, and the power of being independent. They are not taught to be caring, feeling, or emotional, to value relationships, or to care for others. This too has sexist implications.

Today, the primary caregiver of young children is the female. Whether or not there is a male/father who is in the picture for the infant, toddler, or preschooler, it is still the female/mother who fertilizes the seeds of the *prejudicial "isms"* identified as the number-one GenderTrap. These seeds sprout under what I call *momisms*. Sometimes momisms are right on; other times, they are in the wrong place, at the wrong time. Momisms directed toward daughters include (but are not limited to):

Be nice.

Be a lady.

Be good.

Look out for others.

Be sweet.

Let the boys win.

Don't be pushy or aggressive.

Don't make waves.

Don't enter into conflicts.

Look good.

Be careful.

Be friends.

People will judge you by the company you keep.

It's not winning that matters, it is how you play the game.

Good things come to those who wait.

Don't be noisy.

Don't brag.

Take turns.

Eat everything on your plate; there are starving children.

If you can't say it nicely, don't say it at all.

What goes around, comes around.

Your turn will come.

Momisms (and sometimes *dadisms*) for boys include (and are not limited to):

Don't cry.

Be a little man.

It's OK to get dirty.

Your hurt doesn't matter.

Get up and get going (after falling down).

You can do anything.

Fight for your rights.

Don't be bullied.

It's OK to be messy.

It's OK to be rough.

Girls and ladies first.

Get it while you can.

Win.

The bottom line is that boys and girls go through cultural conditioning as they become men and women. Women become distrustful of power and dependent upon it at the same time. Men become relatively devoid of feelings and distant from their families.

One of the most important books published in 1992 on and about women never made it to the best-seller list. Social psychologist Carol Tavris wrote the *Mismeasure of Woman*. Its subtitle is *Why Women Are Not the Better Sex, the Inferior Sex, or the Opposite Sex*. What Tavris is saying is that women are one of the genders; men the other. Listen to what Tavris has to say:

> Equality as acceptance means that instead of regarding cultural and reproductive differences as problems to be eliminated, we would aim to eliminate *the unequal consequences that follow from them*. We ask how to achieve equality *despite* gender differences, not how to achieve equality by getting rid of (or pretending to ignore) gender differences. We would no longer accept the prevailing male norm as always the legitimate one, while trying to find special circumstances to accommodate women or minorities who are trying to measure up to it. We would stop labeling women's experiences as the deviant one.[3]

> *Men and women are different and that's the good news. Pretending there are not differences between the sexes is absurd.*

Women in today's workplace want equality for themselves as well as for men. Equality, though, is not the same as being the same. What women want is to be heard, represented, and paid equitably. Just as men do.

Prejudice: An attitude that is usually preconceived and not favorable or positive toward a race, gender or culture.

TRAP 1:
THE PREJUDICIAL
"ISMS"
Discrimination, Racism, Sexism, Ageism, and Lookism Thrive in the Workplace

- Do you feel that you have been passed over for a promotion or a job because of your gender?
- Do you think that you have been turned down for a position or a job because of your race?
- Do you feel that you have been spoken down to or your opinion/ advice has been ignored because of your gender?
- Do you think that you have failed (or passed) any interview because of your looks?

During President Bush's administration, former Senator John Tower was nominated for Secretary of Defense. Washington, DC was abuzz about his alleged womanizing and drinking. Tower was invited to be on the *This Week With David Brinkley* show. Brinkley was away, and Sam Donaldson stepped in as host. He said, "Well, senator, it's not just alcohol, you know. There have been charges of womanizing." Tower responded, "I'm a single man; I do date women," and then added, "What's your definition of womanizing, Sam?" Cokie Roberts was sitting there with a quasi-amused expression on her face during the exchange. Donaldson turned to her and said, "Cokie, do you have a definition of the term?" Her response was, "Well, I think most women know it when they see it, senator."

So it goes with prejudice. Most women know it when they see it. When individuals harbor prejudices that are out of sync with reality, whether it is in the job market, the salary market, or relationships and perceptions, it can be a detrimental foe to women in their workplace.

THE MUDDY BOTTOM FOR WOMEN

The world is still at war against women. A 1980 summary of a United Nations report found that women worldwide did two-thirds of the work, earned one-tenth the income, and owned one-hundredth of the property. In between, dreams have fallen, market economies have risen, female prime ministers and CEOs have made it to the top. Overall all, it has been a decade of high growth. And still, women are the recipients of discrimination just about everywhere. In 1993, the UN *Human Development Report* found that, nonetheless, no country treats its women as well as its men.

All women work. Some get a paycheck, and some don't. Of the 58 million who work for a paycheck every year, a disproportionate number do housework and cleaning on the side, or after hours. A study released in the fall of 1993 by the Families Who Work Institute, based on a survey of 3718 Americans, found that employed women do 81 percent of all household cooking and 78 percent of the cleaning. Some 42 percent of the respondents had experienced downsizing at work in the past year, and 27 percent had experienced racially motivated on-the-job discrimination.

While violence, harassment, and the glass ceiling hog the headlines, a vital issue for women revealed in the GenderTraps survey centered around bread and butter, not sexual harassment or the glass ceiling. *Women want to be paid what they are worth.* In 1994, *Ms.* magazine found the same results in a survey of its readership. Sexual harassment and the glass ceiling did not lead the list of important issues. Getting paid appropriately was number one.

According to New York's Corporate Board Resource, 6 million women currently hold managerial positions with half in senior management—vice president and higher. The U.S. Bureau of the Census reported that between the years 1980 and 1990, the number of women in managerial positions increased by 95 percent. In March of 1995, the Federal Glass Ceiling Commission released a report stating that even after two decades of women in the workforce, little progress had been made in obtaining the power positions of corporate America. The study found that only 5 percent of senior management positions (i.e., vice president and above) are held by women.

Catalyst, a nonprofit women's research and advocacy group, estimates that the figure for women in senior management is closer to 7 percent, and that within the next decade it will increase to 15 percent. Assuming that Catalyst is correct, the 15 percent in senior management still reflect a population of fewer than 9 million women.

Presently, it is estimated that 58 million women work for a paycheck. Even if those numbers do not increase in the next decade (which is doubtful), there are over 49 million women who are not in senior management. The real question, I believe, is: How many care?

You may argue that more women should be in management. I will agree. But do more women *want* to be in management? Maybe. Maybe not. Multiple surveys of women MBAs have found that within 10 years of graduation, over 20 percent of them don't work. The family/balance issue certainly plays a heavy role in their opting out of corporate America. But I believe there is more to the story.

The glass ceiling that has so grabbed the headlines of the past few years is directed more toward a minority group. In reality, 90 percent plus of the women in the workplace are more concerned about the muddy bottoms and the brick sidewalls than they are about the glass ceiling. Women today are continually placed, and work, in the Velvet Ghetto—jobs that are off the primary career ladder and/or are in female-dominated environments.

Those Velvet Ghettos identified in the previous chapter include secretaries, cashiers, bookkeepers, accounting and auditing clerks, registered nurses, nurse's aides, flight attendants, elementary school teachers, waitresses, sales and retail workers, child-care workers, librarians, receptionists, hairdressers and manicurists, textile sewing machine operators, general office clerks, bank tellers, maids, and computer operators.

In my opinion, the glass ceiling is an issue for many women, but not the majority. Data show that women are thriving in non-Fortune 500 companies. Companies the next level down, the Fortune 1000, employ 20 percent of all the nation's workers. In 1994, the

Department of Labor reported that in excess of 40 percent of managers in these companies are women. Women also do better in new technologies, such as biotechnology and health care.

Then, of course, there are the women-owned businesses. Women head over 6 million businesses, which in turn employ more than the Fortune 500 combined. Women who want to start their own companies are doing it. Other women who find management nonresponsive and unreceptive to their needs opt out of the workforce (as many of the MBAs have) or pull back, rarely delivering to their employers their true talents. At the other extreme, women exhaust themselves by trying to do it all.

This still leaves the majority of the female workforce—the majority who cheer for the women who want to move up the ladder, but for themselves *choose not to*. To paraphrase Rhett and Scarlett, "Frankly, my dears, we don't give a damn."

WAKE-UP CALL TO THE CONSCIENCE

The word *prejudice* is very powerful. To many, it invokes fear. The real fear is the action that can come out of prejudice. When you can identify what actions are derivatives of your prejudices, you can make a conscious decision to stop yourself from discriminating, from incurring racism, sexism, ageism, lookism, or any of the other negative actions that can surface from a prejudice. Your operative word becomes *consciously*.

In *The Empathic Communicator*,[1] William F. Howell identifies five stags of consciousc/unconscious activity. Included are the *unconsciously incompetent*—those individuals who are oblivious to anything and everything around them. They don't have a clue that their actions or activities are inappropriate, out of sync, or just plain wrong.

The *consciously incompetent* individuals are very much aware of inconsistency, of drawbacks, of their lack of skills in dealing with issues both personally and professionally.

The *consciously competent* individuals are tuned into the present, where they are competent, but they have to think of what actions and strategies are needed to bring off what the task is.

The *unconsciously competent* seem to make all the right moves, but are oblivious or unaware of the styles, strategies, and actions that are invoked. They just do it.

The fifth mode is the *unconsciously supercompetent*. You realize that something has happened, but it's as if time were suspended, a timeless euphoria sets in. Magic—it "just happened." Former football great, San Francisco 49er quarterback John Brodie, reported that there were occasions when he would go back to make a pass, and time would be suspended—he would have all the time he needed to find his receiver and complete the pass. Anyone who has watched a football game knows that "having all the time" is not the real world. More like split seconds.

Whenever individuals act in an unconsciously supercompetent state, it is as if a guardian angel had come in and assisted in whatever the feat or task was. Stephanie West Allen is the author of *Triversity Fantasy* and *Seven Keys to Unlock Prejudice*, and a mediator of cultural and gender disputes. She likens Howell's stages to the skill of tying a shoe. In the unconsciously incompetent stage, a baby doesn't know she needs shoes, much less how to tie them. In the consciously incompetent stage, the toddler knows that she needs the shoes, but she doesn't know how to tie them. As she progresses to the consciously competent stage, she knows she needs the shoes, has to think about the process of tying them, and can do it. In the unconsciously competent stage, she has become an expert at tying her shoes. Unconsciously, they are reached for and slipped on the foot, and the tying task is completed by habit.

As you deal with prejudice, it is important to transition to Howell's third and fourth stages of competence. You should strive to become consciously aware of actions created from attitudes of prejudice (yours and others), such as discrimination, ageism, racism, sexism, lookism, and any other "ism" that surfaces. The next step is to become unconsciously competent such that your nondiscriminatory actions are a habit and something you don't have to think about doing. You just do it.

PILGRIMS AND SEXISM

When white women talk about discrimination, their usual remarks are focused on sexism and job and pay discrimination. For women of color, discrimination is usually translated into racism. Angela, a personnel manager, started her career in a large retail chain. Today she works for one of the Baby Bells.

White women have to worry about penetrating the male network in corporate America. Black women have to worry about that and the white network.

According to Cherokee principal chief Wilma Mankiller, sexism is very old. Before she was elected the first deputy chief of the Oklahoma tribe, she endured vicious opposition and distrust for 11 years. Mankiller says:

> Sexism is not a native concept. When the Europeans arrived in America, Cherokee women living in the Southeast were consulted on major issues, attended councils and had an equal vote. The tribe's creator was called the *Mother-of-All-Nations,* and men and women lived in harmony.

> With the arrival of the Europeans, those pilgrims, Indian women began marrying white settlers. Where they had been participants in councils in the past, their new spouses expected them to be quiet. The tribe's creation story was altered, and acculturation assigned women to secondary roles.[2]

When a disease enters a community, it festers and grows until some antidote is discovered and administered. Besides smallpox, Mankiller says that the disease Pilgrims brought over was sexism. Today, sexism is everywhere—the home, the school, and the workplace.

THE PLAYING FIELD "GIRL"

Even today, it is a major put-down for a male to call another male a "girl" in an athletic competition—and the male can be of any age. When it comes to sports, chauvinism vibrates off the playing field. According to Mariah Burton Nelson, author of *The Stronger Women Get, The More Men Love Football: Sexism and the American Culture of Sports,* it is time to "level the playing field," a term that is used frequently by experts in the field of discrimination, sexism, and racism. Nelson says:

> It's appalling to me that little boys are still told, "You throw like a girl," as an insult. Or parents will tell their own daughters that they throw like a boy, and mean it as a compliment.[3]

She proclaims that there is nothing gender-related about throwing. Rather, if you haven't been taught to throw well, you don't; and if you have, you can.

It is not uncommon to see spectators who routinely stand and cheer while players fight on the field, whether it's football, baseball, or ice hockey. Popularity is presently at an all-time high for many of these sports, especially when you think about cheering crowds egging on the warriors. According to Burton Nelson:

> Sports, alone, are not the problem. There's plenty of physical joy, a sense of competence and lessons about teamwork discipline that can accrue from sports. It's the values we bring to them that are the problem. Many are askew.[4]

She is correct. Both athletes and coaches use vocal put-downs that denigrate women or their bodies. Derogatory female terms are used to motivate players. Early on, boys learn negative associations with women's bodies—"You throw like a girl, you pussy," or "What's wrong, are you on the rag?" In addition, they learn to associate athleticism, toughness, and dominance with masculinity.

When a boy who has been ridiculed as being feminine enters adulthood and becomes involved in a relationship with a woman, he may find it difficult to see her as a peer—his whole sense of self, of masculinity, has been defined as superior to women in his earlier training. This, in turn, has the potential for brutalization within the relationship in the future.

DISCRIMINATION AND HARASSMENT

Although only a few of the respondents in the survey reported sexual harassment as one of their top three traps (21 respondents—less than 2 percent) it is still an issue for many women.

Carolyn Allen Zeiger, Ph.D., is a psychologist, coauthor of *Doing It All Isn't Everything*, and a founding partner of the Athena Group, a Denver-based leadership training and consulting organization that focuses on solving gender issues in the workplace. She is quick to note that sexual harassment has been considered by the courts as a form of gender-based discrimination. Sexual harassment also:

- Affects the terms or conditions of a person's employment
- Creates a hostile work environment

According to the Equal Employment Opportunity Commission and Nine-to-Five, the National Association of Working Women, 90 percent of harassers are men harassing women, 1 percent are women harassing men, and 9 percent are members of a given gender harassing their own (see Chap. 5).

The psychological symptoms and effects of harassment are well documented. They include anger, fear, depression, anxiety, and humiliation. Physical effects include headaches, loss of appetite, gastrointestinal disorders, and sleeplessness. According to Zeiger, the behavioral definition of harassment has four key elements:

1. It is sexual or sex-based behavior.
2. It is deliberate and repeated.
3. It is not wanted, not welcomed, and not returned.
4. It involves an abuse of power.

This kind of discrimination may be expressed verbally, nonverbally, or physically. One thing it is not—it is not about men versus women. Neither gender has the right to discriminate against the other in the workplace. As Zeiger says:

> There are no black-and-white rules for exactly what you can and can't say or do. As in all our relationships, it takes sensitivity, good judgment, and clear communication to treat others respectfully.

In fact, it is more of a gray area. In the fall of 1993, the Supreme Court issued a unanimous decision stating that a harassed individual did not have to show psychological injury—the standard for proving harassment in the past. Supreme Court Justice Sandra Day O'Connor wrote:

> Federal law comes into play before the harassment conduct leads to a nervous breakdown. While merely offensive conduct is not prohibited, an employer has broken the law if a reasonable person would find the workplace so filled with sexual improprieties that it became a hostile and abusive environment.[5]

With that kind of support from the Supreme Court, it is probable that an increased number of sexual harassment cases will be filed with the EEOC as well through the lower-court systems.

Any type of harassment and discrimination also produces another victim—business profitability. In 1993, a survey of Fortune 500 companies found that sexual harassment typically cost employers $6.7

million dollars a year in increased absenteeism, higher turnover, low morale, and low productivity.

If sexual harassment cost Fortune 500 companies $6.7 million a year and it didn't register within the top 10 GenderTraps for women in today's workplace, imagine what the cost of anger, fear, depression, anxiety, humiliation, headaches, sleeplessness, and physical disorders totals from problems created from the top 10 GenderTraps. If businesses would put their foot down and say enough is enough, profitability would be skyward bound!

INNUENDO OUT OF PLACE

Many women experience disappearing support. Judy works on the East Coast and is enjoying a new position selling hospital information systems. She reported that, in her previous employment, her manager had initially been very helpful and supportive. That is, until she started doing well. When her sales increased, when her performance was equivalent to and exceeded that of some of the men in the division, her manager became abusive, demanding, and even undermining.

> When I first joined the company, my manager was terrific. Out of 40 sales personnel, I ranked 38th. He kept assuring me that, as I learned more about their products, I would do well, and, as far as he was concerned, everything was fine.
>
> He was right. As I learned more about the product and sharpened my sales skills, I did get more business. I ended up number two out of 40 the second year. Coincidentally, at the same time, he became more difficult to work with and communicate with. He kept telling me I was doing everything wrong; that my methods in presenting and obtaining contracts were off the wall and inappropriate—the same methods that he applauded 6 months earlier.
>
> I knew that there was reorganization, and pressure was being put on our manager from the top. I believe I became his scapegoat; I was the only woman out of 40 people under his management.

When I asked whether any of her 39 colleagues noticed any disparity, she said it was fairly common to find that they were sympathetic toward her, even with comments such as "I don't know what his problem is" or "I can't believe he said those things to you."

It was easier for Judy to attempt to get along in the workplace. The only time that she spoke up was if something really got out of line. The person who was usually out of line was her former manager.

> I was at a meeting, and several of us were talking, including my manager. I saw someone whom I had been trying to get hold of for over a week, and excused myself to go talk to her. When I returned, I apologized for having to leave, but I had something that I had to take care of. My manager said, "I guessed that, or that you got your period." I immediately said to him that any discussion of my bodily functions in public, especially in front of my peers, wasn't a good idea. I didn't appreciate it.
>
> I later took him aside in private and explained to him that what he said was totally inappropriate, and, if he continued, I would tell someone who would make his life hell. In our organization, the managers were supposed to go through a special training course, such as sexual harassment. After the first day of the meeting, he blew it off and didn't want to take part.

Judy's boss is one of the Neanderthals who is, unfortunately, alive and thriving in today's workplace. As long as these toxic bosses and coworkers exist, the workplace will continue to fertilize sexism and harassing remarks.

GENDER BLIND...NOT

Today, Ann is the director of Minority Affairs at a medium-size college. Her primary purpose is to support the students of color. Her training is as a psychologist, and for much of her career she worked internally as one in the educational system. For the past 15 years she has been a management consultant in the human resources area.

Ann recalls that she was quite guarded about speaking up and stating what was on her mind when she started working. Today, she is not so hesitant. She says that in earlier parts of her career, she felt she was in a schizophrenic environment. At work she would dress, talk, and walk as was expected of someone in the corporate world. When she got home, she could let her hair down, put on "her" kind of clothing and music, and surround herself with the people who were more in tune with who she was and what she was about.

She remembers being involved with a major corporation for several years. As a black woman, she usually stood out. She was the only black female at social functions and events, and she was the only black woman with a professional title and responsibilities in all branches of the company. She found that it was not uncommon to see tokenism, sexism, and competency mixed up and confused.

> When I was hired, I was hired to do a specific job. I was the only black woman. The reason I got the job in the first place was that I was exceptional at what I did. I don't think that people intentionally meant malice, but when someone said, after you had accomplished the task that you were assigned to do, "How did she do this?" in amazement, all I could do was shake my head. Especially when you move into the higher levels.
>
> After I had been at the company for 6 months, there was a new product that they wanted to develop. It involved a retirement package, including a training program, that could be taken into companies and presented in either a workshop or counseling format. The project that I became involved in included the production of a manual that would teach people about retirement, help them make decisions, and so forth. What I didn't know was its history. When I went into that meeting, I discovered that it was a project that they had tried to put together for 5 years. Several senior vice presidents had attempted it and never made it go.
>
> At the meeting, there were several of my subordinates including secretaries and staff. I volunteered to take it on. I hadn't been made a vice president yet; I was an associate. In addition to myself, staff, and subordinates, there was the executive vice president and other vice presidents. The executive VP was conducting the meeting. He was enthusiastic that I agreed to take on the project, and would be the primary force in creating the new product for them. And then he added, in front of everybody, "This is going to make or break her in this company."
>
> When he said this, I couldn't believe it. I didn't know what was going on. It seemed like one of the "isms." I didn't know which—racism or sexism. I was furious. When he made this remark, everyone's face dropped in the meeting. Afterward, several people said to me, "I wouldn't want to be in your shoes right now." Instead of getting congratulations, I got, "Oh-oh, do you know the history of this product?"

When someone steps on your toes, makes remarks that are inappropriate or out of context, or makes a statement that could potentially sabotage your position or career, it is normal to feel anger. Ann said she was furious, but what she did was wise. She stepped back and started making connections with people—men and women she was close to—to get feedback. She didn't know whether the VP's remark was directed toward her because she was black or because she was a woman.

> I asked black men and I asked white men, all ages, all different walks of life. The unanimous opinion of every man asked was that it was not racism, it was sexism.

In reality, it could very well have been a combination of both. When women, and women of color, advance up the workplace ladder, it is not uncommon to hear remarks such as "We know how she got there," or "The only reason she's there is because she's a woman," or "She is black (or Hispanic, Asian, and so on)."

COLOR HER SUCCESSFUL

Today, Cathy is the principal of her own insurance agency. She ran into a reverse discrimination situation, as many of the respondents in the survey had. She recalled a situation that arose when she joined another agency 5 years ago, an agency that was family-owned. As with Ann, Cathy was the only black. She felt that she was discriminated against because she did too well and looked too good. She said that when she thinks about what she went through before she left to start her own agency, it still brings tears to her eyes.

> I took a lot of pride in my work, and I did it very efficiently and I was very good. Everyone there wanted to know things about me. I was well dressed at all times, I did my work, and I carried myself very well. The real animosity started right after I bought the Mercedes-Benz. It was like, "What in the world is this girl doing with a Mercedes-Benz?"
>
> They started picking on me. I don't know if they thought I was on drugs or selling them. How could I have gotten the money to buy the car? All of a sudden, the boss came in and wanted to know how I bought the car, and then his wife came to me, and everyone else; everyone in the agency wanted to know how I bought the car.
>
> When I put personalized license plates on it, they wanted to know who gave me that idea. They started to tell racial jokes. They nit-

picked at my appearance and my work. When the boss finally fired me, I asked why he was terminating me. He said, "For something you did 2½ years ago."

The old saying "People stick to their kind" certainly fit in Cathy's situation. She was different, she stood out, she did very well. With her best friend, she started a competing and very successful agency. It still, though, doesn't take away the hurt that she experienced.

THE WRONG FIT

Joyce is the senior analyst at a university. She works in a female-dominated environment. She remembers that during the previous year her department was told that it had to hire minorities. Her supervisor made the mistake of hiring a nonminority person. Because her department was female-dominated, she was told to hire a minority. The person hired was a black male. This black male now became Joyce's new supervisor. He lacked minimum qualifications. His skills were so bad, he was let go after 2 years.

> I had a black supervisor; he was male. After 2 years, he was let go; he was just totally not the right person for the job. I felt he was hired initially because he was black and there was pressure on our department from upper management. We were told we had to have ratios, and if we had too many men, or nonminority people, or not enough, that we had to do something about it. I agree with some of the affirmative action, but I also disagree with most of it. Some people are just not qualified.

Debbie is a training manager in a phone company located in the Southwest. Several of the managers as well as staff members are Hispanic. Debbie is not.

> No matter what I said, the majority of my coworker's—Hispanic males—opinions and voices carried far more weight than mine did. I found that when I had to criticize anyone, the group would band together against me.
>
> As a trainer, I was responsible for understanding the materials that were to be used as well as for having adequate presentation skills. It was not uncommon to be blamed, as a woman, and white, for not being able to communicate effectively.

EVERYONE HAS PREJUDICES

Many believe we live in a color-blind society, that racism no longer exists, and that everyone is on equal footing. To have that belief puts one in la-la land; it's just plain ignorance. It is nonsense to believe that thousands of years of cultural racism can be eliminated in the 30 years since the civil rights movement began. The color of one's skin is still a factor. Someday, we will routinely judge people by their character and quality, but it hasn't happened yet.

Any time we allow ourselves to be pulled into stereotyping a culture, race, or gender, it becomes easy to regress to overt racism. Think about it. It is not difficult to place cultures, races, and religions into a common stereotype. Once you get something embedded into your mind, it's very difficult to alter, much less erase, the programming of years past. Thirty years of civil rights does not undo the hundreds—thousands—of years of inequities among people.

Racism transcends discrimination—even bigotry—because it arises from assumptions and outlooks that most of us are unaware of. In the summer of 1994, ABC's *Prime Time* show did a segment on taxicab drivers—cabbies who would refuse to stop for black riders solely on the basis of visual input—the potential rider was black and standing at curbside.

Cab after cab passed by as the black man in the street continually called for a taxi. Viewers couldn't know what was going on in the driver's mind. It could have been, "He may have a gun, I'm not going to stop," or "He may want to go to a part of the city I don't want to drive to." When someone white further down the block beckoned the same cab that had passed the black person, it stopped immediately.

The driver's decision to stop or not to stop was blatantly racist. Ironically, the white person whom *Prime Time* put out there to beckon the cab turned out to be a convicted felon. The black was a professional athlete! Stereotyping and racism are alive.

SWITCHING SIDES

Racism has an ugly twin. It is called reverse racism. Some minorities believe that reverse racism is impossible; it is merely a form of payback, and should be considered fair play. When we get into reverse racism, which has surfaced as a complaint from some who question the extent of affirmative action programs, almost everyone has a story about an unqualified person who has been put into a position that is either the wrong fit or the wrong skill level.

Dr. Deborah L. Flick is the owner of Flick & Associates, a management consulting firm, and was a lecturer at the University of Colorado at Boulder for 15 years. She conducts assessments for Fortune 500 companies. Flick says that men, particularly white men, believe they can't get promoted or won't get hired, and every manager is looking to feather his or her affirmative action cap. In other words, white men don't have a chance. When she hears that kind of accusation, her response is to roll up her sleeves and probe into the data. When the assessments were done, she and the men who claimed unfair treatment found that, in fact, white men were getting hired and promoted at greater rates than people of color or white women.

> People grow accustomed to seeing people like themselves, white males, or, in some cases, white females, in certain positions, as managers or engineers, for example. What is in fact a privilege, over time, comes to be experienced as something that belongs rightly to one or one's group. Any time someone different occupies a position who hasn't been there before, it attracts extra attention. Even if it's only one example, the perception is, "It's happening everywhere." The fear is that "they" are taking over. The belief is, "What is rightfully mine is being unfairly taken away." I refer to this distorted perception as resulting from the experience of *privilege deprivation*. It can lead to false claims of reverse discrimination.
>
> *Privilege deprivation* is the psychological dynamic that is set into motion when a shift occurs and white women and people of color begin to move into positions previously exclusively held by white males. It is like a Copernican revolution (where the sun supplanted the earth as center of the solar-system universe). If you've been accustomed to being at the center of things, as white males have been, and now you are just one more planet in the orbital field, the adjustment is very difficult.[6]

Numerous companies have put out the word that only women need apply. With all the media directed toward the glass ceiling scenario, some managements have tapped into the fact that they do need to diversify, and bring in something besides the white male. According to feminist lawyer Gloria Allred, "this may be a ticking time-bomb waiting to go off."[7]

When businesses exclude men from consideration of a lucrative managerial post, they risk reverse sex bias, sex discrimination lawsuits. In addition, such exclusion is bound to create a disruptive loss of morale among other male employees.

Kathleen manages various projects for a finance company that has 2000 employees nationwide. Headquarters are located on the West Coast where 400 are based. Only three women hold executive positions in the entire company. She has also noticed that sexism and discrimination are alive and well. Several women have been routinely passed over for men, men who don't have the qualifications and education of the women who were bypassed.

> I don't have an MBA; neither do many of the men. In fact, several who have moved into senior-level positions don't have college degrees at all.

Today, much of sexism is covert, behind the scenes, or coming from a side angle. It is not uncommon for women to be left out of events or have events put together that would not be as receptive to women as to men. Golf has been one of the classic male domains. Within the past few years women have begun to take up clubs, tee off, and head for the greens.

Bonny, an IRS attorney, feels she is very much a minority and left out of the loop.

> It's not that we don't have a good working relationship, but I find that my male colleagues and I have different interests. The only time I'm included when they play golf is when they invite all the spouses.

Anyone who works in sales knows that there is always some type of contest. One of the incentives in any contest is a reward. Many workplaces have tapped into the fact that, not only are women in sales, but they also win the rewards. Unfortunately, sometimes rewards are the wrong fit, the wrong size, the wrong type.

Lona has been in sales for years and has won just about every type of promotion and reward offered. Today in the mid-1990s, she feels that the majority of the sales promotion trips are geared toward the men in the company. Lona reports:

> My company is always surprised when women either win or they are not motivated to compete. Most recently, there was a promotion that was based on production. The prize was a football, an NFL jacket, and a cap. I won the jacket and the cap along with a note from the front office saying that the football was on the way.

Another time we did a water rafting trip. It wasn't really a lot of fun to be on a float trip with 35 men. I finally said to my manager, "You know, I don't know if this would ever happen, but either substitute a day such as a day of pampering for the women, or consider doing a spa day as a reward for both men and women. After all, manicures, pedicures, and massages are good for everybody."

THE ROUND TABLE IS SQUARE

Nancy also grumbled about the recognition generated within her industry. She considers herself very successful as an insurance agent. The second year she was in the business, she made the Million-Dollar Round Table. The percentage of women who make it to the Round Table is very low as compared to men.

When I went to my first meeting, I was shocked to see the faces. Of approximately 4000, an estimated 200 were women. As I walked down the hall I would be congratulated, but with a surprised look, as if, "How could she possibly do this?" For the men, it was a pat on the back and no questioning or attitude or how they did it. Insurance companies' sales prizes are also very sexist. Top prizes are a man's navy blue sports coat and a company looking school ring.

Sexism is often expressed in more subtle and covert ways. It can take a variety of forms. One of the forms is that of exclusion. The golfing, rafting, and jock activities are a form of exclusion. Other forms include when women are left out of decision making, important meetings, or business trips, or when their opinions and suggestions are ignored.

SECOND-CLASS ATTITUDES

Discrimination and sexism rooted in religious beliefs still exist in many workplaces. Gladys worked in management with an Adventist hospital on the East Coast. In her hospital, almost all department heads were men, except nursing. She felt that she stuck out like a sore thumb.

The Adventist cultural value says that women are subservient. I didn't fit in. It's just not my style to be subservient. When they spoke to me I was supposed to sit there, be quiet, speak when spoken to and when I had problems, not to go to other department directors and try to work things out.

I was too direct for them. I was told I would never move up within the organization because I wasn't an Adventist. It did not matter how good I was.

Polly is a web press operator. Her skills produce the sales promotions and flyers that are routinely distributed in the newspapers, particularly Sunday's. There are very few women in her profession. She finds she has to put up with a lot of BS, name calling, and an overall attitude that women are subservient and inferior.

All the men I work with are lazy. They view that, because I'm a female, I can clean up after them. When I notice the other men working together, when one spills ink, either he or the other will clean it up, and they take care of each other. But when I am involved in the team, it doesn't matter who spills or drops stuff, I'm expected, as the female, to clean it up.

It's a tough area to work in. Most of the men feel that women shouldn't be here. The result is that you have to prove yourself, and be determined to stick with it. One of the foremen I worked with always catered to the guys. Whenever I had a complaint, he ignored it.

Subtle—or modern—sexism also surfaces in the annual meeting that many companies have. Marsha attended her company's annual convention. In overall sales, she ranked in the top 21 percent. After about 6 hours of all-male stories and bravado, she left the convention and walked back to the hotel where her husband was. When asked why she left, her reply was:

I'm not going back. I'm tired of the sexism, with both the overt and subliminal remarks. My husband said, "It can't be that bad," and he decided to attend the next session with me. Now, he is from the South, and very much supportive of what I've done to achieve the success within the company I had. After about 20 minutes, he turned to me and said, "Let's get out of here, this is offensive."

STEREOTYPES CREATE ABSURD EXPECTATIONS

Oppression and prejudice are soulmates. Oppression is defined as the mistreatment of a group of humans by society or other groups of humans because of an arbitrary characteristic such as skin color, gender, weight, age, and nationality. In other words, all the "isms" mentioned before are included: racism, sexism, ageism, and lookism.

Upbringing and societal conditioning limit both men and women. Men are conditioned into assuming roles that often deny them emotions and feelings and require them to behave in ways that can be damaging to strong and cooperative relationships between both men and women.

Messages men receive are transmitted by parents, schools, media, movies, TV, friends, colleagues, and so on. These messages create a stereotypical image of what a man is supposed to be in his behavior, his attitude, even his activities.

Messages that women get from the same types of sources are that they are less human or capable than men—the second-class citizens. Pervasive stereotypes about women include that they are not as strong or as capable or as smart as men; that they are emotionally weak, dependent, and easily victimized. Women need men to take care of them, and they're not whole without men in their lives. Women are in competition with one another for the available men as caretakers; women should put others first; and women should be seductive and physically attractive, to get a man. It is assumed by most women and men that women are the providers of nurturing, compassion, tenderness, and emotions.

Female behavior patterns that emerge from these stereotypical expectations include:

- Women devalue their own work and that of other women.
- Women don't take pride in their accomplishments.
- Women often settle for less than what they really want.
- Women will deny that sexism exists.
- Women will discount their own thinking and opinions.
- Women defer to men when they are speaking.
- Women focus on their physical appearance as more important than their personality or contributions.
- Women allow men to touch them or have sex with them when they don't want it.

Male behaviors and expectations that emerge include:

- Men have difficulty in expressing feelings.

- Men are insensitive to the feeling of others.
- Men have fewer close male friends with whom they can share personal information with.
- Men have fewer close, nonsexual female friends.
- Men substitute sex for closeness.
- Men are more likely to misuse alcohol, drugs, and food.
- Men are responsible for the survival and financial well-being of women and children.
- All other men are competitors.
- Men are different from women intellectually, emotionally, physically, spiritually, and sexually.
- Men should be strong and stoic, and the only feelings they show should be those of anger.
- Men must not be vulnerable.
- Men are the disposable sex in the pursuit of higher causes (God, country, and so on).
- Men shouldn't be close or affectionate with women unless it is sexual.
- Men should be creative or expressive only in "male" activities such as sports and business.

Underneath the blanket of society's expectations of the stereotype, a different picture can emerge. The reality is that women are intelligent, capable, and independent, have great courage and strength, can think clearly, can be loving, compassionate, sensitive, and vulnerable—and so can men. The stereotypes that are imposed on men and women as small children, and then reinforced as they grow up, are etched deeply. It takes a lot of work and commitment to change.

SOCIETY'S FULFILLING PROPHECIES

Everyone has prejudices, according to consultant Stephanie West Allen. One of the exercises she does when she presents her Psychology of Prejudice program is to identify different groups, such as women, men, blacks, Native Americans, and Asians. Participants are encouraged to call out "descriptors" of each group. Responses range anywhere from "bad driver" to "manipulator" to the more common "breadwinner." It is amazing how long these lists become.

West Allen points out that the mere fact that these lists are created shows that a conditioned prejudice is always in the background of one's mind. She identifies this as being "mindful." Each of us can tap into what we carry around internally—deep-rooted, internal expectations that can lead to self-fulfilling prophecies which can happen anywhere. Consider the Pygmalion concept in a classroom:

> Two teachers have the same types of kids. One teacher was told that her kids were brilliant, and she would have a great time throughout the year. The other was told that the kids were dumb and to do whatever she could do to get through. At the end of the year the kids were tested. The ones with the teacher who thought they were brilliant performed at a much higher level than the group whose teacher thought her kids were barely functional.

> *Mirroring is crucial. If somebody treats you as if you are a "somebody," you'll begin to act as if you are. If somebody treats you as if you are worthless, over a period of time, you will begin to reflect or mirror those expectations.*

Business and management are reluctant to connect what happens in society—the stereotyping and prejudices—with the workplace. It is impossible to keep the two separate. You don't leave issues, whether they are racism, sexism, or discrimination out on the street when you come through the workplace door Monday through Friday. When the door opens, your concerns, fears, biases, and stereotypes enter into relationships with coworkers, managers, and customers. According to broadcaster and author Studs Terkel, racism is America's great obsession.

> Racism is an issue that has been with us since the first slave ship landed in 1692, yet it is difficult for white society to admit its racism. As one black journalist said, our country, which was founded on principles of enlightenment, practiced slavery. It requires plenty of denial to have those two conditions existing simultaneously. Today racism and its denial are, to this day, indelible parts of our culture.[8]

Terkel is right. Racism is a part of everyone's life and will not go away overnight.

THE WORKPLACE'S DIRTY LITTLE SECRET

So is lookism, another fact of life. Just ask former CBS morning personality Kathleen Sullivan. In 1994, she resurfaced as spokesperson for Weight Watchers. Prior to her reemergence, she had been ceremoniously dumped by CBS because of three widely publicized factors: she'd gained a little weight, she'd gotten a divorce, and, horror of horrors, she'd let her hair go gray.

Her new position got the media's attention. All of a sudden, she was in *People* magazine and wanted by the talk shows. People returned her calls. An interview on Tom Snyder's CNBC show revealed that her exile had been very painful. As I watched her interact with Snyder and take calls from listeners, I was deeply impressed with her intelligence, her wit, and her spontaneity, and was appalled that anyone would want to let this talent go. (By the way, Kathleen Sullivan is a superb golfer.)

Lookism is the workplace's dirty little secret. Unfortunately, women across the country experience lookism as a fact of life. It is quite common for employers to keep a negative stereotype or opinion about race and gender to themselves. When stereotypes about looks surface, it seems to be acceptable. Discrimination against overweight women is the most rampant form of lookism.

Esther Rothblum, Ph.D. is a professor at the University of Vermont and researches attitudes about obese people. One of her studies found that 60 percent of obese women and 30 percent of moderately overweight women reported that they had not been hired or not been promoted because of their weight. One woman in Rothblum's study reported that she gained 90 pounds after being put on steroids for a hand injury. When she physically showed up for interviews, she was rejected. Typical comments were "She wasn't right for the position" and "The position has already been filled."[10]

HYPOCRISY IS ALIVE, AND TOO WELL

Women's weight matters more than men's. Most employment experts say that overweight men are more likely to be hired than overweight women. Terri Smith-Croxton is president of J.D. and Associates, an executive search firm in Arlington, Texas. She reported that she had sent a female candidate who was well-groomed, but overweight, for a position. She wasn't hired—because her weight was a problem. Smith-Croxton says that the company then asked to set up an interview with a male candidate whose résumé she had forwarded. When she told them he was heavier than the female candidate they had just seen, their response was, "That's OK, as long as he's neat."

Unfortunately, many employers view an overweight man as someone who doesn't feel his looks are important, whereas they assume an overweight woman is lazy and has little or no self-control. In 1993, the Harvard School of Public Health surveyed over 10,000 young adults over a 17-year period and found that overweight women pay a price for their poundage. The report, published in the *New England Journal of Medicine,* found that obese women are 10 percent more likely to have incomes below the poverty level.

No matter how well they do on intelligence tests, fat women earn $6710 less a year than other women with the same credentials and job skills. And women who are overweight are vulnerable to being fired, even though the Americans with Disabilities Act covers obesity. In Rhode Island, a federal discrimination suit was upheld in 1993, allowing a 320-pound woman to get her job back.

Overweight people aren't the only victims of this lookism nonsense. Employers can see a woman with gray hair and assume she is not modern and informed about current trends or doesn't know how to run a computer. The opposite can also hold true. A woman may be young or look young and find herself rejected for a position she is well qualified for.

Employers must be educated to the fact that a lot of wisdom can come with gray hair and wrinkles, that many young people have extraordinary savvy, and that some people who carry more weight may be perfectly healthy.

THROUGH THE AGING GLASS

On the coattails of lookism is ageism. With the downsizing of the 1990s, the majority of the discrimination complaints filed with the EEOC are for age discrimination. Retirement and a gold watch at age 65 have become the impossible dream for many.

Among the most likely "layoffs" are people over 50. Primarily, they cost more money. Companies seem to forget that there are substantial monies invested in the experience of a long-term employee. Terminating the over-50 and retaining or hiring the "kid" because of a lower salary could very well come back to haunt the downsizing 1990s.

BIRDS OF A FEATHER

Other forms of discrimination surfaced from the surveys. One was *levelism,* or discrimination against others because they are at a different level or status. Many of the women who worked in positions that would be considered nonmanagement reported experiences in which those in positions above them viewed them as having less worth or value. An example is an administrative assistant who views a receptionist as being in a lower status. Whether the receptionist is a male or a female would not matter. The status of the position is the key factor.

The old adage "Birds of a feather flock together" surfaces in adversive racism and adversive sexism. What was said openly about the opposite sex and another race in the 1970s just isn't said today. There are different standards for acting and talking. Internally, though, attitudes and minds may not have changed. Your internal dialogue can't shout and be bold about its prejudices.

In order to fit into today's societal norms, women and men must curtail their external behavior, not necessarily their internal attitudes. In adversive racism, if you are prejudiced against an ethnic group, such as Hispanics, you would make an effort to avoid being and working with people who are Hispanic, because you have to use extra energy to curtail your attitude and behavior toward them.

If you find that working with men is negative, you would use extra energy to curtail your negative attitude toward them. The result could come out in a type of abrasive or negative behavior. With the expanding diversity of the workplace, adverse attitudes become more difficult to control.

The political correctness arena is also a button pusher. Some of it makes sense, and at other times absurdities set in. The position that equality means sameness is equally foolish. The practical reality is that there are situations where a woman is most likely to be the leader, and other situations where a man should take the leadership helm. In most cases, gender shouldn't have much to do with it. The prevailing qualifiers should be skills and talent.

Most supporters of affirmative action believe that the playing field should continue to be leveled. It is too disproportionately in favor of men and, in particular, Caucasians. Others argue that too many people fill positions who are incompetent and got their jobs solely because of gender or race.

Both views are correct. The impact of change is felt more deeply and rapidly today than in the 1980s and 1970s or any decade prior. With the guarantee of continual change, all businesses need the best talent to lead and manage the way. If you have the best credentials, skills, and talent, the job should be yours. Gender, race or nationality should be a secondary consideration. I believe that quotas are bad business for both employee and employer.

Many of the affirmative action mandates may be coming to an end. In 1995, a backlash began to spread in America: No more quotas. The belief that affirmative action is a gravy train is commonplace. Some people feel it has become a way for minority politicians to take care of their cronies, or a means of getting a job for those who don't have the skills or credentials to obtain one. Those who *are* qualified can't get jobs because of affirmative action mandates.

The ideal way to eliminate the need for any affirmative action measures is to simply eliminate the actions of prejudice and discrimination. Then the people who get the jobs are the most qualified. It doesn't matter where they are from, what their culture is, or what gender they are.

The savvy leader and manager today needs to accept the fact that both men and women have the abilities and vision that stem from both their biology and physiology as well as learned abilities that allow them to cross over and excel in areas that have been traditionally held by the other gender.

That prejudice and its multioffspring are the greatest GenderTraps in the workplace is no surprise. The surprise is that it continues to breed, generation after generation. This is one area that cannot be solved by apathy or denial. Nor can it be resolved by wishing it away. You, your friends, coworkers, and family must strive for making a difference and altering the damage that destructive prejudicial actions promise.

Communications: Translating your message into a clear, concise statement or concept that the receiver understands.

TRAP 2: COMMUNICATIONS BARRIERS

- Have you ever had your "voice" drowned out by louder or more persistent voices?
- Have you ever felt that you understood what someone said and found out later that you misinterpreted what was said?
- Have you ever not spoken up or out about a situation out of concern that others might think negatively about you?
- Have you ever communicated your thoughts, strategies, or concerns to others after the meeting is over?
- Have you ever felt that your turn would come to express your opinion?

When most people think of power, they think of money. For some, that may be true. In reality, power comes in other forms. The real power in today's workplace comes from communicating: being able to speak loudly and clearly so that what you meant to convey is understood, and having the verbal savvy to articulate your words in the right context.

Communication also involves superior listening skills—yours. It always amazes me that when I do a book that involves personal interviews, such as the ones used throughout *GenderTraps*, I often get notes from respondents telling me I am a fascinating person to talk to. Although I don't think I am a dullard, these comments amuse me when I think about the majority of interviews that I do. During an interview, I ask only a few key questions.

In this book, those who were interviewed had completed the initial survey. During the interview, I would recite back what they wrote on the survey, and then add the line "Tell me about it." Then they would start talking. I might probe here and there to get further information, but as a rule my conversation was more along the lines of "mmm" and "ohh." It was my subject who did the great majority of the talking; I just listened.

According to communications expert Dianna Booher, author of dozens of books, including *Communicate with Confidence: How to Say It Right the First Time and Every Time*:

> Communication is the soul of management: analysis and solid decisions translate into clear messages that influence people to act and feel good about their performance.[1]

Booher goes on to say that whether it is a valid or invalid measure, the lack of communications skills tags people as being less confident, less attractive, and less qualified as leaders. In her book, she has over 1000 tips (actually 1042) on how to communicate effectively with anyone about anything at any time and anywhere.

According to the dictionary, *communi-* means together; *-ation* means duties or responsibilities. In other words, *communication* means together, duties or responsibilities. If communication is going to work, there are duties and responsibilities for both the listener—receiver—and the speaker—activator—of the dialogue.

THE LANGUAGE OF SILENCE

For 6 years, I had the opportunity to work with the Miss America Pageant as a member of its Women's Advisory Council. Most of my work was behind the scenes as a speaking coach. I've had the opportunity to work on speaking style, mannerisms, phrasing, and stories—with the media and with several of the Miss Americas. I've learned about the inner city, AIDS, education, domestic violence, and the homeless.

In 1995 Miss America was Heather Whitestone, a woman who was extraordinarily talented and a fabulous communicator. What made her so good? She spoke with her eyes, her gestures, and her body language. Heather learned early on that over 90 percent of communication is nonverbal—which was an important asset for her. Why? Because Heather Whitestone is deaf.

It's ironic that many in the deaf community expressed anger at Whitestone because she chose to speak, rather than solely "sign." Here was a talented young woman who had stretched and overcame an adversity.

The deaf should have joined millions of others who applauded Heather Whitestone's tenacity and vision. Instead their voices actually sabotaged her and undermined her value within their community.

At the news conference, the morning after she was named as Miss America, she had to tell the reporters to stop talking and stop "flashing." All of them were clamoring for attention, speaking at the same time. Heather said, "You are all talking so loudly, I can't hear you." To those with cameras, she said, "Please stop taking pictures. I can't hear because of the flash." Heather reads lips. With everyone talking at the same time, she couldn't hear. With the cameras flashing, she couldn't see to hear.

Communication is much more than just words. Tone, inflection, and facial expression account for approximately 93 percent of your message—words, a mere 7 percent. The key components of nonverbal communication include body posture, eye contact, distance and physical contact, vocal tone, inflection, volume, gestures, facial expression, even clothing.

When I have coached the various Miss Americas as well as several friends who speak professionally, I've had to learn about their topic, listen to their stories, ask what they want to project and get across, and find out what their comfort levels are in speaking as well as where they are willing to stretch. Then, and only then, can I make suggestions on how to rework, rephrase, restyle, and recommunicate with their audiences. It's really no different for you—whether you are communicating with your family, your coworkers, or individuals you don't know on a personal level.

BEING A RESPONSIBLE COMMUNICATOR

When it comes to any speaker, her first responsibility is to speak loudly enough to enable the listener to hear whatever the message is. The listener's primary responsibility is to hear or receive the message generated by the speaker.

The second responsibility of the speaker is to speak clearly. For the listener, it is to understand what the speaker is saying.

The third obligation of the speaker is to communicate in terms and words that will be of interest to the listener. When possible, the speaker should use their jargon, their word phrases, and examples that can be easily identified and related to. The listener's responsibility is to appreciate the message. This doesn't mean the listener must necessarily agree with what the message is, but must appreciate that it is coming across in a communication style and language that is understood.

Finally, the speaker must be specific. Don't just fill the air with words; be prepared to ask for help, deliver a plan, and so on. For the listener, the responsibility then will be to participate in the request and act on it. This means the listener may not agree and may choose not to comply with the request.

According to communications expert and author Bert Decker, in *You've Got to Be Seen to Be Heard,* it is imperative to understand that most communication is nonverbal, with the majority coming from gestures, tones, and body language. This means that, as a speaker, the last thing you want to do is to speak or present in a straight-faced, dull, monotone, statuelike delivery. Guaranteed, within seconds, at the most minutes, your listeners will be looking over shoulders, at walls, at other people, at their hands, or through their notes, or doing anything else that is deemed an alternative to listening to you.

Listeners listen with their ears and their eyes. Within an audience, they also listen with the sensing of those around them. It is not difficult to pick up whether others are agreeing or disagreeing with, enjoying or not enjoying, what is being presented.

No one is born or, for that matter, wakes up suddenly and decrees they know how to communicate. Communication is a learned behavior. The first component in becoming a terrific communicator is to learn how to be a terrific listener. And with that comes an understanding that men and women, cultures and races, have different communication styles.

COMMUNICATING CAN BE A FOREIGN LANGUAGE

Marlene is a controller of a manufacturing company on the East Coast. There are two men beside herself in senior management of the company. At times, she thinks they speak a foreign language.

When we have strategy meetings, a lot of the times I feel my goals and the things I would like to see done are never understood or heard. I don't believe the other two—the men—are tuned into the communication differences between men and women—me. There are too many times when I don't think they hear what I say.

Holly, a director of customer services, faces a different type of communications problem. She reports that working within her organization is comparable to walking on eggshells. Communication is poor to nil. While her company is presently financially healthy, she finds communication between management and her employees so bad that she feels someday soon all the small fires will explode and grow out of control. The majority of Holly's staff is under 30—the Generation Xers.

My staff is fantastic. They work long and hard hours; they increase the volume of customer contacts and routinely exceed quotas set by senior management. The problem is that management doesn't recognize the staff. At least, they don't recognize the staff the way the staff would like to be recognized.

Managers here seem to be stuck in a time warp. When employees reach specific goals, management's style for rewarding them is to buy them lunches every 2 or 3 months. In the summer, there is a picnic; and in December there is a Christmas party. One time, the staff people got a sweatshirt; another, they got a watch. But that's not what the staff wants.

What they say is, "Keep your money, keep all your toys and trinkets; just talk to us. Listen to us. If you want to recognize us above and beyond, either say so with a bonus—money, even a few dollars—or simply say 'Thank you, you did a great job.'"

Now, the staff is not asking for a lot of money; they could use the bonuses. What they don't want is to have money wasted on lunches, especially when lunch is presented as more of a spur-of-the-moment thought. One time, I didn't know they were going to give a "reward luncheon." A majority of us were in the cafeteria and lunch was actually delivered to the tables where we were sitting. We'd already paid for our own lunches.

Holly has several legitimate complaints. First, few people have telepathic skills. Unless management communicates clearly and directly that there is a "reward," employees will continue to do what they have done in the past. In the case of the "reward lunch," if managers are going to treat employees to lunch, at least they should say so ahead of time.

Second, the reward that management chooses to deliver doesn't appear to be a "fit" for the employees. It wouldn't be difficult to ask them what their "druthers" were if certain levels of performance were achieved. And when those levels were attained, management could acknowledge it and deliver the appropriate reward—a simple action that can create harmony in the workplace.

Miscommunication and noncommunication can create tremendous conflict in the office. Brenda is an office manager for a construction firm in the Midwest. She grumbles that senior management thinks she has telepathic skills. Her frustration levels increase when she is caught between senior management and the subcontractors: Everyone expects her to know who says what to whom, even if she hasn't communicated directly with any of the parties involved.

> My department is responsible for preparing documents called submittals, in which subcontractors have to give to the main contractor or the owner of a facility specific specifications, diagrams, and instrument lists. The raw data for the submittals must come from the engineers. My department is the final step. When they are received, they are proofed, compiled, and then delivered to the main contractor.
>
> When the main contractor doesn't get it in a timely basis, they are immediately on the phone—or physically in my office and demand to know why they don't have what they need. My response is that I can't go any faster. If the subs don't supply the information (or the contractor) on what I need to go after, I can't move it any faster.
>
> What is also difficult is that there are many times when I'm not included in meetings when changes are made or information and concepts are created. This makes everyone in our department crazy. We assemble the various packages and find out after our work is completed and delivered that some procedures are no longer in effect. The package is, therefore, wrong. I have no problem being a traffic cop; I just have to know which direction traffic is going to flow.

Throughout the interviews for *GenderTraps*, it was not uncommon to hear a phrase such as "I was zinged" or "I was zapped" by someone. Typically the issue wasn't noncommunication, but rather misconstrued communication. Melanie is a nurse manager in a large hospital in California. There are three other managers who work in the emergency department. All report to one director. It is not uncommon for a manager to compile various problems and wrongdoings—various gnats of the workplace—put them into her complaint bag, and take them to the monthly meetings.

> It is routine for one of the managers to gather up various problem situations, most of them quite minor, such as "Suzie was 10 minutes late to work," and bring them to our monthly manager/director meetings. All the problems would be unloaded at that time, and as a result the director began to believe that we couldn't handle anything on our floors.

> The other nurse manager and I would respond to her that it would be much more helpful to resolve whatever the problem is by bringing it to us immediately, or at least by the next day when it involves another shift. Why hold it off for several weeks and put us on the spot as if we were incompetent?

> It wasn't uncommon for me and the other nurse manager to zap her back with a laundry list of problems. Finally, after attending a program where we heard you speak, we decided to bring it to a head and explain how it felt to be zinged. Initially, the manager denied it. But we were prepared; we cited various examples. We finally all agreed that we did have communication problems, and have agreed to keep talking to try to resolve it. So, it's a first step.

THE FIRST STEPS

Melanie indicates that talking it out is a first step, and she is correct. She and the other manager waited over a year before they finally confronted the third manager on her methodology of identifying and presenting problems. Many problems were construed as minor ones that should have been dealt with immediately, before they had the opportunity to mushroom. If minor salvos of the workplace are not dealt with, they become ammunition. In Melanie's situation, they became ammunition that was delivered in the monthly meetings with the director.

When one individual zaps another, whether it is a staff employee or someone in management, it definitely leaves a bad taste. A common—and in some places, expected—reaction is to zap back. The zinging and zapping become a vicious cycle, and if not nipped in the budding stages, are likely to infest the workplace, turning it toxic. Morale and cooperation plummet.

Another factor that is insidious within the workplace is gossip. Both men and women gossip, but women tend to be more probing and to obtain more personal information that can be spread about. As the health services administrator at a jail on the West Coast, Deb feels that workplace gossip is counterproductive and extremely negative. She constantly counsels her staff not to feed into it. In keeping ongoing communications on line, Deb has supported an open-door policy. She has found that innocent, casual statements have been misinterpreted and circulated among those in her workplace.

> In the past, it wasn't uncommon for me to respond to anyone who came to my office door to come on in and sit down. When they started to talk about their family and what they do on their days off, I would listen and make casual comments. The next thing I knew, everyone in the jail knows what I like to do, where I live, and what my hobbies are. I learned that it is very easy to be misquoted.
>
> I've learned to document everything I say. Before I call people into my office, I write it out. I then say only what is on the piece of paper. After I tell them whatever it is I need to tell them, I have them sign the paper when I finish, so there is some basis for agreement upon what was said—and what wasn't said.

Unfortunately, most people are on automatic when they communicate. Sometimes the brain is not put in gear before the mouth opens. Speech patterns are learned early on and engaged with little thought. Childhood speech characteristics are deeply imprinted by the time a woman reaches adulthood. A native speech pattern, whether it is stuttering, having your speech littered with "umms" and "ahhs," or even slurring words, can damage your credibility.

APOLOGIZING, HEDGING, AND QUALIFYING

Another factor that appears to have a greater drawback for women than for men is the use of "polite" speech. On one side, it shows a high regard and respect for another. That's not bad. Some cultures covet this behavior. But there are times when too polite speech lacks the necessary assertiveness or forcefulness. In almost every book on communication, there is mention of women's use of "tag" questions or qualifiers. Whether women use them more than men do, is not clear. There is a debate. The important fact is for you to be aware if you do use them. Typical "tag" questions include:

"This needs to be completed by four o'clock. Is that OK with you?"

"We need to be at the meeting at 10 tomorrow morning. Is that a problem for you?"

Where the first sentence is declarative, the second sentence—the "tag"—can be interpreted as a window for choice. The receiver of the remark may say, "No, it's not OK with me." Other factors of nonassertive speech patterns that can get you into trouble include the use of qualifiers.

Qualifiers are often interpreted as a form of discounting what is being said. Qualifiers are hedges—words or phrases that make you sound uncertain: "You know," "Sorta," "I guess," "I suppose." When you are uncertain, qualifiers are perfectly legitimate. But as fillers or hedges, they lessen your power when communicating with another. Well-known examples of beginning-sentence phrases are:

"I'm not sure that this is a good idea, but…"

"You may think this is dumb (stupid, silly, idiotic)…"

Women also get into trouble when they use too many adverbs or adjectives. The result is that their speech is sometimes trivialized. Two examples are: "It's so lovely and wonderful to be here today" and "I think this is so very wonderful, exciting, and fabulous. I know it's going to be beyond belief."

Sometimes, women feel inhibited to ask for something boldly. So as not to appear so bold, it is common to soften a statement. Let's say you want to go to lunch. Instead of saying, "Let's go to lunch," to a coworker, you might say:

"Gosh, I'm famished, and I've been so busy: would you like…Oh, you're probably really busy too, and don't have time to take a break…Or do you think you'd like to get a bite to eat with me?"

Because many women are process-oriented in their relationships, they are that way with answers and explanations as well. When someone asks you something, it's not uncommon to tell the reasons in detail of how you arrived at your answer. Some people love to hear all the details; others don't. They'd rather you focus on the bottom-line impact.

> *Women need to learn goal-oriented language in order to relate their messages more effectively.*

When people apologize, it is usually an expression of regret at having done something wrong to another. Unfortunately, women are harder and more judgmental of themselves when it comes to accepting or taking on blame. Men tend to apologize only when it is expected or when it can't be avoided. In fact, sometimes men never say "I'm sorry." Instead, they make another statement with the "I'm sorry" implied, as in "I screwed up."

One of the reasons men avoid apologizing is that it tends to put them in an inferior position. Since women are often people pleasers, being apologetic doesn't make them feel put down. According to Deborah Tannen, Ph.D. and author of *You Just Don't Understand:*

> There are many ways that women talk that make sense and are effective in conversation with other women. When in conversation with men, they appear powerless and self-depreciating. One such pattern is that women seem to apologize all the time.[2]

One thing to keep in mind is that it is not necessary to apologize over a situation over which you have no control. If a land mine is exposed (or explodes), it's sufficient to state whatever the problem is (minus any apologies), followed by recommended solutions to fix it. What Tannen implies is that when the issue is between women, it's OK to apologize; in fact, it can be advantageous in creating a bond and even encouraging intimacy. For men, though, apologizing may be construed as a weakness.

Another common speech faux pas is inviting disagreement. When you have a strong opinion about a situation, or you require someone's participation, it doesn't make sense to preface your statement or request with a disclaimer:

"I may be wrong, but..."

"You may not like what I'm going to say, but..."

Not only do such statements lessen your speech and presence power; they also invite your listeners to move into a defensive posture, and disagree with you before you have a chance even to make a statement.

Being friendly can do wonders in the right place at the right time, but it also can be a distraction. Don't chit-chat excessively.

Women tend to disclose more personal information than men do. Personal talk and disclosure may indicate that you are friendly and open, but it also can work against you. Too much self-disclosure may dilute whatever messages you are attempting to get across. If your objective is to talk to your boss about a raise, you will probably be most effective by saying "I deserve a raise because...." Then lay out the points that support your request.

If you need to take a day off, whether for a personal appointment or for mental health (e.g., because you are exhausted), the request "I need tomorrow off" carries far more clout than something like "I know you are really busy, and I hate to bother you, but do you think it would be all right if I took tomorrow off?" Most bosses will appreciate it if you just say what you need. If they request an explanation, give one. Otherwise, keep it short and simple.

MANNERISMS TO AVOID

Unassertive-type mannerisms can get women into trouble. As a rule, women are more inclined to create eye contact with the person they are talking to. That's the good news; don't avoid it. Good eye contact is a communications gesture that should be mastered early on. With it, you are more likely to be taken seriously. If you constantly hop around with your eyes, rarely connecting with the person you are talking to, your remarks can easily be interpreted as meaning you're not serious, or you're nervous. A subtle message can be sent that your concern, opinion, or statement is not important. When you don't make eye contact with someone, you can signal fear or submissiveness, or even invite interruption.

In groups consisting of all women, women interrupt one another. In groups consisting of all men, men interrupt one another. But in mixed groups, men are far more inclined to interrupt women than women are to interrupt men. Keep your gaze steady and firm when in conversation. The person you are communicating with is far more likely to take you seriously than when you let your eyes wander every which way.

In addition to using speech patterns that are unassertive, women are far more likely to smile inappropriately, especially during times of conflict, than are men. It is not uncommon for both men and women to interpret a smile during a stressful or conflicting time as a signal that it's OK, you're OK, and the problem or stress is not as big a deal as you feel it is. It is also not uncommon, during stress-ful and painful times, for women to laugh or, worse, giggle. One of the best things that a woman can do is learn to keep a straight face, especially when it comes to business.

Remember when Anita Hill testified at the Senate hearings, before Clarence Thomas was affirmed as a justice of the Supreme Court? During those hearings, when various questions, innuendoes, and even accusations were directed toward Hill from the committee members, it was not uncommon to see her nodding slightly or bob-bing her head. That type of mannerism sends off confusing signals.

Normally, when listeners nod their head up and down, most people assume that they agree with the speaker. Not necessarily so. Women appear to be more inclined to nod their heads during a con-versation than do men—even though they don't agree with what's being said. It's more of a mannerism of taking information in. I sus-pect that during the Thomas hearings, the thoughts in Anita Hill's head were probably more along the lines that several of the senators who questioned her were actually bozos. Head bobbing and nodding can make you appear submissive, or that you agree with someone, when you actually aren't or don't.

The Communications Savvy Quiz in Fig. 4-1 is designed to bring up your awareness on gender differences. Answer true or false to see how well you understand women and men. A score of 19–21 is excellent; 16–18 is good; 13–15 is fair; 14 or less is big trouble. If you score less than 15, it's critical that you go back to basic Communications 101. Ask a close friend to give you honest feed-back about your speaking and listening styles. You need help.

CONFLICTS HAPPEN

One of the myths of the workplace is that conflicts are an indication of poor management, poor relationships, and at times general chaos. Granted, these factors surface with conflicts. But they are created when conflicts don't get resolved. In reality, conflicts are normal; it is how they are managed that makes the difference. Too often, communications barriers are the culprits in the fueling of conflicts within and outside the workplace.

Let's say you have a communication style that is different from several other people that you work with. It is unlikely the differ-ences are genetic; rather, they are learned as children and carried

1. __ Men tell more jokes than women do.
2. __ Women avoid verbal confrontation more than men.
3. __ Women speak more politely than men.
4. __ Women tell fewer stories than men.
5. __ Men look at women more frequently when talking with them than women look at men.
6. __ Men talk about their feelings more often than women do.
7. __ Men would prefer to talk about things rather than people.
8. __ Men talk more on the phone than women do.
9. __ Men accept words at their face value more often than women.
10. __ Women brag about their successes more often than men.
11. __ Gaining respect is more important to women than to men.
12. __ Men gossip more than women.
13. __ Women smile more than men do in conversation.
14. __ Women and men use the same set of words.
15. __ Men are likely to repeat requests more often than women.
16. __ Men interrupt others more than women.
17. __ Men's faces are more expressive when they speak than are women's.
18. __ Women make decisions quicker than men do.
19. __ Men tend to be more apologetic than women.
20. __ When a woman is in conversation with another, she tends to nod her head in approval of the speaker.
21. __ Men use vocal put-downs with others more often than women do.

Quiz Answers

1. True	8. False	15. False
2. True	9. True	16. True
3. True	10. False	17. False
4. False	11. False	18. False
5. False	12. False	19. False
6. False	13. True	20. False
7. True	14. False	21. True

Figure 4-1 *Communications Savvy Quiz.*

into adult life. You have your own style—one that is comfortable for you, effective, and noticeable, and still, I believe, one that needs to be recognized as humane. Others have their own style.

Today, it appears that many people get stuck on whether something is too feminine or too masculine. The key factors should be whether you are good at what you do and how you do it, and whether you have a communication style that is comfortable and effective for you and those you work with. There are times when you are going to have to be cooperative and friendly, and even give in; other times, you may have to go for the jugular.

The United States consists of multiple regions—ethnic and cultural—that are compounded by political and philosophical beliefs. It mirrors the rest of the world. The 1990s workplace has been receptive to men with multiple communication styles. At the same time, women have been expected to stay with the more traditional feminine style—soft and submissive. Consider the classic *Gone With the Wind*. In it, Scarlett O'Hara displayed every tendency imaginable. At times, she was soft. She could be manipulative. And she could run over anyone as if she were a Mack truck.

Miss Scarlett was as competitive as any men that she encountered. She was assertive, innovative, creative, pushy, and at times vindictive in order to get what she wanted—just as some of the men were. In other words, Scarlett did what she had to do to get what she wanted. The men were no different. One of the *momisms* mentioned earlier is that "Your turn will come." Scarlett didn't believe that her turn would come. She had to create the path to get there and make it her turn.

Some people are direct in their communications—the bottom liners; some are data gathers—the more info they get, the better; some react and speak intuitively and emotionally—they use their gut reaction; some are more interested in keeping the peace—they never raise their voices and try to get all sides heard; some communicate in multiple channels—they jump around and have difficulty focusing on any one topic or person at a time; and some are silent, almost passive—they take it in, but have difficulty articulating what they want or what their concerns are.

YOUR GUIDEPOSTS

The following guidelines are intended to assist you in getting past some of the cultural barriers that are out there. To get communications back on track—whether you are staff or management, or act in any other capacity—you should learn to read other people and be able to adapt and use their communication styles when dealing with them.

• No one communication style is the best. Contrary to your own belief, you may think that your style is the preferred way. Wrong. Depending upon the situation and the circumstance, other styles may be preferable. Learn to respect the strengths and weaknesses of each. There are parts from each style that might assist you in communicating better with another.

• Because of upbringing factors, many men arrive at decisions more quickly than do women. Women are more likely to want to build a consensus before they get to a decision. The reality is that there are times when men would be more effective if they worked first on consensus building, and women would be equally effective if they came to quicker decisions.

• A stereotypical communication style can lead to trouble. One of the traps that President Clinton encountered was his atypical male style of seeking consensus. Hillary Rodham Clinton's style was more direct and to the point. These personal styles became GenderTraps for each. When people do things that are unexpected or nontypical as the President did, it is bound to create concern and even lead to ridicule from those who are the observers of "normal" power.

• When working with a bottom-line, get-to-the-point type of communicator, give details and clarification only if asked; otherwise, keep your comments brief.

• When working with someone who is a detailer and an analytical communicator, be prepared to give reams of written as well as verbal backup. Make sure that adequate time is allowed to "crunch" what you have relayed.

• It is not uncommon for coworkers, subordinates, or even management to ask a lot of questions. It is also not uncommon for questions to surface after a meeting or an encounter is over. Before you move on to another point or terminate a gathering, ask how various members of the team, or the individual you are interacting with, will approach whatever the issue is that you are discussing. The point is not to make them defensive. Your questioning is not meant to be offensive. Rather, you are saying, "Let me know what your game plan and strategy are."

• A difference between men and women is that men usually don't ask a lot of questions during a conference or after it. Women often don't ask questions during a conference, but will raise them afterward. One way to help sidestep this phenomenon is to create and introduce questions that you believe might surface internally in people's thoughts and/or on the outside as they talk among themselves. Some may think you are clairvoyant.

• If one or two participants at a group meeting always have a lot of questions, anticipate their behavior on the basis of past patterns. Make sure that you ask others in the group if they have questions, and you yourself ask questions of them. Avoid letting anyone dominate a meeting.

• Know how the group works. Some groups take turns, one member asking the question, the other waiting for the response. Other groups are comfortable with interruptions. Whatever it is, "Go with the flow." You will build cohesiveness among the participants, and they will come away feeling that you are working with them, not against them.

• If you are someone who talks a lot, you most likely use language—whether verbal skills, body gestures, or tone—that may intimidate others. Take a break and let someone else speak, and practice the art of listening. A word to the wise: In any negotiation process, people who know how to listen usually come out ahead when the negotiation is over.

• There's a myth that if you ask too many questions, you will be viewed as weak, stupid, or incompetent. The reality is that there are few stupid questions. Don't be afraid to ask them in order to head yourself in the right direction. In this case, it is results that will count—they will speak loudest. If the questions you ask put you on the trail to the successful completion of a project or lead to the results you or your manager desired, you will be considered brilliant, not stupid.

• If you are more likely to act on an intuitive or gut feeling without gathering up a lot of information before making decisions, proceed with caution. Your style may not always work. If colleagues, coworkers, or senior managers are detail-oriented, they won't listen to your hunch. They need facts. A good communicator recognizes that and will deliver information in the methodology that's appropriate for the receiver.

• Don't be afraid to clarify. There is nothing wrong with asking your listeners to rephrase or repeat back what their understanding is.

Barbara Fielder is a communications expert and author of *I'm Communicating, But...Am I Being Heard?* She believes that many people develop a hearing prejudice, another type of self-inflicted barrier.

> In this case, you already know what the other person is going to say; therefore, you don't have to really give it your voice or listening system. I find that many people make believe they are listening. Too many times, we are on a mental vacation, we wake up when we hear our name or something of interest. It is then time that we begin to focus on the conversation.
>
> One of the biggest areas of failure in communication is not being a proactive listener. Most people have biases and prejudices, and internal noise going on. It is not uncommon to think that you already know what is going to be said, that you already know the information that needs to be known, and, therefore, you don't have to listen.

WHAT KIND OF LISTENER ARE YOU?

When I conduct interviews, I work hard to limit my comments. I listen and wait, hoping to hear a nuance or one of those "gems" to which I can say, "Ahah!" Listening is hard work. Do you know what kind of listener you are?

- When someone is talking with you, do you doodle, take phone calls, or rearrange your desk?
- Have people ever said that you don't pay attention when they are talking to you?
- When you meet people, do you ever look over their shoulder for someone else when you or they are talking?
- Do you interrupt people before they finish their sentence or thought?
- Do you find yourself thinking about other items that need to be dealt with while another person is talking?
- Do you have a policy that allows or encourages others to interrupt you when you are talking?

If you answered yes to any of the above questions, you are a one-way communicator and most probably a poor receiver. In communicating, it is critical to let others know how you best receive information so they can adapt to you. On the other hand, you need to know how they best receive so you can adapt your style to match theirs. In the end, you both win. As it stands now, you both lose.

BEING ASSERTIVE GETS YOU HEARD

The ability to be assertive is the basis of clear and honest communication between you and another. Most communications and behaviors fall into three categories: assertive, passive/submissive (nonassertive), and aggressive. Aggressive behaviors can be divided into direct and indirect.

People who are nonassertive are most likely reluctant or unable to confidently say and express what they feel, believe, or think. When you cross the line from assertiveness—confidently expressing yourself—to outright aggression, you enter troubled waters. There's a big difference. Granted, you are able to express yourself, but the method in which it's done often involves intimidation, degradation, or even demeaning another.

If you demonstrate confidence and respect for yourself, being assertive is rarely difficult. When you have low confidence and feel that your opinions or beliefs are of little or no value, you often find yourself as a "doormat." Others may view you as someone they can easily work over and push around. If you appear or act with low confidence or passiveness, your behavior is easily interpreted as being a "wimp."

In 1975, Stanlee Phelps and Nancy Austin published *The Assertive Woman*. In it, they described the various behaviors and communication styles of women you work with, play with, and have within your family. They explored doormats, indirect behaviors, assertiveness, and aggressiveness.

It's time to revisit the styles that Phelps and Austin introduced (see Table 4-1). Today, you could identify four types of communicators: Assertive Andrea, Pushy Paula, Confusing Connie, and Wimpy Wilma. It is important to point out that these behaviors are not exclusively female; there is always a male counterpart, whether it is Wimpy Walter, Pushy Paul, Confusing Charlie, or Assertive Arnold.[3]

Do you recognize what type of communicator you are? Are you assertive, passive, confusing, or aggressive? Recognition is a big step toward making your communication style a more appropriate and accurate display of what you want and how you feel. There are four

TABLE 4-1   Women's Behavior Styles

	PUSHY PAULA	CONFUSING CONNIE	WIMPY WILMA	ASSERTIVE ANDREA
Attitude	I'm right; you're wrong.	I'm not sure if you're OK or not; therefore, I'll keep you up in the air.	I'm never OK.	I'm OK and so is everyone else.
Decision making	Makes decisions for everyone.	Indirect— makes decisions behind the scenes.	Lets anyone else make decisions for her.	Makes her own decisions and lets others make theirs.
Possible traps	Makes promises she can't keep; claims to know all when she doesn't; is rash in making decisions.	Appears two-faced because of indecision and nontrust-worthy because of indirectness; professes belief in areas she doesn't really believe in.	Never takes the rose-colored glasses off; leads with emotion; is everyone's mother.	Says yes too often and is caught in the Superwoman syndrome.
Sense of humor	A master at put-downs; is angry if she is the butt of a joke; has a difficult time laughing at herself.	Indirect; uses innuendoes; sometimes is caustic; uses mockery.	Is often the butt of a joke, even encouraging it; is usually teased within the workplace by others.	Is willing to be funny; loves a good story; is able to laugh at herself.
Receiving feedback	Immediately defensive and fearful; feels hurt if you don't support her.	Both suspicious and confused when others tell her how they feel or how they perceive a situation.	Feels defensive, angry, and abused when given negative feedback.	Is positive; even negative feedback can be construed as support or encouragement from others.
Tenacity	Hangs in there, though likely to blame others if things go wrong; is sometimes pig-headed.	Will move ahead but covers up her fear of failure.	Prefers sympathy and rarely stands up for her beliefs and convictions.	Is not paralyzed by conflicts along the path; is willing to take risk.

(Continued)

Table 4-1   Women's Behavior Styles (*Continued*)

	Pushy Paula	Confusing Connie	Wimpy Wilma	Assertive Andrea
Give-ups	Has few friends; viewed as the "bad guy"; teamwork never seems to pay off.	Is rarely trusted; is often retaliated against.	Shows minimal, if any, self-respect and self-confidence.	Places undue pressure and unrealistic expectations on self.
Gains	Displays control, visibility, and authority.	Is whimsical and fun; viewed as being clever.	Likes attention and having people feeling sorry for her.	Enjoys responsibility and integrity.
Burnout potential	High; overworks herself and others.	High; puts a lot of energy into covering up duplicities and the games she plays.	High; doesn't take care of herself because she could never say no; ends up being a doormat.	High; tries to do it all; rarely sets limits; because she is competent, more gets piled on.
Power	Is often obnoxious and egocentric; decides for others, even when they don't want to participate.	Controls by using manipulation, women's wiles, even tears or being cute.	Uses powerlessness, helplessness, martyring, and even guilt to control others.	Is comfortable with power and with others having power; is true to self.
Career persona	Is financially successful but a miserable overachiever.	Once her manipulative style is exposed, her career hits a roadblock or plummets.	Does what she thinks she should do or what others think she should do even if she doesn't want to do it.	Is successful and happy and feels she can do anything she sets her mind to.
Bottom line	Is lonely, angry, and "ticked off."	Loses trust and respect; if she does get it together, is viewed as suffering from the lone wolf syndrome; no one believes she really needs help when she asks for it.	Creates a full-time career as a martyr.	Has balance and peace of mind.

parts to effective and assertive communication, especially when your objective is to change a behavior or an outcome:

- A nonjudgmental description of what you want changed
- A disclosure of how you feel
- A clear description of the impact and effect of the other person's behavior on you
- A description of what behavior you desire

Changing to a more assertive communication style doesn't happen overnight. It takes time to become a master. If you are really intent on practicing speaking up, you might start along these lines.

When you...   state the other person's behavior nonjudgmentally

I feel...   disclose your feelings

Because...   explain how the behavior affects you

I prefer...   describe what you want

This approach works whether you are a beginner or feel that your skills are quite good. Every master always goes back for retooling. When you speak clearly and succinctly, you are far more likely to gain the admiration and respect of others. But that's not a 100 percent guarantee; there are always those who will respond to your assertiveness with put-downs or other demands. Those who do are usually insecure and are attempting to put you in your place—so that they can maintain theirs.

When you are communicating a problem, make sure you communicate the real issue and the factors within the problem; and make sure you communicate to the right person. One of my personal mottos is "Don't take no from someone who does not have the authority to say yes." If you are communicating a specific issue that you desire to be changed, make sure you communicate it to the person who has the capability of making the changes.

THE BOTTOM LINE

What is the bottom line when it comes to communication? First, moving beyond miscommunication, noncommunication, and uncommunication is critical. Second, neither men nor women are the "better" communicators. Both women and men must learn to be more flexible in their styles of speaking as well as in their interpretation and understanding of speaking. It is absurd to pretend or ignore the fact that there are communication differences between genders as well as cultures.

Here are some key communications differences:

- Women tend to play down their power. Rather than make demands of their subordinates and coworkers, they are more likely to couch or soften their requests and suggestions.

- Men's humor is often based on put-downs, whereas women's humor is often self-depreciating or mocking. Such behaviors get misinterpreted: Women often view men as being hostile via their put-downs, and men view women as having lower self-esteem because of the self-depreciating style.

- Women are more likely to empathize when coworkers have a problem. Men jump in and offer solutions. When a man offers solutions, women view him as not listening to what they are saying. The reality is that both genders interpret situations differently.

- Both genders like power. Men seek it. From an early age, boys are taught to be competitive. As adults, they have no problem telling others what to do. When men are on the other side of orders—receiving them—or are being criticized, they are less likely than women to view the communication as a personal assault. Women are more likely to personalize any type of criticism.

- Women don't brag. In their efforts to play down their own power, they rarely draw attention to what they accomplish, or take visual or vocal credit when tasks are completed. Men are more boastful and aggressive about touting their successes and accomplishments. They often get promoted and moved along because of their vocal visibility.

There are two sides to communication: the speaking and the receiving. As the receiver or listener, it is your responsibility to clear up any potential misunderstandings. The speaker knows what she or he wants to communicate—what he or she means. If you are unclear as to what is said or meant, you must clear it up. Try:

"I'm sorry. I'm, not sure what you meant. Is it...? If not, would you be more clear?"

By encouraging others to do the same, you will significantly reduce miscommunication, noncommunication, and wrong communication in both your workplace and your personal life.

Sabotage: The undermining or destruction of personal/professional credibility. The end result is the erosion or destruction of self-esteem and confidence.

TRAP 3: SABOTAGE Caution, Women at Work

- Has anyone ever passed on or exchanged information about you that was untrue?
- Has anyone ever taken credit for work you have completed?
- Have you ever been with an individual or group that has identified a problem and committed to seeking a solution to it, only to discover that there is no one to support "your" problem when you discuss it with a manager or supervisor?
- Has anyone consistently criticized areas or items in your work without acknowledging or applauding the positive tasks you complete?
- Has anyone ever told someone else personal information about you that you had shared confidentially?

Lucille was grateful for the support of her staff when she was in the hospital. The fresh flowers, phone calls, and visits assured her that her clientele was being taken care of after she had collapsed in her beauty salon one day. After a week of tests in the hospital, the doctors could not explain or identify what malady had befallen her. To her close friends, she confided it must be overwork. Her friends weren't so sure.

For several years, Lucille's salon had been one of the "best" in her city, as rated by the general populace. She had supported all kinds of groups and causes in her community over the past 15 years by donating haircuts, facials, and manicures for the asking. Whatever group needed to raise money, she was there to support its cause.

While in the hospital, she appreciated the employees who visited her daily. Maria went out of her way to be helpful—bringing paperwork from her office, tracking inventory, even giving Lucille a rundown on the types of services rendered to the salon's daily customers. Maria would even drop tidbits of the latest gossip that circulated within the shop.

When Lucille was finally discharged, the doctors strongly advised her to stay away from work for a month. Impossible words for someone who is also the owner and the one who is usually the first to arrive in the morning and the last to go home at night.

During Lucille's convalescence, Maria reported that Sandra had tried to add all the new customers and changes of address to the customer file on the computer, but was having trouble opening it. Appreciating the extra help, Lucille gave her the password. That one word shut down Lucille's business.

When Lucille got wind of what was going on from a former employee, she went to the shop and learned that it basically had been raided. Maria, Sandra, and another stylist had walked out, carrying the detailed records of a 15-year-old business. They had opened their own shop, knowing the details of Lucille's business and the name, address, and phone number of everyone who had been in the salon in the past 5 years.

Lucille's computer was still there, with a few modifications. Names and addresses had been deleted, inventory depleted, and thousands of dollars in bills for merchandise (including $1800 in flowers) ordered in her name. The pile of bills was unbelievable. To ice the cake, a virus had been entered into the computer, infecting all the files.

At its peak, Lucille's thriving business grossed $750,000 a year. After Maria's handiwork, the business wasn't so thriving. Eventually, Lucille declared bankruptcy. When she discovered Maria's duplicity, she felt betrayed, used, and angry. All rightfully so. With her health weakened, Lucille felt she had no energy in her to confront, much less combat, her foe. Rebuilding a business takes time, drive, and positive support. She just didn't have it.

Painfully, she closed her business and took what customers she had left to another shop in town. Some of her remaining employees went with her; the others found a "new home" as Lucille contacted her friends in the trade.

Lucille was sabotaged by Maria, an employee she had hired 5 years before. Maria had relished the flexibility Lucille offered so that she could pursue her passion of skiing in the winter. What compounds Lucille's experience, and the sabotage reported by many, is that Lucille and Maria work in a female-dominated workplace. Does this mean that sabotage is worse in a female workplace? Is this a woman's issue?

EVERYONE PLAYS

Yes. But, men do it, women do it, and men and women do it differently. Women are more inclined to undermine and sabotage their own gender. If a man is a saboteur, gender is not an issue. The target can be either sex. Sabotage is derived from the French word *sabot*, a wooden shoe. The act of sabotage gained its name when French machinists protested working conditions by throwing their shoes—their *sabots*—into the machines to stop work. This action resulted in severe damage to whatever equipment was the target of a machinist's footwear.

Today, men and women don't take their shoes off and throw them into machinery, but they do engage in sabotage that can be just as damaging. Mayhem, destruction, betrayal, treachery, and seduction are all synonymous with it.

In 1987, 1993, and in 1994, I conducted surveys of men and women in the workplace, querying them as to whether they had experienced undermining and sabotaging practices. In 1987, 53 percent of the women responded that they had been undermined by another woman, while 63 percent of the women responded that they had been undermined by a man.

In 1993, significant changes were noted. A slight decrease of men undermining women was reported, with 58 percent of the respondents reporting as such. However, sabotaging behavior, woman to woman, increased significantly. Seventy-one percent of the respondents said that they had been undermined by another woman—a 34 percent increase from the 1987 study.

The 1994 study, undertaken for this book, showed that sabotage—woman to woman—was the third greatest problem the respondents were experiencing. In fact, sabotage almost tied for second with communications problems as a major GenderTrap.

It is also important to note a difference between men and women in their methodology and style of delivering behavior that could be deemed as sabotaging, undermining, or unethical. Men are more inclined to be assertive, direct, and overt when they engage in any type of sabotage. Women, on the other hand, are more inclined to be covert and indirect when sabotaging another.

THE BULLY ON THE STREET

The most common reasons women undermine other women are that they are envious, jealous, lack confidence, and have low self-esteem about their abilities. They may be fearful that someone is after their job. Saboteurs are, in effect, bullies. Bullies are masters at determining who has less power than they have. A bully/saboteur attempts to gain power by putting others down. It is much easier to win—to put someone down—when the target has less power and less confidence than the perpetrator, the saboteur.

Since only 6 million of the 58 million women who work are in management positions, it is fairly safe to assume that if a woman has any positional power in the workplace, that power will most likely be over other women. Therefore, if a woman attempts to dis-empower another, the target of her action will most likely be another woman, not a man.

Sabotage weighs heavily in the cost arena. Embarrassment, emotional duress, and loss of reputation, self-esteem, jobs, promotions, and money all rank high when women talk about being undermined by another woman. Women report that they, and society in general, expect men to display inappropriate, nonsupporting, and undermining relations in the workplace, as in "What else is new?" Almost stereotypical. So, if men do it, what is the big deal when it happens woman to woman? The answer lies in stereotypes and the momisms: Women are supposed to be nice, to be friends, to take turns, to be caring, and on and on.

The reality is that there are not only a lot of jerks out there, but also lots of jerkettes. There are men and women with whom you have no business sharing your hopes, your concerns, your fears, and your dreams. Women are more inclined to be too open, too soon—sharing information that a potential saboteur, who may not have their best interests in mind, can use against them. Information that they have freely given can be used in personal and work relationships with men and women, as well as within the overall workplace environment—with coworkers and management.

When one person undermines another, the saboteur seeks to gain something, while the sabotaged, in turn, loses something. The gains that most saboteurs make are in reputation, promotions, and jobs. Their own self-esteem gets enhanced—at the expense of the individuals who were sabotaged. And the employers are not left out; they lose too. They can lose in their reputation, loyalty, productivity, credibility, team growth, and effectiveness. All are fallout factors that affect the bottom line.

MORE THAN ONE IS A CROWD

Women are far more likely than men to work closely together physically. It's called *crowding*. Because of the nature of women's positions in the general workplace, or in one of the many Velvet Ghetto environments, women's jobs are often viewed as having less or lower status. The fact is that lower-status individuals get less space. With few exceptions, those who are in upper management are more likely to have their own offices.

Secretaries and clerical workers often get no more than a partition if they are lucky, and are placed in a bullpen environment. Criminal psychologists have noted that crowded living conditions in small spaces have a negative mental effect, and are considered factors in the criminal's life.

Ongoing research shows that those who work under high-density conditions which include high-level interactions are more likely to feel hostile and aggressive. This is usually the case for women. Imagine the secretarial pool. Women are more likely to be accessible, even leave their doors open if they have them, which leads to a higher interaction level with others at work.

Much of the sabotaging and angry behavior that women engage in today is primarily a result of their social conditioning in the cultural context of the workplace. Situations are created in which women feel hostile, aggressive, and angry, and they take out their aggressions in a covert and subtle way. This compounds their feelings of low power and low self-esteem.

When a woman is in a low-status, low self-esteem position, she is more likely to be a target—a scapegoat—vulnerable to the workplace bully. One of the survey respondents wrote that her office had Friday meetings at which someone would be designated as "it." Actually, "it" would be selected early in the week by the manager, so that cutting remarks and innuendos could be bantered about by coworkers until the meeting day arrived. Thus the group could direct anger, remarks, and negativism at the person of the week, deflecting any from others. The "it" girl was got!

Women are the most likely scapegoats when anger surfaces. They are typically the low-status members who have less power to protect themselves. They are "it." They're the easiest choice. Women don't sabotage and undermine other women because of genes or gender-linked characteristics.

With the significant changes resulting from the reorganization and downsizing of the 1990s, a classic situation arises: the survival of the fittest. Battles will be fought by both overt and subtle manipulations. Many of the players of the workplace, women and men, will be rendered obsolete. Some will come away dismayed and distressed; others will look at the battlefield as an opportunity to grow and expand in whatever they are doing.

ARE WOMEN REALLY BARRACUDAS?

The fact that sabotage—women undermining and/or not supporting other women—ranked number three among the GenderTraps doesn't surprise me with the repetition of feelings of betrayal, anger, and hurt from women across the country. It does, though, pain me. Susan, a registered nurse, reported:

> I didn't want to believe it was happening. It was one of those times in our lives I didn't listen to myself. I kept pushing it down, saying, "This isn't true; it can't be happening. She's really not like this." When I finally opened my eyes and ears, I found that everything she did was for her own benefit. There really wasn't any effort to do anything as a team member or a partner.

When I quote Susan from the platform as a speaker, I am amazed by the number of women who tell me those could have been their words exactly.

One of the most common forms of sabotage is gossip—no special skills or tools are needed. Just how prevalent is gossip in the workplace? In 1993, a *Self* magazine survey found that 74 percent of its readership liked to gossip. When respondents were probed as to what they usually talk about, 61 percent said goings-on at work, 44 percent said their friends' personal lives, and 40 percent said people they disliked.

When it came to what they thought about gossip in general, 64 percent of the respondents said it was a harmless diversion and usually a lot of fun. Only 26 percent felt that it was destructive and malicious, and 22 percent regarded it as petty or a waste of time. Fourteen percent of the respondents felt gossip was a practical way to get the office scuttlebutt (totals exceed 100 percent because of multiple answers). The old adage "Sticks and stones can break your bones, but names can never hurt you" is a myth. Words do hurt. When words are passed on irresponsibly, whether verified as a validity or not, it is almost impossible to undo the damage.

WHO'S THE MESSENGER?

One of the most important ways to stop rumors is to identify who the key messenger is. For Lucy, the message was accompanied by a letter threatening to sue her for slander. Lucy worked in a small Southwestern hospital. The letter and the messenger's sharp tongue didn't exactly make her day.

> I was the charge nurse of our unit. One day, one of the nurses handed me a letter. When I asked her what it was about, she said, "You will find out." When I read it, it was full of charges that I had spread rumors and that I had gone to the supervisors with a series of complaints about the nurse and the work she performed within the unit. The letter said I would be hearing from her attorney.
>
> I didn't know what to do, so I thought the best thing was to go directly to my charge nurse. When I did, he said he would check it out. The next day, he told me she wanted nothing to do with me, and she didn't want to talk to me. My response was that I really didn't understand what it was all about, since the letter wasn't specific about what the complaints that were made, were.
>
> Finally, one of my friends came to me and said, the reason the nurse was going to sue me was that I had complained about her friend. The whole thing kept escalating, and finally I was told that she could be fired with her continued, unfounded threats toward me. Now, I didn't want this to happen. I felt the whole thing was ridiculous and was embarrassed telling anyone about it.

Lucy went on to note that she spent endless time and energy defending herself for something she was never directly involved in.

She felt that both her productivity and morale were knocked down, and she was angry that her charge nurse did not step in and say, "Enough is enough."

SABOTEURS IN YOUR MIDST

Sometimes the messengers of sabotage are not so blatant as to deliver a letter. In our workshops, we developed an 11-point questionnaire to identify a *saboteur in the midst* (see Fig. 5-1). They are questions you can ask yourself to assist in uncovering someone who may be setting you up or who is actively involved in some type of perpetration. A yes answer to any of the questions demands that you be on the alert.

After you have identified possible or probable saboteurs, the next step is to deal with them. Two things need to come into play here. The first is to document; the second is to develop good confronting skills. When you do confront, you need the facts to back up whatever your accusations are. Most saboteurs will do just about anything to avoid public exposure. They will rarely commit anything to paper, so you will need to have the facts.

Once a saboteur is identified, it is important to sidestep her games. Being a saboteur takes a lot of time and commitment. Over time, she—or he—will be less productive. The longer the game goes on, the less she produces, and the more likely she is to be exposed to others. The jig is eventually up. Until that happens, the workplace may feel like a battlefield. Dealing with confronting and confrontophobia will be covered in the seventh trap.

Figure 5-1 *Is There a Saboteur in the Midst?* From Judith Briles, *The Briles Report on Women in Health Care* (San Francisco: Jossey Bass, 1994).

> 1. *Does anyone encourage gossip?* Most saboteurs are messengers—they can hardly wait to pass along damaging information about anyone or anything.
> 2. *Does anyone keep a tally sheet?* Everyone makes mistakes—saboteurs usually keep count and can make a brouhaha out of any small incident.

3. *Does information ever pass you by?*   A typical strategy of a saboteur is to isolate others. The most common practice is to withhold information or interrupt an information pipeline that is relevant to your work.

4. *Does anyone feel her job is in jeopardy?*   Whenever there is fear and anxiety, such as that created by the downsizing and reorganization of the 1990s, many people overreact. For some, paranoia sets in.

5. *Does anyone stand to profit by another's mistake?*   Any time someone makes a mistake, saboteurs relish the opportunity. They will be players in passing along the "error" and may eventually benefit by a promotion or bonus, or at the very least by an enhanced reputation because of the mistake.

6. *Have new coalitions formed on your team?*   It is common-place for saboteurs to continually realign their "friendships." With each new realignment, they are often in the center, similar to the "movers" in a high school clique.

7. *Is anyone on your team sometimes too helpful?*   Until you really know how a group or team operates, an overly helpful or zealous player may not be what you think she is.

8. *Does anyone routinely deny involvement in activities, yet know all the details?*   Saboteurs are masters at working the grapevine; they are also chameleons. They initially claim no knowledge of any specific incident, yet somehow they are able to pass along the details and information to anyone who asks, and, in some cases, doesn't ask.

9. *Does anyone encourage others to take on tasks that appear impossible?*   When you or another fail at a task, saboteurs derive great pleasure from it. Your failure makes them look good, and even more savvy, for not taking on the impossible.

10. *Does anyone bypass your authority or go over your head?*   Saboteurs will do almost anything to look good, including sidestepping a leader's authority or ignoring other team members' contributions.

11. *Does anyone routinely take credit for or discount yours or other coworkers' contribution to the workplace?*   Saboteurs rarely compliment or give credit openly for another's work. Their style is more likely to discount participation by other team members or take credit for themselves. Women are more inclined not to speak up or out when someone hogs the limelight and/or takes credit for another's work.

RUMORS AND INNUENDOS

Whereas Lucy (the hospital charge nurse) experienced rumors directed at her professional ability to do her job (or personally, at her relationships), Danielle was hit with rumors whose objectives were to sink her business. She's in her third decade of work, and is a successful owner of a thriving day-care center. When she began, hers was the only center in a medium-size city in the South. Like most cities, hers has experienced significant growth. One of her competitors set out to put her operation, and several other day-care centers in the city, out of business. It all started with rumors and innuendos.

> Two little boys who had gone to my center had been switched to my competitor's. The mother had said that one of the boys was scared of the dark after he came to mine. The woman reported me to the licensing authorities, telling the state that I had locked him in a closet. When state authorities contacted me, there was no reason for me not to be completely cooperative with them.

> In the meanwhile the harassment was stepped up. My competitor reported there was a truck out by my place, and said that we were taking kids in the truck on trips—which of course, was not true. Then she started to make phone calls—you know, the type when someone is on the phone for a few seconds and then hangs up. I wasn't the only one who received them. Members of my staff got the same treatment, as well as people at the other centers.

> Eventually I called my lawyer, and we contacted different sources to find out what my options were. The telephone people helped out right away, and we were able to track where the phone calls were coming from. Needless to say, all of us were getting a little depressed.

> Finally, I went to my minister and asked him for help. I asked for him and his prayer line at the church to pray for a person who was having a great deal of difficulty. Of course, the person was the woman who was harassing us. I never gave her name. In the meanwhile, I had my own staff do morning prayers for this woman. Within 2 weeks, the harassment stopped.

> It wasn't too long afterward that I found out she had a nervous breakdown. She still owns the building, but now someone else manages and directs the day-care activities.

> I try to make it a point not to listen when people talk about the other facilities in town. What I do say is that I'm trying to make my center the best I can make it, because I care about the kids.

My objective is not necessarily to please the parents—I try to do what is best for the kids in terms of their safety, their health, and their welfare. Then, I'll go to the parents and try to please them. But I let them know up front that their kids come first.

FROM COWORKER TO BOSS

When I spoke with Jessica, she was actively looking for a new position. She had worked most of her adult life, had always had good evaluations, and was stunned when she received an employee warning a week earlier. Her immediate supervisor, who had issued the warning, was fairly new in the position. When the office manager retired, she had been given the job. Prior to that, she had worked part time with the company. Jessica said that there was very little that her supervisor liked about her personally or workwise.

> My new supervisor continues to cut me down to the boss. She blows every item out of proportion, complains that I won't ask for help on the computer—when I did so the previous week, she was very sarcastic and didn't want me even working on it. What I've learned from her short term as the new supervisor is that she wants everything underneath her thumb. In fact, all of a sudden she is a mother hen, telling us what to do and glaring at us when we speak up and question anything that she says.
>
> I'm not the only woman who has experienced her criticism and put-downs. The general manager has sat down to discuss what is going on. This makes her crazy, because I'm there to defend myself when she makes accusations. For me, I'd rather just get out. I know I'm good at what I do, and there are other jobs that are available. It is just not worth the hassle.

Jessica is caught up in an interesting scenario. It is quite common for someone who receives a promotion from an internal group to move from the inner circle to the outer circle. As a rule, the inner circle closes up, literally excluding the former colleague. There are also times when someone with new-found power doesn't quite know how to control it, as you'll learn in reading about the power play trap in Chap. 12.

Whether Jessica is a contributor to the problem with the supervisor, I don't know. I do know, though, that there may be some wisdom in her decision to scout around for another position. Too often women hang on and stay within a disruptive and demoralizing workplace, surrounded by toxic coworkers and toxic bosses, and feel hopeless and helpless. Jessica feels that she has value and that her value can be transferred to another workplace.

SHUT OUT

In Mary's case, she felt that her work was pulled out from underneath her. In addition, Mary ran into the *Patty Principle* when another woman affiliated with one of the hospital's foundations came in to run a surgical unit, an area the woman had not been involved in for many years.

> Initially I had worked for a very competitive man who was quite direct. He told me that when he got promoted, he would recommend me to take over his position. His promotion did come. He did recommend me, but I did not get the job. Prior to the naming of the new head, I was responsible overall for the unit. I was told at that time by two women in the administration that there was "no way" I would be interviewed for the position. Instead, they were going to hire from the outside.
>
> I believe my new supervisor was threatened by me, and all of a sudden several things that I was in charge of and working on disappeared. I was left out of all meetings, literally cut off from the internal network.
>
> When the showdown came, she accused me of saying something that I hadn't said. Her accusations usually took the form of remarks such as "I always hear you say this" and "I'm always told you say that." When I would ask her if she heard me say it directly, her response would be, "No; someone told me that. And if someone told me you said it, then you must have." My response to her was, "Here is my 2-week notice. I quit." When I went into work the next day, I got my final paycheck, and was told I was no longer welcome.

DEALING WITH A MESSENGER

One of the things that Mary had experienced was really quite classic: the old "Someone said you said this" or "Someone said you did this." If you find yourself in this kind of situation, here's a technique that works:

1. When someone tells you that Mary Lou said such-and-such about you, your response should be, "Will you go with me to Mary Lou to validate what she said to you so that I can discuss it with her?"

The most probable response from your messenger will be no. She may add, "It's not really a big deal; I just wanted you to hear." Or something along the line of "You know, she talks about everybody." Don't let it stop with a no.

2. Ask your messenger: "If you won't go with me, can I use your name when I approach Mary Lou with what you've told me?" Again, the most likely response you are going to get back is no, possibly with the add-on, "I don't really want to get involved, and you may be making too big a deal out of this."

Your messenger is displaying a classic female tendency in not wanting to be a party to potential conflict. ("Don't make such a big deal; it will go away.") The reality is that when gossip is not checked, it doesn't go away. It only escalates and builds. Usually, you don't even know the originators of the gossip—those anonymous sources.

Shortly after Whoopi Goldberg hosted the Academy Awards, she was a guest on the *Tonight Show* with Jay Leno. Because our media are so Hollywood-oriented, there was a lot of chatter of her hosting skills, even of her dress and hairstyle for the evening.

Of course, most of those comments didn't have names attached to them. They were delivered—cited—anonymously. Her response to Leno when he brought the subject up was, "People who stab you anonymously aren't real people." So it goes with the gossip pool, especially when the tattlers hide behind another.

3. If your messenger declines to go with you or to allow her name to be used when you go back to Mary Lou (whom you believe to be the original source), your next statement should be: "If I can't use your name, and you won't go with me, then it's not a problem."

Letting go is another issue that seems to surface when women work and deal with other women—letting go as in not being willing, or in some cases, not being able to let go. Many women feel that if an issue is being dealt with and an agreement has been reached, whether it is between two parties or the consensus of a group, it is time to move on. For some, though, that is impossible. They keep coming back to recheck if that is what everyone in the group really wants. The other side is that at times, when women don't confront a situation, they tend to "carry it" with them in their pocket. An issue can resurface that many thought was dealt with—and over with—long ago.

WOMEN'S INHUMANITY TO WOMEN

When I first started writing about sabotage in the workplace, and after the first printing of my book *Woman to Woman,* it was not uncommon for me to get letters and phone calls from women in various parts of the country. Story after story would unfold, some tales so ludicrous that you couldn't believe that someone could be so caught up or so naive. Other stories were so painful that you wished you could reach across the phone lines and hug the caller, giving support and caring as well as shelter from any additional onslaughts.

What continues to amaze me is women's inhumanity toward other women. And with that inhumanity come the parallel game playing and denial, in which a perpetrator can display either a conscious or an unconscious reaction to the chain of events that unfold.

In the thousands of interviews that I have done at this point on women who have been undermined by other women, there are a few that stand out above the rest. One such individual is Rita Lavelle. I first met her in 1986, when she was serving time in a women's prison in northern California. She had once held a key, visible position in the U.S. Environmental Protection Agency. Her crime was that she had "lied" to Congress four times. She had told the same lie to four committees. Congress charged her with perjury, and off to the slammer she went.

I find it almost ludicrous that Congress can charge anyone with perjury with all the nonsense and baloney it feeds to the American public. But, indeed, Congress did. The saga of Rita Lavelle displays deception, manipulation, and almost a blind faith that you can support another woman just because she is a woman.

When I appeared on the *Oprah!* show in 1987 to discuss women and sabotage in the workplace, Rita Lavelle was one of the guests. As she was telling her story, I waited behind the curtain prior to my introduction as the "expert" on the topic. The security guard said as we both viewed the monitor, "You women just don't get it." When I asked him what "get it" meant, his response was, "When we men set people up, we take care of them when they get out."

I never forgot his words. In 1992 when Ross Perot appeared on the *Donahue* show during the presidential campaign, Phil Donahue asked what Perot had told Oliver North during the Iran-contra hearings. Perot responded, "I told Ollie to tell the truth. If he went to jail, I would take care of his family, and when he got out, I would guarantee him a job."

Now, how did that security guard from Chicago, Illinois know what Ross Perot from Dallas, Texas knew? The security guard knew that if there was a scapegoat or a fall person, one of the rules—unwritten—is that you "take care of them when they come out." Why didn't women know this rule?

Almost a decade has passed since Rita Lavelle set her foot inside a prison. She is still trying to put her life together, this time with the word "felon" attached to her name. Lavelle's lie to Congress concerned a date. She couldn't pinpoint the exact date of meetings because her calendar had mysteriously disappeared. Was there one? Indeed. It showed up in the back of Ed Meese's safe when he left the Reagan administration. Too late.

Today Rita Lavelle is the founder and CEO of a company called Nutech, a California-based company that specializes in evaluating and implementing strategies for getting rid of toxic waste in private industry. During our conversation in the fall of 1994, she told me that it isn't unusual to be in strategy meetings that include other groups competing for the business. It's also not unusual to have derogatory comments or innuendos made about her when women are on the opposing team. The quality of her work carries an excellent reputation and speaks for itself. There are never questions, innuendos, or inferences from men—*only from other women.*

On the *Oprah!* show in 1987, she said, "The whole experience was equivalent to an out-of-body nightmare." When Oprah Winfrey probed as to why she covered up for her boss, Anne Burford, she responded, "It was to help a sister. There were very few of us back there (Washington, DC)." Lavelle also said that if she had been told that she was to be the sacrificial lamb, she would have been able to tolerate the situation and understand it better than she did.

Meanwhile in Colorado, her former boss continues to make headlines. She has been picked up several times for drunk driving, and faces a lawsuit filed against her by the city and tenants for being a slum landlord. In 1994, newspaper headlines declared that the Colorado courts had turned down her claim against her ex-husband's estate. Burford had attempted to obtain assets from heirs and creditors, since she was the latest surviving spouse, even though it was in the "ex" status.

Rita Lavelle's dream is still to clear her name and be pardoned. Whether she ever gets her pardon, only time will tell. President Reagan sheltered the wrong woman.

JUST OFFICE POLITICS

Prior to a speaking engagement in one of the New England states, I did radio and television segments and public relations to support the event. One of the television segments was to be aired on the five o'clock news. After being introduced to the TV anchor who served as the reporter for the segment, I was given a series of questions (actually, statements) referencing sabotage in the workplace.

The TV reporter's position was that sabotage was normal, and it was just basically office politics. I said no, it is beyond office politics. There are differences in the way women and men engage in sabotage. Also, women tend to overpersonalize and react in a more personal basis when it happens. The end result is that no matter what, when sabotage occurs, productivity, morale, loyalty, and even profitability for the employer are affected.

Over the 3 days I was in the city, I was scheduled to make three different speeches: one on *confidence,* one on *money,* and one on *women and sabotage.* The only thing the anchor-reporter wanted to talk about was sabotage—something that I really hadn't expected. I had hoped to focus on confidence and crisis since, at the time, thousands of men and women from the local army base were in Haiti.

She wasn't interested in talking about crisis and its impact on one's personal life. It was sabotage—office politics—or nothing. After I left the studio, the PR director for the sponsoring hospital told me that this same anchor had recently been suspended for 2 weeks for harassing a younger reporter at the station. The anchor had written unsigned letters telling the younger reporter that she was dumb, that she didn't know how to be a newsperson, that she never looked right, that she didn't know how to speak, and that she was too big-breasted.

It was later brought to light by a third party that the anchor-woman was the culprit; alas, the suspension from her position.

When I heard the story, my first response was that it was improbable that my presentation on the topic of sabotage would be mentioned on the five o'clock news. Our anchor wouldn't want to remind the community of what she had done, nor would she want to support a program on a topic that she had been suspended for. I was right. Nothing appeared, and the women of the community lost out. They hadn't heard about the program scheduled for the following day.

SHARK ATTACKS

When women report that they are undermined by other women, it is like being attacked by a snake. A quick strike, sometimes not knowing what hit you. Or like swimming with sharks. Everything seems quiet and peaceful in the waters of life, and then, all of a sudden, you are bitten. Sabotage and women undermining women will continue to grow unless women stand up and speak out when the situations occur.

Scientists estimate that the chances of being bitten by a shark are 10 million to 1. The odds of encountering a shark in the workplace are far greater. With the continued reorganization and downsizing of the 1990s, the odds are even more enhanced. Women who undermine women—the sharks—are far less likely to undermine those who speak up for themselves and their rights, and who display confidence—swim assertively. When there are so many fish in the sea, why waste time on one that could possibly bite back? Yet striking back is what you must be prepared to do.

Now, sharks come in both genders. Keep in mind what the research shows. Men are inclined to be unethical, though not discriminatory, when it comes to sabotaging and undermining coworkers. Women are equally unethical but more inclined to direct their energies toward other women—the easier targets, the ones with less power and often weaker skills in fighting back.

The reality is that some of the momisms ("Be nice, be fair, your turn will come") make a woman more vulnerable. One of the biggest mistakes women can make is to believe that if they "lower" themselves into the office politics arena, they become tainted, even sleazy. The other thing women do is believe that if they work hard, they will be noticed and be justly rewarded.

BEING FRIENDSHIP-SAVVY IN THE WORKPLACE

The Friendship-Savvy Quiz in Fig. 5-2 identifies 10 questions that you should ask yourself regarding women in the workplace, women

1. Would you feel uncomfortable if you needed to criticize a friend's work?
2. Would you allow her extra time to complete tasks or projects?
3. Would you feel hurt or be angry if she took another position without telling you about it first?
4. Would you feel left out if she transferred to another department or moved to another city?
5. Would you feel excluded if she went to lunch with another coworker and didn't invite you?
6. Would you feel overlooked or forgotten if she forgot your birthday?
7. Would you feel bad or uncomfortable if she criticized your work?
8. Would you feel betrayed if she told someone else a personal story or revealed anything that you considered intimate?
9. Would you feel uncomfortable competing for a position or promotion with her?
10. Would you cover for her if you knew she was having personal problems?

Figure 5-2 *The Friendship-Savvy Quiz.* From Judith Briles, *The Briles Report on Women in Health Care* (San Francisco: Jossey Bass, 1994).

with whom you may develop friendships. If you answer yes to any of them, it indicates that your personal expectations of others carry a "strings attached" awareness when you develop or build friendships in the workplace.

Women need to recognize that a healthy relationship is a necessity and that friendships are a luxury. It is also imperative for women to understand that not everyone is friend material.

The questions in Fig. 5-2 are applicable whether you manage other women or work alongside them as a colleague or coworker. A yes answer doesn't mean that you shouldn't develop friendships in the workplace; it just means there are some hooks—those attached strings. A yes or several yesses mean that you may have to be sensitive to your relationship; hurt feelings may spill over. The domino effect could (and most likely will) impact your work, your friend's work, and the work of others.

THE TEN COMMANDMENTS OF CONQUERING SABOTAGE

In addition to being able to identify a saboteur in your midst and determine whether or not developing friendships may have strings attached, there are 10 steps that you can take when sabotage occurs. These steps, or commandments of conquering sabotage, have been developed over the years from my observations, experiences, and input from readers and audiences—in other words, from people like you. When it comes to sabotage within the workplace, your objective should be not just to survive, but to remove yourself from any attacks in the future.

1. *Acquire confidence.*   Self-esteem is the reputation you have with yourself. Confidence is the power to create, expand, and grow that reputation. Women and men who sabotage others are bullies. They are also abusers.

People who are bullies and abusers focus their attention on others who they believe are weaker and less secure than they are. In fact, saboteurs usually have low self-esteem and self-confidence, are insecure, and are often riddled with envy or jealousy. Their "druthers" is to direct their attention to others who they believe are as miserable and insecure as they are.

Saboteurs and bullies want to win. When you demonstrate insecurities or low confidence, you become vulnerable—the new target. In most cases, when you respond assertively, the bullies will back off. They begin to realize that you will not succumb to their pressure, innuendos, and overall nastiness. If you don't show strength and act assertively, future attacks by the saboteur can actually expand and increase in number as well damage.

Acquiring confidence is not an overnight phenomenon; it takes time and desire, and it begins with an attitude—yours. Do you walk your talk? Are you true to yourself? Do you treat others as you would like to be treated? Do you treat yourself as you would treat others?

In the nationwide study for *The Confidence Factor,* we found that the number-one builder of confidence for the group identified as Accomplished Women was facing crisis—in fact, facing multiple crises. Confidence also comes from stretching and learning new things, and being able to pat yourself on the back. Sometimes, you may be your own best audience.

2. *Don't confuse friendliness with friendship.*   Women continually fall into the friendliness pitfall. Men don't. Women are more inclined to talk too much, be too open, and tell too much about themselves, their fears, and even their weaknesses too soon in any relationship with another woman. Just because a woman is friendly doesn't mean that your life saga needs to be shared up front. Wait. Review the Friendship-Savvy Quiz in Fig. 5-2. Forget the momism "Be friends with everyone." It's a flaw that many women perpetuate. For every jerk, there's a jerkette. Friendships in the workplace should be construed as bonuses, not requirements.

3. *Be discerning with your trust.*   Before you open up, determine what types of values, desires, concerns, and feelings you and another woman share. This won't happen overnight; it will take a period of time. If there is commonality, then and only then should you consider sharing anything that might be construed as being personal. Otherwise, information about you will end up floating around to be refiltered. By the time it gets back to you, it might not be recognizable.

4. *Speak up and speak out.*   In other words, confront the saboteur. The single most important step to take after you've been sabotaged (or figured out that you've been at a later date) is to confront the saboteur. Rarely is this fun; nevertheless, it is critical so that you can move on. Women have not been encouraged to engage in conflicts as men have.

If you don't confront the saboteur, you are setting into play a series of factors that will enable the situation to perpetuate. When you don't confront you are saying, "OK, keep doing it." And you might as well add, "Keep doing it to others." Because women are more inclined to internalize anger, they can reexpress it in a variety of unhealthy ways, some of which can make them quite ill. Chap. 9, which examines the *confrontophobia trap,* identifies techniques that will help you become a master of confrontation.

5. *Get a mentor and be a mentor.*   Every organization has skeletons and ghosts. A mentor can point them out, acting as a coach, an adviser, and a teacher. A mentor is not a mother, ready to jump in and fix whatever needs fixing if a crisis or problem occurs. A mentor will guide you through the office hierarchy.

She (or he) can be someone who has been with the organization for several years or someone who is just a step ahead of you, possibly being in your position within the last year or two. Or it could be someone who is a peer. People who have been in an organization for a period of time know where all the dead bodies are, and the traps.

In any mentor relationship, it is important to be respectful of the time that's been dedicated to your professional development.

As a rule, most mentorships are positive experiences. There are those times when changes come about; you may outgrow your mentor, or you could decide to move in another direction where the mentor's guidance and expertise are not as anchored as you need to have. There are also times when a mentor relationship can turn toxic. Your mentor could perceive you as a threat and after her job. This is most likely to occur in the mentor who is just a few steps ahead of you.

Your mentor could also fall out of favor in the organization. A variety of factors could come into play, including the situation where the mentor headed a project that met with a dismal failure and became a political hot potato within the company, or the mentor was sabotaged by someone else. No matter what, the toxic effects can spread. You end up with a poisonous aftertaste.

6. *Communicate the unwritten rules.*   There are only a few written rules of business, ones that anyone can identify. Go to work, do your job. For most of us, those are the big things: going to work and doing our job. But there is a lot more. Each organization has a series of unwritten rules (as do families and relationships). There can be just a few; there can be hundreds.

You learn these rules by watching and experiencing, by being there, listening. Sometimes, I think people pick them up by osmosis. It's not going to be the 1000-pound gorilla that gets you; it's going to be the gnats, those pesky critters you try to swat away, but they just keep swarming around. Two of the most common unwritten rules are to make a new pot of coffee when the last cup is taken, and to switch the copy paper back to regular after colored paper has been used.

Imagine you have a rush project. You have to make several copies. You set the copier up to make 300 copies and go back to your desk to complete several phone calls, confident that the project will be done when you are off the phone. When you return, you discover it is done, but on fuchsia paper. The net result is that you are going to be ticked off, time is running out, and you are ready to hang the person who didn't switch the paper back. Do yourself and your coworkers a favor and begin to compile a list of unwritten rules—the rules that make your workplace slick, click, and tick—and post them. You will be amazed to discover that some of them are antiquated and should have gone out when word processing came in.

7. *Give credit where it's due.*   And, if it's due you—terrific—give credit to yourself. If you don't pass on credit to those who have earned it, they may become resentful, even plotting a get-even-with-you down the road. When you praise, use the "atta girl" approach. Men know all about this. Whether in sports or in the workplace, men routinely vocalize their applause for another's performance. Women's style is to go up on a one-on-one basis and give applause. That's dandy, but it's not as effective as acknowledging and cheering in public so others can hear the applause.

8. *Don't become invisible.*   One of the classic momisms is "Don't brag." In today's workplace, it's important to understand the art of bragging and taking credit for your accomplishments. It is also essential to maintain your visibility. Whenever a company reorganizes, downsizes, or reenergizes, those who survive or move up are usually the ones who are visible.

When you come across land mines in your workplace, a normal response is to pull yourself out of it—in fact, to withdraw almost as if it's an "exit, stage right." Don't. You need to stay forward. People are watching you, how you react, how you continue with the day-to-day activities. Granted, you feel wounded, but you are going to need to heal those wounds, often in the public eye.

Behind closed doors, you can share whatever pain you are going through with someone who is extraordinarily close to you. Seek out someone who is caring, supportive, and nonjudgmental—a spouse, a relative, or a best friend. Most likely, it should not be someone within your workplace.

9. *Create and maintain allies.*   There is always safety in numbers. Your allies should be coworkers and colleagues as well as supervisors and managers within the organization. It usually pays to be pleasant toward anyone in a superior position. Those in higher positions have mastered techniques that allow them to be "Artful Dodgers" of saboteurs in their past. Building alliances also enables you to let supervisors and managers, including those who don't manage you directly, know of your accomplishments and achievements.

Remember, don't confuse friendship with friendliness. Allies are the people you build strong and supportive workplace relationships with. They are not necessarily those you open up and share your personal life with. When you have strong allies, it is difficult for someone with saboteuring and shark tendencies to attack you. Your coworkers will be as tuned in to her techniques as you are, and can sound off warnings as well as head off any attacks.

10. *Learn to be more overt.*   Men are more direct than women. Women need to learn to be more overt and less covert. If you haven't honed your assertiveness skills or read a good book on the topic, do it now. When it comes to women sabotaging women, it is sometimes difficult to determine who did what to whom, and when it really happened. Women have been trained since childhood to be less direct—to act coy and appear nice, almost at all costs, to get what they want.

This learned behavior—another momism surfacing—leads to behind-the-scenes action. Early on, boys learn that it's OK to grab, push, or be blunt and act directly for something when they want it. Any bruises they receive along the way are a part of growing up. In the end, it makes them stronger and ready for the real world. By learning to be overt, you let others know where you stand, whether it's yesterday, today, or tomorrow.

UNITED WE STAND

Today's pressurized workplace has created a cut-throat climate for some. The ability to protect yourself becomes a critical survival skill. Individuals who have been laid off, or have lost their jobs, are often victims of backstabbing who did little to protect themselves.

> *No matter what, when you deal with a saboteur, it's important to keep your cool. Have your facts—whatever documentation you need to support yourself, your position and/or your opinion—along with a healthy dose of self-esteem.*

The last thing you want to do is to plot revenge, or malign a coworker, boss, or company. The effort is self-destructive, and can almost guarantee a visit to the unemployment lines. You may end up being labeled a malcontent, or even deserving of your fate. Your model should definitely *not* be "Don't get mad, just get even."

A healthier approach is to reframe the situation and determine what kind of learning experience you can derive from it. In the end, many saboteurs' successes are not as sweet as they envisioned. The deceit and sabotage that enabled them to win an early victory may, in the end, block them from a goal that they sought in the long run. The adage "United we stand, divided we fall," definitely applies to women and their sabotaging actions toward other women.

Management Chaos: What persons directing a business or organization create with a disorganized and disruptive style.

TRAP 4: MANAGEMENT CHAOS
Trouble on Top

- Have you ever been in a situation where management said it would support you, and later you found out it didn't?

- Has a manager ever given you instructions to follow and then given others on your team different instructions?

- Has a manager ever criticized your work in front of others?

- Has your management group ever set up a quality assurance program and then not supported it?

- Have you ever been asked by a manager or supervisor to complete a task ASAP and then, when you had done so, discovered that it sat in a pile for weeks before it was ever looked at?

Each year Nine-to-Five, the National Association of Working Women, sponsors a contest to identify the best—and the worst—bosses of the year. It's the good news–bad news approach. In previous years, winners of the Good Boss award included a small business owner in Dobbs Ferry, New York, who created a family-friendly work environment in which children were welcome, workers were allowed to make their own schedules, and the boss picked up the tab on all work-related college courses for employees.

Or consider the plant manager from Des Moines, Iowa who believed in a real team concept. His strategy was to share all information with staff and fight for raises for workers. The result was that his group was the most financially successful plant in the corporation. Then there's the city engineer in Minnesota who endured threats and sabotage because he chose to help the women on his staff by ridding the department of various acts of pay disparity, reprisals, and harassment.

These managers know what managing is all about. Unfortunately, they are more the exception than the norm. Read on.

The unbelievable Bad Boss winners included a doctor from Rochester, New York who demanded that his nurse immediately return to his office—even though she had just found her baby sitter dead on the living room couch. Or the supervisor in Maine who not only allowed but encouraged sexual harassment against all women in his male-dominated workplace. His management rewarded him with a promotion. Then there's the casino manager in Las Vegas, Nevada who terminated a pregnant employee because she could no longer fit into her uniform, yet issued larger uniforms for women who had breast implants.

In Mount Prospect, Illinois, an office supervisor fired her consumer relations associate of 3 years just a few days after the woman's baby was still-born. And a Tampa, Florida law firm canceled a pregnant associate's insurance shortly before the birth of her child because the associate's pregnancy wasn't part of the firm's business plan.

THE NUMBING FIELD

When you hear about bad bosses, bad managers, or bad workplace environments like the ones described above, it's easy to rationalize that yours may not be so bad. Any time there are extremes, there is usually an offsetting positioning. If nothing at your workplace is as bad as any of the above, then there is no big deal if management gets out of line with lesser-type abuses. It becomes a numbing field—you tolerate the little stuff and with each "so what," the field of tolerance expands. Before you know it, it takes a tornado-type assault to get your attention.

What happens when employees, and in particular women employees, feel that management doesn't listen to them or solicit their input? For Barbara, her solution became obvious. She left.

Barbara describes herself as a career women. She doesn't have children, and she is married. For 26 years, she dedicated herself to a teaching career in the mental health arena, and then in higher education, before she began her own successful company specializing in career counseling and relocation. She routinely works with individuals who have been fired or laid off. She also subcontracts with firms to service their outplacement and training needs with layoffs and reorganization. Barbara's own relationships with management and bosses have been tenuous at best.

Barbara's a classic case of what happens to competent, creative, and assertive women. She had no intention or vision of going further within the university that she had worked for. Her "druthers" were not to be school chancellor but rather to create a cohesive, leading-edge program within the university system. The glass ceiling was not the issue; it was the brick walls and the muddy basements that so many women find themselves immersed in and surrounded by.

When she left, she created a new organization with 19 employees. The good news is that she is in control, has full autonomy, knows where she's going, and is quite successful. Her employees—men and women—are encouraged to stretch, are allowed to make mistakes, and feel empowered. The bad news is that businesses and the various bureaucracies of the workplace lose big. The people with the talent needed to take bureaucracy into the next century respond, "Screw it, I need these hassles like I need another hole in my head." And managers at all levels (including the university chancellor, in Barbara's case) are impotent. Their efforts to cut through the "office politics" of the toxic workplace carry no weight. These top-heavy and lopsided organizations will someday go the way of the dinosaur.

THE TOXIC WASTELAND

Sheila was also ensconced in a toxic workplace, overseen by toxic management. She was a counselor for students at a small college. Sheila was mainly involved with personal and career counseling, on-campus recruiting, and a variety of stress and career-related workshops. Most of her time was spent working with, or for, the students. One woman vice president ran, in large part, the daily operations of the college. Sheila believes that Dana set out to destroy several of the teams that worked under her. She finally concluded, along with several other employees, that this woman was in serious need of mental health counseling.

Three years ago, our entire campus worked as a team. Then Dana, one of the vice presidents on campus, stepped in and her philosophy has seemed to be "divide and conquer." In the past year, she has hired another woman to replace my old boss. Unfortunately, this woman is a lot like Dana—controlling, manipulative, rude, with poor managerial and personal skills, and, many times, displaying unethical behavior. When Dana advertised for the position, she custom-wrote a job description for her friend, the woman who became my new boss. Many of Dana's comments inferred, "I want *this* woman in *this* position. We'll advertise it because that is the legal requirement, but she's going to be hired."

Dana showed little respect for the hiring process. Many individuals applied for the position, including two excellent candidates. As part of the interviewing committee, we were asked to share written comments about each candidate; however, we knew that our input was useless since Dana's friend was going to be hired anyway.

Dana's main objectives have been to gain control, power, and authority. She often turns two managers against each other by giving them must enough negative information (usually contrived) about each other. That way, teams eventually break up and at least one manager sides with Dana, leaving the other to fend for him/herself. The underlying theme of Dana's orders is, "You'll do what I say, or you'll be fired." If she does not agree with someone's opinion or input, she usually accuses the individual of being insubordinate and writes it up. Most of the employees on campus know she keeps personal files on each of them.

Evidence of Dana's objectives appeared after she worked for several years on turning the board of trustees against other administrators, including the president of the college. Eventually, all top administrators and the president stepped down. Other teams on campus began to disintegrate as well. In the wake, Dana remained the only person at the top.

We began to wonder if we were reading too much into Dana's actions. Then we came across a book entitled *Too Perfect* by Allan Mallinger and Jeanette DeWyze. It described Dana very accurately and caused a sign of relief from those of us who felt *we* might be the crazy ones.

My previous boss, who has been replaced by the woman who is very much like Dana, was recently promoted. She now has to deal with Dana on a daily basis and has much more patience than I have. Dana and her friend began to have trouble relating with each other on a managerial level soon after the woman was hired. I ended up being caught in the middle on several occasions. My previous boss finally took me aside and said, "Sheila, you've got to understand that this isn't you. They are having a power struggle and you are the one who has to bear the outcome of each battle."

I believe that Dana didn't like the fact that I am my own person. I stick to my ethics, I like being treated like a professional, and I speak my piece. I have respect for her position, but I don't have respect for her, which she has made obvious—she dislikes. My old boss once told me Dana disliked me because of my independence and self-confidence. After seeing so many teams disintegrate, and after struggling with the inherent sickness of Dana and the woman she hired, I realized I had to leave that very unhealthy environment. (Interesting, within 6 months, so did the three other people with whom I worked.)

THE ILLNESS OF HEALTH CARE

Sheila's experience with the toxic president of the college is not unusual in the overall workplace. As more and more organizations downsize, rightsize, and reorganize—whatever you want to call it—anxiety and the fear of change impact just about everybody. With the cry of health-care reform of the mid-1990s, fear and anxiety have been common occurrences in the health-care environment. Hospitals have been dramatically hit, and nursing has been particularly affected.

Any time there is fear and anxiety, sabotage levels increase. Just a few years ago, a nurse could take a position with a hospital across town, and actually get a signing bonus. With the charge of reform, all concepts of bonuses have disappeared. Thousands are lucky to receive 2-week notices. The cry has become "Cut corners, cut services, and cut expenses in every direction." An aura of penny-wisdom and dollar foolishness permeates the air.

Several respondents in the GenderTraps survey were from the health-care industry. In fact, several nurses from the same hospital were interviewed. They worked in the recovery room of a hospital in the New England area. The common theme of their complaints was directed toward management—or mismanagement, nonmanagement, and, in some cases, wrong management.

Dorothy, Evelyn, and Dianne are all staff nurses. Dorothy initially wrote that information was routinely withheld, and that the manager of the recovery room rarely gave credit to any of the other nurses on her day staff, which usually numbered a dozen. The manager was also confrontophobic. Dorothy recalled the time when she was up for her annual evaluation. After she had completed her review, which showed no discrepancies or problems, the manager tossed out a comment as she got up to leave her office.

> My evaluation was considered average—nothing spectacular and no problems. The one area I consistently rate high in is my ability to work with patients' families, especially when there are problems. I have a knack for dissipating anger, so I end up with a lot of the difficult patients.
>
> At the end of the evaluation, my manager added, "By the way, I've had complaints about you." When I asked about what, she responded that I didn't hold up my share of my responsibility. I again asked who's saying that I didn't do my share. She responded that she didn't want to give names, but she was getting complaints from every shift.
>
> Well, I was taken aback. When I came back from my break, I went back into her office and said, "I really don't like what you said. You've hit me below the belt. That was not really a good way of telling me; it was such a blanket statement." I also told her that I wanted the specifics and that I realized people make mistakes and they can improve. But without any specifics, it would be difficult if not impossible to improve in the areas that I supposedly don't take responsibility in.

For her manager to say only vaguely that there were complaints is absurd. Dorothy was open for her evaluation and for suggestions on how she could improve her skills and techniques. Her manager offered her none, hiding behind blanket statements. Her manager's response that there had been several complaints—without identifying the specifics, or even the people complaining about Dorothy's work—has a twist to it.

THE CAT'S MEOW

Several of the women who work within Dorothy's group stated that they had a problem with the favoritism their manager directed toward the sole male in the group. Although he was hired to be a staff nurse, just as they were, they found he routinely did not do staff work. Instead, he practiced his computing skills, updating and inputting various programs on the manager's computer. He became adept at doing the various scheduling and rescheduling requirements that the recovery room went through as the demand level changed.

It was not uncommon for him to check out hours before their shift routinely ended, saying that he would be working on scheduling at home. He then got paid a full shift. Whether he worked on the schedule or did other, related work at home no one knew. Evelyn, one of Dorothy's coworkers, specifically noted this situation in her interview:

> Our manager thought he was the cat's meow. She put him in charge of scheduling and inventorying the needs within the unit, and he got a whole 8 hours. He also got to go home early, saying he was working on the total quality management program. He would leave the hospital at five or six o'clock but sign himself out until nine o'clock, getting paid for the entire shift.

> We had an incident where a narcotic was misused and it was obvious that he had mistakenly opened the morphine and thrown an unused portion into the disposable drug box. If any of the women on the floor had done it, we, at the minimum, would have been verbally counselled. She said nothing to him.

> Our manager bends over backwards for her favorites. Unfortunately, most of the women on our floor are not her favorites. Several of us approached her to try to figure out how the morphine got misplaced. He had been involved with patient care during the shift where only one patient received morphine. When we approached the manager about the sloppiness, her response was that it was just a mistake and we should let it go at that. He continues to get special favors.

MONEY SAVER

Dianne feels a lot of support from the nurses she works with. In fact, she feels it's the only thing that keeps them going. She believes the manager is kept on because dollars are saved. She buys the cheapest of any specific items and holds on to outdated equipment, even when replacements can no longer be obtained and improved, newer versions have been introduced.

Evelyn concurs with both Dorothy and Dianne. She believes that their manager works in a parent-child style, controlling her employees by power threats and manipulations.

I don't think that she'll be leaving her position any time soon unless she creates a tremendous mistake. Her people skills are minimal. If her position became open, I doubt they would fill it with anyone like her again. She hasn't kept up with management training or education in her field.

We had a situation where we needed some new cribs in the recovery room. All the nurses had looked at the catalogs and identified several models that would be acceptable. The one we unanimously said no to, was the one that was ordered. Why? Because it was cheapest. It didn't matter that one of the sides couldn't go down— a necessity in our department.

A common problem for many women is that they seem to swirl in a conspiracy of silence. When they see things that are outrageous, inappropriate, and out of place, they rarely go directly to the person, senior management, or even the CEO, all of whom can make some changes. Women's style is far more likely to result in a complaint about a significant situation within a tighter circle of co-workers or even friends, rather than to resolve it.

THE WRONG TIME

After several years on staff, Sheryl had an opportunity to move into management. Her supervisor offered her the position as the manager of a growing unit. As would be expected with the increased amount of responsibility from staff to manager, she found herself working 60-plus hours a week. At year's end, Sheryl finally came to the conclusion that she didn't want to continue at that rate. The hours were too long, and she had other stresses coming in from her home life. When she approached her supervisor about some of the stress that she faced, she was told that she would get through it.

I found that she wasn't really amiable, and wasn't willing to be flexible in working out some of the time constraints that I was under. I realized that I didn't want to be in this particular position any longer, so I began to look for someone to take my place. The person I found was eminently qualified. When I turned in my resignation, I gave the supervisor the other person's name as well.

She was not happy; in fact, she was angry. It was as if to say that she took a chance on me and I failed her. I told her that the job was not what I thought the position would entail; I did not want to work the 60 hours a week; and I didn't want to be mom to all the adults on my staff. Her attitude toward me changed significantly.

Future opportunities seemed to disappear. I am in my forties and I have young children. I noticed that there seemed to be the assumption that anyone who has young children isn't interested in any other types of management. Since my resignation as manager, other nonstaff positions or management positions have either been made unavailable or denied to me. To deal with it, I've developed an alternative network of people who keep me aware of potential new positions. Meanwhile, I continue working and continue with special projects, and wait and see.

I received interesting comments from management regarding my family, such as "You wouldn't be interested in a specific profes- sional meeting or subject because you have a family." Or "You wouldn't be able to find time." I learned that I have to be very spe- cific and state something along the lines of "No, you need to give me that opportunity; I still make decisions for myself." I even found some skepticism over my nursing skills after I had my fami- ly. The assumption was that somehow the division of my time between work and home would make me less competent.

The situation that Sheryl identified is not uncommon. Many people in management, and it doesn't matter which level they are in, often assume things that shouldn't be assumed. In Sheryl's situa- tion, she was in the wrong place. When she was the manager of the unit, she discovered she wasn't willing to put in a 60-hour week along with the level of stress it generated.

Sheryl's style and skill could very likely have been better served in other management areas within the hospital in which she worked. Senior management, though, chose to ignore any further attempts to place her within the management field because of her previous rejection of the position that she held. The fact that she took it upon herself to identify someone with the credentials and skills to step into her position strongly indicates that she is a team player, that she has the overall needs of the hospital in mind, and that she is willing to say that she was the wrong fit for this particular position.

COMPASSION IS NOT THE PSALM

Joan is a bookkeeper for a Catholic church in the South. Prior to that, she was the secretary for the church for 5 years. She and her husband

were attending a wedding reception when he suddenly collapsed. His
heart stopped for almost 4 minutes. If it hadn't been for the bride and
two other nurses who were guests, her husband would not be alive.

Her husband was in intensive care for several weeks and, while
there, underwent multiple surgeries, including the amputation of
his leg. He was given a 10 percent chance of living. When her husband emerged from the coma, he needed bypass surgery. This
required him to be transferred to another hospital. During that
time, Joan continued to contact her employers, the priests. They
told her not to worry. When her husband was transferred back to
their home city, they would sort everything out. They didn't wait
until she returned; they fired her instead.

> My husband had just turned 50, and we were attending the wed-
> ding of one of his coworkers. After several dances, we switched
> partners, and that was when it happened. All our friends surround-
> ed him and I was held off by strangers. I was so angry that I stood
> up on a chair so I could see him.
>
> By then, they had cut off his suit and were giving him CPR. If it
> wasn't for the three nurses who were there, one being the bride,
> he wouldn't be alive. They worked on him for 45 minutes, and the
> paramedics worked on him for another 45 minutes before he was
> transported to the hospital. The priest had given him the last rites.
>
> When he didn't die, the doctors said that he would be an invalid
> for the rest of his life and would never work again. They were
> wrong. He survived the surgeries for the blood clots and the
> amputation of his leg and he came out of the coma. The hospital
> transferred him to another hospital 2 hours away where the bypass
> surgery would be performed.
>
> I had been on my job for almost 5 years. The second week my hus-
> band was in intensive care, one of the priests told me I was fired.
> Ironically, the person they gave my job to was, I thought, my best
> friend. You would think that the Catholic Church would have
> more compassion. I had asked for a leave of absence and was
> denied it. I was told that the parish was too small, and that I
> couldn't be given any time off.
>
> When I learned I was several months shy of 5 years—at which
> point I would have been fully vested in the pension at the dio-
> cese—I almost lost my faith. Three parishes later, another priest
> hired me and was able to get his diocese to give me credit for the
> $4\frac{3}{4}$ years I had already put in. At least I'll get a pension.
>
> I've been back to my old parish a couple of times, and several of
> the people—the parishioners were mostly older—were like adopt-

ed parents. When I saw them, they would hug me and say, "Oh, Joan, why did you leave us?" And when I told them I didn't leave, that I was fired, the priests weren't too happy.

My husband's boss encouraged me to file for unemployment compensation. I finally did, but the priests fought me. After months, they dropped the case and I was able to collect before I got my current job.

During my husband's hospitalization, I tried to call my former bosses several times. When I finally connected, they said not to worry, that we would talk when he got out of the hospital. When we did, it was very cut and dried. They had gone through all my personal belongings, and half were destroyed or missing. All that remained had been piled in a corner of a back office.

I said I wanted to talk to my direct boss, and I was told I needed an appointment. They said they would get back to me. When I got home that afternoon, there was a message saying that my boss could see me in a week and a half. I learned that the three priests together had decided that I was to go.

The priests' response—management's response—to Joan's personal crisis was totally inappropriate. Initially, the odds that her husband would survive were extremely low. The things that Joan needed most were compassion, understanding, and support—none of which she got—from her employers. The fact that they were also her religious support makes her experience more outrageous. Today, Joan is a bookkeeper. When her husband became ill, she was a secretary, a position that could easily have been filled on a temporary basis from an agency. Her treatment, and her husband's, as an individual and as an employee was inexcusable.

BIG MAC RUINED HER DAY

Deborah is a supervisor at a regional discount chain. She is the overall manager of the video department in several of the stores in her region. Prior to this position, she had been manager at one of the busiest McDonald's sites in the South for 10 years. From that position, she was terminated for misconduct.

After 10 years, I was sat down one day, given a 30-day probationary period, and told that after that period I would most likely be fired. Now, this was out of the clear blue sky—no warnings, no previous pink slips, no nothing.

My supervisor told me that the store was run by a bunch of bitch-es who didn't get along and that the nastiness was going to cease. I felt that there was more to it. In fact, I felt that it was directly related to the fact that the supervisor and my head manager were close friends. She and I had never really gotten along well.

She had progressively moved up through the organization for sev-eral years. She worked at one store and I worked at another until we both worked at the same store and she became my head man-ager. It was at that time that she and my supervisor both sat me down and said that my time was up.

I felt I was going to have a nervous breakdown. My doctor suggested I take a few weeks off. I took it as sick time. When I got back to work, I was fired that day. I was never placed on a probationary peri-od. On looking back, I felt there was little that I could have done.

It might be construed as a personality clash. I had been with the company for 10 years, and never had a problem, nor had received a pink slip. The company handbook listed specific steps to be taken if a person was to be terminated. There was a pink slip, a verbal warning, a written warning, and so on. Everything had to be documented. In my file, there was nothing.

What is ironic is that I had planned to resign in October because of the problems I was having with this specific manager. They both begged me to stay. At that point, I had turned in my resigna-tion, giving them a 2-week notice. Another job had already been lined up. Giving in, I said OK, I'll stay. A few months later, I was fired. I felt I was set up.

Deborah could very well have been set up. Her termination within a few months of her announcement that she was leaving after a long history of success within the overall organization is sus-picious. It might even be likened to a jilted lover getting even with her for her rejection.

MANAGEMENT IS AN IDIOT

Several of the respondents wrote on their original survey, "Management stinks." In follow-up interviews, they were probed for examples of what management had done to earn this verdict. Examples were far-ranging: everything from communications to per-sonality styles to saving substantial sums in the budget and then being forced to terminate a needed employee—and a good friend—to literally coming in and rearranging an employee's office furniture.

Jackie, a free-lance writer, found herself in a unique situation. Over a period of time, she was fired five times by her boss. Prior to her going to work for him, she had done free-lance work on an occasional basis. When several employees quit, he asked her if she would come to work for him on a part-time basis.

> When I walked in, I discovered I was replacing two people. I was to do their work part time. The workload was tremendous. He started to tell people that I did artwork, and assumed that I could do it, since writing is an art. I did have skills in production layout as well as some photography work. But art, no.
>
> At one time or another, everyone in the company was fired at least once. I remember saying to him, "Look, explain to me how you can run an advertising production company if you have no one to do the work—all the writing and the artwork that I do. I also work directly with the clients, so explain to me how you can let me go and get all the work done without having to stay in town and do it yourself." Well, he didn't have any response to that. In fact, when I left the office, I came out with a promotion.

When Cindy wrote that her boss's management style "stinks," she was referring to the many times she felt that multiple problems had been created by her boss's style.

> I believe strongly in the chain of command, and I appreciate it when the people under me use it as well. My boss would often come into the department and make changes when I wasn't there, or she'd come in with criticism directed toward my staff but never addressing me. I felt that she continually undermined my authority in an attempt to make me look foolish. One time she came in after hours and rearranged furniture in our day-care facilities.
>
> She said she had had some complaints from parents. I don't believe she understood what their complaints were about. She didn't take any of them up with me, merely started to move furniture around on a whim. Her objective was to line up the furniture a certain way so it looked like there were actually fewer infants being cared for within the center.
>
> Now, this woman doesn't work in my building. What she would do is see people walking the hallway and seek them out, asking if they thought everything was OK in the day-care center, or if they had anything to complain about.

When she found out that all the furniture had been rearranged back to its original positioning, I got a call. When she kept saying it had to be put back, I responded that we needed to sit down and talk about it. It was like a broken record; she kept saying that we had to change everything back, and I responded we needed to talk about it. I refused to do what she said, at least until we had the opportunity to sit down and talk. Eventually, she dropped the subject and never brought it up again.

I felt the real problem was that, when she was given the responsibility of our department, she didn't really understand it. She rarely came over to the center, nor did she attempt to familiarize herself with how we worked with the parents as well as our own teachers. She often complained to my teachers, but rarely to me. When I made appointments with her, with the intent of bringing up her complaint, she rarely kept them. It was almost impossible to communicate with her.

THE GOOD-GUY, BAD-GUY ROUTINE

Helene is in charge of promotions and publicity at a small advertising agency. She found herself caught in a good-guy, bad-guy scenario. The two studio partners would constantly fight and use her like a ping-pong ball, not physically, but mentally and verbally. When she was initially interviewed and hired, she was told that a variety of career paths would be open to her once she was on board. Wrong. She learned that the carrot dangled was different when she joined the company.

> When I interviewed, one of the partners gave me a list of job responsibilities and the career paths they would take me to. It turned out to be a complete lie. He had no interest in promoting me anywhere. I would hear remarks like "If she thinks she is going anywhere, she has another thing coming. She should be happy doing what she is doing because that is what she was hired to do."
>
> I was stuck for over a year, and then someone left. I was interested in the position so I approached the two partners. One of them would say that he wanted me to have the position, but Sam didn't. Then the other would say, "I want you to have the position, but James doesn't." So it was a good-guy, bad-guy situation.
>
> They began to interview other people for the position and didn't inform me of the status. Finally, I just went in and said, "If you are not going to interview me for the position, you can find someone for

mine, because I'm giving notice." They caved in and gave me the position. Then they added that they felt I couldn't handle the job.

If I ever made a mistake or had difficulty with any segment of the job, the usual comment was, "Damn, I knew she couldn't handle it." There just wasn't any support. To my face, they said they did, but behind my back, it was just a crock!

TEACHING FROM THE PAST

Patricia Noonan is a consultant with expertise in management groups from the top to the bottom. Prior to being self-employed, she was the manager of organization and development for a Fortune 500 company based in the West. She believes that most managers have one foot in the 1950s and the other foot in the year 2000—even if they're only 30 years old. The reason is that most managers come through a business or school system in which the professors were trained in the 1950s and, in many cases, have found it impossible to let go of the old ways. In Noonan's view, the experiences of some of the women described in this chapter are not uncommon or unusual.

One of the problems coming from traditional business and management courses is that the professors rarely understand the newer concepts, much less what the real workplace is like in today's market. Most have done nothing professionally other than teach. Hands-on or practical experience is nonexistent. Most of these professors teach from textbooks whose research, data, and cases are often outdated. As Patricia Noonan points out:

> Textbooks are still based on "Let's go through the management theories and see how they work," and then "What you should do if this circumstance should occur." They rarely teach flexibility, compromise, how to look at a work group, see its diversity, and know what its value is. They teach you numbers and a formula and an outcome of X. This may be one of the reasons affirmative action hasn't been as effective as it should have been, at least in enhancing the bottom line, as management perceived it to be.

WHY AFFIRMATIVE ACTION CAN'T WORK

In applying affirmative action, management tried to get a formula for a certain percentage, whether it was female, black, Asian, or

Hispanic. Rarely did the leaders of corporate America look at affirmative action as a part of integration, as something that would redefine the rules and change the overall atmosphere of the workplace. Instead, they thought of it as merely a numbers game, and once they had the right numbers in the right slots, everything would be better. Their upbringing, their learning, was from Finance 101—the same finance courses that use the standard textbooks. When will it change? According to Noonan:

> Any type of affirmative action program can't work until management starts to think that the bottom line involves the ability of members of the workforce to get along with one another. In addition, the management structure must be flexible.
>
> For the most part, management comes from the same dynamics that families do. Most management is dysfunctional. Whatever we learn at home, we take to the workplace—unless someone sits us down and says, "The workplace is not home. You don't compete against one another; you are here to make the company successful."
>
> When there is competition within the workforce, sabotage often occurs. Most employees play a lot of games that they learned in school and at home, and they don't relearn. Management is no different. Managers don't understand that they too play games. They honestly don't view it as "This is not OK to do." That is, until they hit a crisis. Then they call in the consultant.

EQUAL DOES NOT MEAN THE SAME

When consultants like Noonan are brought in, it is rarely at a calm time in a company's life where everything is going smoothly. It's when crises hit. She finds the key to unscrambling most problems is nothing more than group dynamics—determining how the group makes decisions, how its members work together, how they accomplish anything that is real. Noonan feels that it is all basically simple stuff, areas that are not complicated and shouldn't have major problems attached to them. But there are. In her consulting work, Noonan finds that management is genuinely confused. It doesn't understand that being flexible and working within the needs of employees is not interpreted as being inconsistent.

> Managers can't get it until they understand that flexibility doesn't mean inconsistency. It's a real key. Managers tend to think that if

they're flexible to the needs of any one individual, much less of a group, they will be viewed as being inconsistent. They are afraid of being called on the carpet for not holding people accountable.

A common thread that managers heard in their classrooms and family dynamics is to treat everyone the same. And management doesn't get it—equal does not necessarily mean the same.

Prior to her consulting practice, Noonan worked for a company that had a tremendous desire to help its employees. And that's the good news. The only drawback was that it was in a paternalistic mode. There was a strong component of "family feeling" at work. And how the company delivered help to its employees was more from the standpoint of being the parent. The company would take care of you, almost as if you couldn't make your own decisions.

> The format the company used is much like how you would struc-
> ture your kids' summer camp program. "We'll pick out these activi-
> ties for you, and we'll help you do this; we'll give you guidance,
> and, of course, we'll pay for it." The company decided that all the
> employees should join a bowling league because it would be a
> great way for them to socialize. Company leaders couldn't under-
> stand why the employees weren't grateful. After all, they had iden-
> tified a fun activity and agreed to underwrite it 100 percent.
>
> Company leaders did it with the best of intentions. Unfortunately,
> they did it from the standpoint that they knew better than their
> employees on how outside time should be spent.

Noonan hits on a critical point: Many in management treat their employees as if they are not adults. Those in traditional manage- ment have been told from the time that they graduated from col- lege, and from the time they entered management, that one of man- agement's functions is to make the decisions for its employees—or, in some cases, for the rest of the world. It's not unusual for manage- ment to forget that the reason they work for a particular company is that they wanted/need to work, not to have decisions made for them. Noonan also believes that, as managers mature and move up within the organization, their attitudes are reinforced.

> As you get higher and higher in an organization, you begin to
> believe that your decision-making powers are so much better than
> those of the people who work for you at the bottom of the organi-
> zation. In some cases, you treat them as if they were children. You
> want them dependent on you. And, then, as in the parent-child

relationship, children grow up and want their independence; they
want to make decisions and be responsible. It is as if the workers
are acting out; management throws up its hands and asks why
can't employees behave like adults.

I feel one of the biggest challenges in the management structure is
to say, "I'm going to treat my employees, not as children, but as
adults. I'm also going to behave as an adult."

If management forms the attitude that it doesn't always know
best, a major transformation in the workplace can occur. It's almost
like a "cosmic goose" (i.e., an event or happening that zaps you with
one of the "ahas" of life). Management all of a sudden realizes,
"Wow, my employees can think, they have great ideas, and they
actually have an understanding of what their own needs are.
Remarkable."

Have we seen the last of layoffs? Not likely. According to Al
Neuharth, founder of *USA Today*, most CEOs have the save-your-
way-to-prosperity philosophy. Their strategy has been to fire long-
time, loyal employees without much remorse or regret. In the early
1990s, IBM, AT&T, GM, Sears, and GTE laid off more than 325,000
men and women. Initially, the strategy gained favor among Wall
Street analysts because of the significant decline the layoffs would
have on the expense side of the ledger. But it doesn't always work.

Losing a position is usually not good news for most workers. In
fact, many have feelings of anger, shock, even disbelief. Many managements have participated in what could be called brutal firings.
When this occurs, there is likely to be some type of backlash.

In 1994, a Connecticut jury awarded a $105,000 settlement to
an employee who was fired, according to the jury, in a brutal way.
Helen Barratt had been employed for 7 years as a social work manager in a New Haven hospital. With her termination notice, she was
forced to leave her personal belongings in a plastic bag. She was
then escorted out the door by security guards in full view of gaping
coworkers.

Her supervisor had told her that if she returned to the office to
gather her personal effects, she would be arrested for trespassing. At
no time during her employment or during the severance experience
had she ever displayed, or had there ever been allegations of, any
criminal wrongdoing or other indications of disloyalty.

A few years ago the accounting firm of Ernst & Young laid off 37
attorneys and 200 support people in its legal department. It had
posted security guards in plainclothes to prevent the destruction of

files and computer equipment. The reaction from the newly unemployed workers was anger and disbelief.[1]

Virginia King is the author of *Never Work for a Jerk*. She feels that managers are often uncomfortable about their roles. Many of the problems generated by management—in particular, the noncommunications or miscommunications from management when times are tough—are a pure and simple result of the fact that few managers involve their employees. Most people are quite resilient if they have the data behind unpopular decisions. For example, "Earnings have plummeted 50 percent and we need to make cutbacks in order to meet payroll."

MANAGERS DON'T GET IT

Many managers and supervisors don't "get it." They don't realize that they don't have to be mean, rude, or abrasive to employees if they don't create what employees think they should. Unless they have totally bent personalities, managers don't need to display lunatic reactions. Yet many do. As a number of GenderTraps respondents reflected, "My manager's style stinks."

One of the biggest problems for management is its lack of ability to use and develop the talent of its employees. According to a 1992 study by the Oechsli Institute of North Carolina, 80 percent of the 487 respondents said they were not held accountable for their performance on the job. More than two-thirds said that when they did not meet standards, supervisors did not deal with them.[2]

Organizations will be far more productive and competitive if their managers do *set* and *enforce* high standards that can be measured. That means that managers have to develop skills and resolve to demand that their employees do their best. It is a two-way street. Many managers sidestep the whole issue of accountability. Somehow, they perceive and believe that their employees know exactly what they are supposed to do.

Also, too many managers today hide behind trendy programs. Technology and slogans are expected to save them. Many of the GenderTraps respondents felt that the concepts of total quality management (TQM) and quality assurance (QA) were a farce. They all sounded and looked terrific with the bells and whistles. But when it came down to supporting and working with the program, management (specifically, upper management) simply dropped out.

GenderTraps respondents felt that management's philosophy was "Do as we say, but not as we do." The reality is that employees must be accountable, and managers and leaders at every level within an organization must be equally accountable.

Some managers take the opposite approach. They believe that if they are softer or nicer in their styles, using phrases like "I hope you do better," then the employee will be less threatened and thus more likely to perform. In some cases, that is a myth. If there is less threat, and management is vague about overall goals, it is easy for people to get lazy.

Instead of telling someone, "We hope you do better," a manager needs to be far more specific. Employees need to know what is successful in terms of amounts, deadlines, and responsibilities. People should not have to second-guess what they are supposed to do.

When there appear to be many problems for both employees and managers, it is easy to get paralyzed. A wise manager should attempt to deal with one problem at a time. Problems to be dealt with should be identified with employees' input. The message becomes, "We are dealing with a problem that is critical to everyones' success, possibly even the company's survival." By isolating a common problem, one that everyone has some input into, a manager can instruct employees to look for measurable actions that can be identified in the process. The objective becomes getting to a result that carries high impact for the organization.

When Debi Colman took over the MacIntosh manufacturing facility for Apple Computer years ago, it wasn't difficult to step into the physical plant and see it was a mess. It was disorganized, looked dirty, and overall was an unpleasant place to work in. The mess was a common problem. Everyone knew it. The physical plant became the first thing Debi would take on, starting with an overall gutting, cleaning up, and a lot of paint. She identifies it as one of the first steps in the major turnaround that she shepherded. The results became evident immediately. Coleman saved Apple's bacon.

MANAGEMENT CLUES

Two other areas are imperative for any manager. The first is to *communicate*. One of the biggest mistakes management consistently makes is to fail to share information. This means sharing the good news along with the bad. Have short and frequent meetings; marathons are not necessary.

The second is to *acknowledge and reward employees*. Give them feedback; everyone needs it—both managers and employees. The attitude that you don't need to thank others—as if they knew they were doing their jobs well—doesn't work. Everyone needs a few strokes.

When employees do their work, they should be paid for it. They should be paid decently, not in an inequitable form, as too many women reported in the survey. When a company is successful and the pay is fair, employees obtain a sense of security. Few people work well when they are under pressure about whether they are going to be able to pay their rent, or if they have a job the next month. That kind of worry reduces productivity.

> *Many managers are clueless about how to manage their employees. The objective is for you to manage your boss, who in turn will learn how to manage you.*

Some of the actions, reactions, and misactions of management are traceable to this fundamental issue. If you think your manager is deranged, or a potential candidate for lunacy, there are several strategies that you can evoke. In Chap. 9, I identify five management styles in dealing with conflict: *competitive, collaborative, compromising, accommodating,* and *avoiding*. It makes sense to know not only your style of dealing with conflict but also the style of the person you are having the conflict with.

The remainder of Chapter 9 is devoted to *managing conflict styles*. Answer the questions as if you were the "other person"— namely, your manager. Understanding who your manager is means that you see her (or him) as she actually is, not as how you would want her to be. There are five steps to enhancing your effectiveness with your manager.

1. IDENTIFY STRENGTHS AND WEAKNESSES

In addition to understanding your manager's style in dealing with problems and handling conflict, answer these questions about her.

It's improbable that you will know all the answers. Keep your eyes and ears open as you gather information.

- What kind of pressure is she under? Is her group (section, division, etc.) meeting the company's financial goals?
- Outside of regular pay, does your manager get bonuses or other perks?
- Does your manager share good news with your group?
- Does your manager share bad news with the group?
- Do you know who supports her within the organization?
- Does she have a mentor or is she anyone's protégé?
- Do you know who doesn't support her within the organization?
- Is your manager a morning or an evening person?
- Does your manager like a lot of information before she makes a decision, or does she seem impatient if you give her too much data?
- Does your manager issue a lot of memos, or does she like to receive them?
- Does your manager prefer one-on-one or group meetings to discuss various issues, or does she prefer that issues be presented in memo form?
- If your manager has young children, does she have problems with child-care needs?
- Is your manager able to juggle a lot of things at one time, or does she handle one task at a time?
- Does your manager have strong opinions, or does she ask the opinions of others before she comes to a conclusion?
- Do you know anything about your manager's previous employment?
- Do you know where she went to school, or where her skills were developed?
- Do you know anything about her outside interests?
- Do you know what bugs her?
- Does your manager tell you what you should think, or does she ask your opinion?
- Does your manager give you feedback—does she give it in person or in memo form?

- Is there anything that your manager hates to do?
- Does your manager like to work with people?
- Does she stay focused on one project at a time, or does she juggle several at a time?
- Does she enjoy her job?

Now reverse the object of the question by substituting yourself for the manager, as in "What kind of pressure are you under?" The purpose of this exercise is to look for areas you have a lot of information in, as well as commonalities with your manager. One of the best ways to develop a positive relationship with anyone is to have similar likes, dislikes, strengths, and weaknesses.

In addition to reversing the above questions, add a few more that specifically have to do with you:

- What do you like best about your job?
- How do you differ from your manager in experience, education, age, and family responsibilities?
- Do you need a lot of feedback on your performance or on projects as they progress?
- Are you a good listener?
- Do you put off any type of task within your job?
- Is there a part of your job that you like better than others?
- In what areas have you had fair to poor evaluations?

2. MEASURING UP

The next step is to see how you both measure up. Can you identify your and your manager's five greatest strengths as well as weaknesses? Do you note any areas where there are conflicts or contrasts? (For example, you are a morning person, and she prefers the evening shift.) Are there any specific areas where you work well with your manager? Are there any areas where you don't work well with her?

Imagine that among each of the married couples you know, the partners were alike. Both were outgoing, fun-loving, involved with a lot of different projects (rarely completing one), outspoken and talkative, reluctant to ask or take instructions from anybody, and addicted to self-help books.

In reality, if two people got together with all the same traits, same objectives, and same passions, they'd end up competing and knocking each other out. There is truth and wisdom in the saying that opposites attract. Sure, there are some commonalities, but it is the opposites—the weaknesses that complement the other's strengths, and vice versa—that make the partnership work.

The workplace isn't any different, and in a management-employee situation, it's the wise employee (and manager) who knows his or her individual strengths as well as weaknesses. And wise employees know it for themselves as well as for those they work with, work under, or work over. The match of strengths and weaknesses enhances the ingredients for completing a job.

I'm good at creating energy and bringing vision to a project, but weak in the details of the execution. An ideal partner has my weaknesses (details and execution) as strengths. It works the same way with a manager and coworkers on a team. By identifying your manager's strengths and weaknesses, and learning how to work with those strengths and weaknesses, you can almost guarantee a transition from lunacy to sanity.

3. MAKING IT WORK

> *The savviest thing that you can do is identify areas where your manager is weak. Then offer a remedy or solution that sidesteps her weakness.*

Let's say you are terrific with follow-up and details. Your manager hates that part of the process; she just wants the project completed and done in the shortest period of time. You can ask to take over the details of reporting, even offering to handle some of the problems and snafus along the way. The likely outcome is that your manager will be highly appreciative of your contribution.

If your manager wants to hear all the details of a project—in the beginning, and along the way, as well as at the end—give them to her. It may drive you crazy to put together the paperwork to deliver that information. But I guarantee it will obviate an abrasive situation. Give the good news as well as the bad news as the project progresses.

If your manager prefers to have employees vocalize their progress, but your style is to write everything down, you'll need to switch gears. You need to communicate in the best style that gets you heard. If your manager is a morning person, and you aren't in full power until noon, you need to get your brain and your energy level to wake up a few hours earlier. Try taking a break and a brisk walk to give your adrenaline a quick start.

Or suppose your manager is a very hands-on person who wants updates routinely. You may feel that you are spending more time making reports than actually doing your job. If your manager's vigilance is driving you crazy, you may end up feeling resentful, and acting out your resentment by coming in late, leaving early, and taking longer to complete various projects. You need to back off from the personality clash. Remember, she is the manager and you are the employee.

Whatever changes that are to come will most likely be initiated by you. If a better working relationship is one of your objectives, then a shift is in order. By setting up a regular status meeting at which you can discuss every project down to the tiniest detail at a specific time each week, you'll end up ahead of the game. Why? Because your manager knows that you will show up every Thursday morning between 10:00 and 10:30 to update her on everything that's happened since the preceding meeting. The result is that she'll view you as cooperative and team-oriented, someone who pays attention to details (which is vital for her) and someone who is important to the organization. She needs you.

One of my strengths is speaking; I do it professionally. I am also quite good at developing stories to make and support a point I am trying to make. It is not uncommon for me to be approached to help in structuring an opening story for an important meeting or activity. Does it make me feel good that someone asks me for my assistance? Sure. I also know that during the process of putting the story together, I learn more about the other person and we expand the bond—whatever it is—between the two of us.

If you have a talent for speaking or writing, you are quite valuable to your manager. Most managers make presentations and write reports as part of their jobs. When you know your manager doesn't like to do it, you could offer your assistance. Is this what some people would call "brownnosing"? It could be, if you look at it that way; and if you do, your actions may backfire. But if you are honestly attempting to develop and expand your present working relationship, it will pay off, and your manager will most likely be supportive of you down the road. A win-win-win. For you. For her. For the organization.

4.   THE ART OF CHANGE

At some point in any relationship, the issue of change surfaces, whether it's personal or professional. Today's talk shows are filled with outrageous stories about people who tried to force their partners to change and failed. Or the shows are riddled with shouting matches: "If only he would do this" and "If only she would do that."

When it comes to a change, the only truth is that you can't force someone to change; that person has to instigate it. Unless a cosmic goose zaps someone into facing reality, change is often difficult. What you can do is change yourself, and the impact of whatever it is you are changing will produce results that others can see.

In a professional relationship, if you create change for yourself and the results can be measured positively in the workplace, you will get your manager's attention. She may be tough to work with, abrasive, opinionated, overtalkative, unwilling to admit she has made a mistake or is wrong, vindictive, overcritical, and even nosy. A pain in the neck.

Nonetheless, your manager must make the decision to change. Herself. That doesn't mean that you can't help lay the groundwork. First of all, you need to decide in what areas should she change. If she's overcritical, it's most likely you would prefer to have her less critical. You may want (need) more feedback, seek inclusion in a decision process, or desire that she talk less about her personal problems than she presently does.

Your purpose in identifying how you want your manager to change is to isolate one or two important areas that you can work on. Your objective in getting your manager to change is called *behavioral shaping*. It takes a great deal of persistence, patience, and sometimes the overall force of your personality to achieve.

5.   REWARDS PAY OFF

As any pet owner knows, all pets, especially young ones, do lots of things that you don't want them to do. As puppies evolve through the chewing, scratching, digging, and peeing stages into adult dog-hood, most owners attempt to teach them to respond to commands. Every day that I am home, I take our new puppy for a walk the first thing each morning. Sasha knows that when the phone rings just once in the morning, and I sit down to put my shoes on, a walk will occur within a few minutes.

She begins to race around the house and stands on her hind legs as I slip the collar and leash over her head. She is ready. As I meet my neighbor, we proceed to walk up to the canal with our dogs (they are brother and sister). Along the way, they are told to heel, to sit, and to stay at various points. When they perform, they get a dog biscuit and a pat on the head or side. They are also told that they are "good dogs."

Sasha knows that if my tone changes and I'm not happy with her, she won't get her reward—being told she is a good girl, getting a pat on her side or her ears scratched, and receiving a dog biscuit are things that she likes. Whatever she is doing that displeases me, she comes back into line—heeling, sitting, or staying. It is a cycle, and it perpetuates because of behavior shaping—the reward.

People are no different, whether they are managers or employees. Behaviors can be reshaped. If you feel that your manager is overly critical, and she is in the process of tearing apart your latest project (or, at least, that's the way it appears to you), when she pauses, it's time for you to speak up. The shaping goes something like this:

> I know that my work is an important part of the project, and I can understand your concern for it to be completed on time. Sometimes I feel that I'm being overly criticized. I understand that you need to identify trouble spots. It would, though, be encouraging to me if you would identify the areas that are working and that I excel in. By getting support for what works, I can work better and produce more.

One of the savviest management books was written by Michael LeBoeuf, Ph.D. In *The Greatest Management Principle*, LeBoeuf points out that in order to develop a good relationship with your manager or boss, you must build on both of your strengths and accommodate your weaknesses. He's a strong proponent of rewarding any type of displayed behavior that supports you and any project that you are involved in. LeBoeuf writes:

You can't give your boss a promotion, a bonus, or a piece of business, but you can give her a lot. Keep in mind, however, if you want to change your boss's behavior, you must reward her in a way that is mutually beneficial. The surest way for you to get what you want, is to help your boss get what she wants.[3]

When your manager does acknowledge your work with less criticism or, at least, with equal spoonfuls of criticism and praise, you need in turn to reward her. Most likely, dog biscuits won't work. A simple thank you for acknowledging your work will do wonders. Bear in mind that managers need strokes too. Just as you need feedback on how you are doing, so does she. Some of her behavior may be a direct result of the pressure that she is getting from her manager.

Women must practice the art of praise and be generous with it. Not just giving praise one on one, but vocalizing it so others can hear your recognition and support. When managers hear through the grapevine that you have acknowledged and applauded something they have done, you make points. Keep your antenna up for any ideas that can be used within your department to save money or ease the path of a project you are working on. By just opening your ears and your eyes, you can be the lightning rod for change within your organization.

LIKING IS NOT ESSENTIAL

Before Tom Peters, Stephen Covey, and Harvey MacKay, Peter Drucker was the best-known management guru. He has written dozens of books on the subject. Drucker spoke at one of my management classes when I was working on my master's degree at Pepperdine University. His wise words were:

> You don't have to admire or even like your boss. You do have to manage him so he becomes your resource for achievement and accomplishment.

Much has been discussed and written about differences between boys and girls and men and women, with particular emphasis on their communication styles. Another area that is repeatedly noted and generally agreed upon concerns relationships. Women look for connectedness and building relationships, whether it's in their personal lives or in their work lives. Being connected or building relationships, particularly in the workplace, is not something that men have put energy into developing.

Women do seek connectedness at work, and when being connected does not occur, they may feel detached and insecure. As women share parts of their personal lives with coworkers, they feel that they are developing their networks. Men also have networks, they just don't base them on bits and pieces that evolve out of their personal lives. A man's style is to focus more on work, and keep personal details to himself.

As a very frequent flyer, I have learned a lot about men's and women's styles. When I sit next to a man, a stranger, and we talk, it will be about business—rarely, if ever, on personal topics. If I sit next to a woman, I may end up knowing about her personal life, her love life, what kinds of problems her children are having, even medical procedures that are planned for the coming week. This information is really none of my business, but somehow women feel they need to share on a personal basis to establish some type of common ground.

Unfortunately, as discussed in Chap. 5, on the sabotage trap, being too open, too friendly, and too trusting in any type of relationship can create problems.

If your manager leans toward the male model, being focused and keeping personal details to herself, don't discount her skills or value because she doesn't want to share her personal history with you. Most likely, she's not interested in your personal history either. Don't take it as an affront. Women often feel that they need to be friends with people they work with or for. Friendship is a bonus in the workplace, not a requirement.

ROLE MODELS AND MENTORS

Women in management are role models for women who work for them and around them. The manager of today needs to be more like a mentor. A mentor is a teacher, a sponsor and adviser, a coach, a guide, and a counselor. Being a mentor involves an interactive relationship with a "mentee." A good mentor nurtures the evolving mentee, but she does not mother her.

Good mentoring relationships are always reciprocal. The mentee, the woman who receives guidance from her benefactor or sponsor, responds with support for her mentor. She receives information and ideas. Coworkers and managers benefit as the ideas are implemented.

Managers who mentor, and employees who seek mentor relationships, are important ingredients in eliminating the land mines of the workplace. When managers act like mentors, they serve as guides for their employees. They must, though, respect the fact that employees are capable of making decisions.

All relationships evolve. The mentor–mentee relationship may eventually end because of a change in employment or in career objectives, or it just may no longer fit.

KEEPING CHANNELS OPEN

In order for employees to put their best efforts forward, they have to be able to see what the issues are. When a two-way dialogue is kept open between manager and employee, the workplace has a far better probability of thriving and growing.

In the end, your manager is your manager, with all her quirks and idiosyncrasies. You and she, as well as your coworkers, will approach problems and situations from different perspectives. It is possible that your manager has a totally opposite style or attitude from yours, and if you had your "druthers," you would choose not to work with her.

You will also encounter problems that aren't worth the drain on your energy to resolve. When you work in a toxic environment, or with toxic bosses, managers and coworkers, it is as important to know what battles not to engage in, as well as the ones you want to take on. Many of the problems relating to toxic bosses and managers, as identified in the GenderTraps survey, can be reduced or eliminated by simply understanding the differences in conflict styles, personal strengths, and weaknesses and by keeping communications open.

If you are new in your workplace, keep your eyes and ears open. Determine who is respected, has skills, savvy, and power—both in your present environment as well as the one you aspire to. Your future mentor is someone you would want to emulate.

After you determine who the "right" one is, request a fifteen-minute appointment or invite her (or him) for coffee—don't forget, you pay! Keep in mind that this person is busy.

If she agrees to act as your guide and advocate after you ask her to be your mentor, let her make the rules. Remember, you need her support—it's her game.

Pay Inequities: A policy whereby business chooses to pay individuals with equal skills and performance at an unequal rate.

TRAP 5: PAY INEQUITIES
Unequal Pay for Equal Work

- Do you feel you are not paid adequately for the job you do?
- Has anyone with lesser skills than yours been paid more?
- Have you had to train anyone to do a job and, at the same time, been paid less than what the trainee is paid?
- Do you think that management has viewed women as being less serious and committed to their jobs than men are?
- Does anyone do the same job that you do, have the same skills and credentials that you have, yet make more money?

Throughout the year there are recognition days, weeks, months, and sometimes the whole year: Bosses' Day, Breast Cancer Awareness Month, Women's History Month, and, of course, the inevitable Secretaries' Day or Week in April. When the television series *L.A. Law* was alive and well, actress Susan Ruttan's role as Roxanne, secretary to a divorce lawyer, was a weekly feature. For several years, the series was in the top 10. Actors were rewarded with financial bonuses and increases per episode.

Although many story lines evolved around Ruttan's character, her "real" pay increases were minute in comparison with those of Jill Eichenberry, Michael Tucker, Corbin Bernsen (her boss, Arnie, in the series), and others. When she objected to the small increase, the producers' response was, "You're just a secretary." They weren't kidding. Susan Ruttan was penalized for playing a secretary in Hollywood. Imagine what happens in real life.

STANDARD EQUIPMENT: ONE SPITTOON

When times were simpler, most businesses were neighborhood bases, and most secretaries were men. Before the Civil War, young, literate white males performed all clerical duties. That meant that they filed, took memos, and learned what the business was about. They even married the boss's daughter. Back in Civil War times, it was not uncommon for a secretary's desk to be accompanied by a spittoon.

The economic revolution from 1860 to 1880 gave birth to railroads, department stores, banks, and the bureaucracy of the federal government. A combination of events altered the clerical workplace: war, factories offering better pay, and paperwork becoming overwhelming. When the men went to war, the women went to work everywhere. And commerce continued to march on.

In the nineteenth century, it was assumed that women could be hired for less than men. As we enter the twenty-first century, not much has changed. The wages that women earned at clerical jobs in the early 1900s were superior to what they could earn as schoolteachers, the other acceptable profession for women who worked for pay.

Today, there are 3.6 million secretaries; 98.9 percent are women. Many are highly educated. According to the U.S. Bureau of Labor Statistics, 41,000 female secretaries hold master's degrees, and 6000 hold Ph.D., J.D., or M.D. degrees. Why would women take jobs that were clearly below their educational level? Because, for many, health benefits were attached. According to Judy Rosener, author of *America's Competitive Secret: Women*, "Many want an 8–5 job, especially if they have kids. So often these women are just marking time."[1]

In 1861, female secretaries who worked for the federal government—the first group to hire women in great numbers—tediously cut Treasury bills with scissors. Their pay: $600 a year. Their male counterparts also tediously cut Treasury bills with scissors. Their pay: $1200 per year. Has the government changed much? Not really.

There are slightly under 4 million secretaries in the United States. Their average income is less than $20,000 per year. Some experts report that the work secretaries do is appreciated. Many are paid on the basis of their tasks and duties, rather than on their rank as "secretary" to the person they work for. Overall, women who do their jobs everyday don't see their situation getting any better.

One of the gaps that is closing between the genders is the number of full-time workers. Today, almost 50 percent of women work full time, compared with 70 percent of men. In 1972, only 35 percent of women were full-time workers, compared with 75 percent of men. In part-time work, the gap expands. Women are more likely to combine a number of part-time jobs to equal a full-time job. Part-time jobs rarely carry full benefits—health insurance, life insurance, or time off for illness and vacations.

Like the producers of *L.A. Law*, the recent administrations of Reagan and Bush appeared to live in a world of make-believe. They were oblivious of women's real circumstances. During their watch, more than 4 million families headed by women struggled to survive below the poverty line—an increase of more than 25 percent between the years 1980 and 1990.

DO AS WE SAY, NEVER AS WE DO

In February 1994, the Gannet News Service did a study of the personal staffs of senators and representatives in Congress. Women hold 50 percent of the congressional jobs, yet men dominate the high-paying power positions. Women tend to be relegated to the clerical and support staff. On average, women in the House make less than 82 cents for every dollar that men make. In the Senate, women earn about 80 cents for every dollar earned by men. In reality, the women are enclosed in a brick box.

When two Senate senior staff members get together, they both have the same concerns. They'll be worried about their senator's image, about the scheduling of key pieces of legislation, and about the best way to respond to the constituents in their state. If both staff members are women, the odds are that they are getting paid fairly equally. If one staffer is male and the other female, the odds are that the man is getting paid considerably more to be concerned and worried about the same things his female counterpart is.

The Gannet survey revealed that the average female Senate staffer makes $30,400 a year compared with $37,800 for male staffers—a 24 percent disparity. Of 17 job categories in the Senate, women earn the same as men in one category and more than men in only five of them.

When it comes to party preference, the Democrats pay both men and women slightly more than the Republicans pay their men and women. As in the regular corporate marketplace, men dominate the best-paying jobs. Among staffers who earn less than $30,000, 63 percent are women; of those making more than $70,000, only 25 percent are women.

Overall, women comprise 60 percent of the Senate staff. Ironically, nowhere in the private sector would a "fox"-guarding-the-hen-house enforcement scheme be tolerated. Until January 1995, Congress was able to find a way around most work laws. That ended when Public Law 104-1 was passed—the Congressional Accountability Act of 1995. It seems rather absurd that our lawmakers have been able to throw away any type of measuring stick for themselves for so long. Congressional personnel records carry no identification as to gender and race. The philosophy seems to be not only "Do as we say, not as we do" but also "You can't miss it if you don't measure it." The men and women in Washington, DC can't continue to scold the American people in reproach when their own house has been such a disaster.

ROBBING PETER TO PAY PAUL

The situation is not so much a case of wanting to move up through the glass ceiling, as has been bandied about so frequently. Rather, what women in America are saying is that they want to break through the brick wall that surrounds them.

Emily is in a management position. Prior to her current position, she worked in the Governor's office in a southern state. She recalls several men with similar positions and responsibilities who made $8000 to $10,000 more a year than she and the other women did. Not only that, it was not uncommon to rob Peter in order to pay Paul.

> There is a big brouhaha internally about the pay discrepancy between the men and women about halfway through the time I worked there. A lot of the men accused the women of having sour grapes. I guess the governor's budget didn't have enough money to pay all these people, and there were a lot of people. It was no big secret that we were paid using another department's funds.

If men want to call women complaining about pay disparities sour grapes, so be it. But sour grapes are difficult to feed a family on. According to the U.S. Bureau of Labor Statistics 1994 findings, there are just two fields in which women earn more than men: registered nurses ($34,476 versus $32,916) and food preparers ($11,700 versus $11,076). In just about every other field, there are discrepancies—some small, others huge.

ESCAPING THE MUDDY BASEMENT

How do women get out of the muddy basement, whether it is in female-dominated workplaces, or just the workplace in general, where there is a disparity between men and women? The first step is to dig up information. Ann, who is director of Minority Affairs at a college, said it is important to know what other salaries are.

> You are always working in the dark, so you don't really know exactly what others make, but you can get an idea. When you are looking for a job, or even negotiating increases within your own job, it's a good idea to network and get your feelers out there. That way you learn what the ranges are.

There's a lot of debris, dirt, and even garbage in the muddy basement. And it comes from all directions: from management, from coworkers, and from municipal, state, and federal laws that are not supported or enforced. The basement depicts the low of the low; it's underneath the ground, much different from a floor, which can be very high in some structures. And it's powerful. Imagine a tall building. When was the last time you were in a revolving restaurant on the top floor—the floor that gives a sweeping view of the city, the view that is designed to impress? In corporate America, the higher you go, the more powerful the floor—the level—is.

Next, as you dig up information, not only on salaries but on other positions that may be opening up and available, go ahead and apply. Even if you don't think you qualify for them yet. Another tip is to practice the fine art of bragging. Men do this well; women need to learn how. Write down all the things you have done in reference to your work, including any special projects. Your goal is to obtain visibility. You let management know that you are serious about moving up and expanding your duties, which in turn should mean that you expand your pay.

THE ART OF NEGOTIATING

The other element is to hone up on your negotiating skills. Most women have not been taught how to negotiate. Women traditionally ask for less than what a job is offering, or they ask on the low side. Because they ask on the low side, and they get it, it is harder to catch up. Many women in the GenderTraps survey shared experiences around the issue.

Whether you are negotiating for a new job, a pay raise, or an exit/severance package, you need information. How do you find out what salary ranges are? First, by asking around; you may know people who are in the position you seek and can give you a range—the high and a low.

Second, most companies, industries, and occupations have national associations. For example, I am a speaker, and I belong to the National Association of Speakers. I also work a great deal in the health-care field. Therefore, I belong to the National Association of Women Health-Care Professionals. I'm an honorary member of the Association of Women Surgeons and have been a member of several other associations that include fields in which I have worked—namely, finance and marketing.

If you live within a big city, there may be a branch or local chapter of an industry association. Besides looking in the Yellow Pages, you might try to call the information operator (800-555-1212) to see if there is a national listing. Don't forget your public library. Using its reference books and computer, you'll be amazed at all the information you can pull together. And it's free!

The National Trade and Professional Associations of the United States (NTPA) publishes an annual directory which identifies main offices, people in charge, phone numbers and addresses, membership objectives, dates of annual meetings, and more, for each trade group. Check with your local library to see if it has a copy. This one directory can give you a substantial amount of information. Call and say you are a student doing a research paper (well, you are; you are on a quest for information) and you are looking for salary ranges for whatever occupation you have an interest in. NTPA can be reached at 202-898-0662 or write Columbia Books, Inc., 1212 New York Avenue, Suite 3305, Washington, DC 20005.

Once you identify what the top of the range is, ask for more than that in a salary discussion. In that way, you have room to move down. According to Nichol Shapiro, author of *Negotiating for Your Life,* don't talk money unless you know what the range is for the position you are seeking. Shapiro advises not to discuss dollars *until the position is offered.* She also advises *what not to say.* Don't say, "Joe Smith gets $—. I'm a woman, and I should get $—." Never do a salary negotiation with a legal threat behind it.

Another item that is helpful when you go into a salary negotiation is a prepared list of things that you would accept in an ideal compensation package. Some organizations are on very low budgets, but they may have some goodies—perks—they can offer. These can include life insurance, health-care insurance, club memberships, extra time off, more sick days (or preferably, personal days to be used at your discretion), extra vacation, flex time, job sharing, and a modem/computer hook-up at home so you need not always come in 5 days a week.

The downsizing of the 1990s has had a major impact, especially on women. Be aware if there has been downsizing, and don't be afraid to ask if the company is at its "right size." Walk in the company's shoes. Be prepared to describe how your work and your input will make a difference. In other words, identify the value that you bring with your employment. Most managers and employers will state that you'll be up for review in a certain period of time. That's fine, but don't agree to be reviewed for that future time, unless you get a written statement of what specific criteria you will be judged by at that time.

JOBS ARE NOT PERMANENT

In 1993, the profits of America's 500 largest companies grew by 14 percent. Personnel shrank by 1 percent. As the economy continues to recover from the recession of the early 1990s, there is bound to be continued change. In 1994, workers put in more overtime, some paid and some not paid, than at any point since the reconstruction period following World War II. Many of the positions that have been created in the past year are for lower-paying service or part-time positions.

Jobs are not permanent in the 1990s. They keep shifting; there is more flexibility; and the part-time arena is expanding. It is not surprising that America's largest private employer is a temporary employment agency, Manpower, Inc. In 1993, the Milwaukee-based company employed approximately 600,000 people in the United States. That's more than the combined work forces of McDonald's and General Motors. Some 75 percent of Manpower's employees are women, who are primarily placed in clerical and secretarial positions. (Why didn't they call it Womanpower?)

As companies downsize, they need some support help on a short-term basis. Repeatedly, they turn to the temporary help agencies. It is not unusual to pay temporary help more than permanent help on a per hour basis. The rationale is that it's only for the short term—a few days, a few weeks. Of course, there are adjustments because no benefits are given to the temporary employee. Temporary or contingent (as they are known in the trade), part-time workers, are usually less productive than full-time employees. After all, few employees want to work hard if they can get thrown out at a moment's notice.

When negotiating for money, whether it's a new job or an increase in your present position, be prepared to walk away before you begin your discussion. Many times, companies have budgets to pay for specific duties and tasks. If you're being interviewed or reviewed for situations that encompass only one or two functions, the reaction may be that there is no money.

They think you would do a terrific job, but you are at the top of your pay level. Don't be afraid to bring in your other skills, your other traits. Describe how those skills and traits can translate into other responsibilities, responsibilities that may have budgeted dollars attached to them.

A common fear many women have is that this is the only job. In reality, it isn't. There are others; it may take some probing to find them. Employers will pay you what they think you are worth. Your responsibility is to be able to prove, as in a show-and-tell with documentation and ledgers, exactly what you are worth and why you are worth more.

PAY INEQUITIES ARE NEVER EXCLUSIVE

Pay inequities within the political arena are not exclusive with Congress. Marie is involved with politics but at a different level. She is an administrative director for one of the state arms of the Republican party. She is responsible for the overall office management as well as keeping track of who contributes—donates—how much and when. Her first real involvement with the political system was in college, where she worked within one of the Republican organizations.

After graduation, Marie worked full time for one of the campaigns that led to the position she currently holds. When she was hired, she received $9000 less than the man she replaced. In a follow-up interview, after the GenderTraps survey was completed, she noted:

> This place has been through hell since I filled out the original survey. I have gotten a raise of a few thousand dollars, but it is not what *he* was making. I believe that I got the raise because the chairman of our state party believed that I would leave. When I started, I was offered $25,000. At the time, I didn't know what the salary ranges were. Now I do.

Marie confirms a point. When you are interviewing for any new position, it is important to know what salary ranges are for that type of work. Women consistently get roadblocked on this point, believing they can't get "inside" information. It is not necessary to get the information from the specific company. As noted earlier, your local library can help out—it has the latest information from the Department of Labor on salaries for almost every field imaginable.

THE WINNING COACH IS INVISIBLE

Gender inequity does not impact only the Velvet Ghetto. One of the male ghettos is coaching. Women in coaching are few and far between, and they definitely make less than their male counterparts. Female coaches of women's basketball teams earn 61 percent less than coaches of men's basketball programs, according to a 1994 survey by the Women's Basketball Coaches Association (WBCA). The WBCA survey also found that 75 percent of the women's coaches have contracts, compared with 92 percent of the men's coaches. The average budget for a women's team is $148,194, compared with $252,922 for a men's team.

Basketball is the most cited example of pay disparities between men and women in sports. There aren't women's football teams in colleges and universities. There are, though, tennis, golf, volleyball, swimming, and baseball teams. But basketball brings in the crowds, and gets national media recognition as well as participation. According to Vivian Stringer, coach of the number-three-ranked Iowa women's basketball team:

> My accomplishments, not my sex, should determine my salary. If I won 5 games and lost 22, I have no right to come up and ask that they pay me the same as the men's coach (if he's had some successes).
>
> I want to be recognized as well as him, and I want to work as hard as he does. It is nice to say, "We certainly appreciate you." But, in America, I don't think male coaches say, "Hey, just pat me on the back, and I'm going to be pleased."

Stringer is one of the exceptions. She's paid the same as Iowa's men's coach, Tom Davis. According to the WBCA, base salaries for college basketball coaches average $44,961 for women and $76,561 for men—a 59 percent disparity. In basketball, men and women do the same thing. They have the same academic rules and the same regulations. It is one sport where apples can be compared with apples.

Some of the female coaches have filed lawsuits. They've learned that the only way they can bring about some resolution is to speak up and speak out. Sanya Tyler sued Howard University, claiming pay and Title IX. Title IX is a provision in the federal code that makes actions illegal that discriminate against anyone based on race, color, creed, gender, age, or physical disability in public education. A jury concurred and awarded her $1.1 million. She had been a women's basketball coach since 1988, and had led the team to six conference titles. Her pay? Forty-four thousand dollars. The men's coach was hired in 1990 and received $78,000 and a car as part of his package.

Some universities and colleges have heard the wakeup call. The University of Colorado's women's coach, Ceal Berry, received a 20 percent raise, with a guarantee of $95,000 for the 1994–95 season. This matches the men's coach base at $93,000. Iowa finally signed Vivian Stringer to a 5-year contract in 1993 that pays her $117,860, which is the same as Tom Davis earns. And Pat Summit, who has taken the University of Tennessee's women's team to final-four playoffs 11 times, saw her base increase from $70,000 to $110,000 in 1993, while the men's coach gets $100,000. Summit's performance matches her pay.

VOCAL MAKES THE DIFFERENCE

Rosalynn is a university professor and does training and consulting for the Peace Corps. When she began working at the university, she realized that men were brought in at higher salaries. At first, it did not bother her, but then that changed.

> I started thinking, "Well, I have the same amount of education, and more experience." One day in a meeting, I brought up the subject. I told the others we need to look at the way that we bring men in at higher salaries than the way in which we bring women in.
>
> I know that this goes on in other departments. Mine wasn't the only one. But it wasn't until I started thinking about the situation, and I thought differently about myself, that I was of equal, if not better value. In the end, I gave myself more self-worth. I also got a raise.

Rosalynn works in Washington, DC and does see some changes coming. She believes that, if women continue to become more vocal and talk to one another about pay and other differences, they can form support groups and go forward as a unified front.

UNEQUAL JOBS, UNEQUAL PAY

Forget gender pay differences. What about paying more for seniority, even when the lower-paying position requires more skills and greater education? Joyce is a senior analyst in a large multieducational campus system. An administration analyst who is several levels lower than Joyce makes the same amount. Why? She's been there longer.

> I'm at the lower end of my pay scale. Because of the overlapping of the two, she makes more—even though she has less responsibility, less work, and less education than I have.
>
> In our department, an analyst is making $40,000 plus; a senior analyst, $38,000. It's like a double-whammy.

Joyce identifies a not too uncommon problem. Some will rationalize that employees who have been there for a long time—say, 20 years—deserve more. Why do they? This is like saying someone who is a janitor should get the same pay as the senior analyst who has been there for only 3 years.

At some point, pay gets maxed out. More education, additional responsibilities, and new duties enables an employee to transition to another level. Pay should be based on work performed. Longevity is a different matter.

WELCOME TO THE ZOO

In late 1993, I did the keynote address for a national association of professional child-care directors. Prior to the speech, I learned what directors and employees made in this field. I was stunned.

> *The average child-care provider—the person who has the most hands-on care for your child—makes less than someone who feeds animals in a zoo.*

Individuals, primarily women, are paid on the lower end of the income scale, some bordering on poverty level, to care, to nourish, to develop, and to encourage our most important assets, our children.

Diane is the director of a large center. She discovered that child-care directors, in general, are paid less than other department managers in the hospital where she works. In addition, she feels that in her position she carries far more responsibility than some of the other department managers. In her view, the employer's rationale for the pay disparity with other department managers comes with the territory—or in her case the facilities, which are state of the art.

> Most of us who enter the field of child care are nurturers. We also tune in to the fact that having pleasant environment and surroundings are a plus. In our case, we have a big, new, multimillion-dollar child-care center. My salary is just under $50,000 a year. A department manager in the hospital, outside of child care, starts at $60,000. It doesn't matter if you are male or female.

Diane does feel some optimism. Over the past several months, the administration has begun to look at the volume of work along with the responsibility of work. One of its goals for the coming year is to do a readjustment for all managerial roles. Diane is, though, not speaking exclusively for herself. She says the readjustment needs to be made for the entire child-care staff. Pay is just too low.

June is the telecommunications manager for a Fortune 100 company. Her responsibility includes the management of all voice and data equipment for the West Coast. The company's head office is in another part of the country. She has been with the company only a few years, but she has progressed in her skills and has taken on a substantial amount of responsibility.

When dealing with a big company, one that is both big in size and many years old, new personnel often have difficulties transitioning through the policies that have been set in place in years past. Women, and men, who are in the fast track often don't get paid equivalently for what work they produce compared with employees who've been around holding another type of position for several years. Even if those "old Berthas" are dated in their skills and slower in work production, they get paid more. According to June:

> A company like ours has rigid time, grade, and salary requirements. Even if you put in a substantial amount of work—quality work—it means little. If you haven't been there long enough to pass through their various grades at the appropriate times, it takes an act of God to get a salary adjustment.

PROFIT SHARING FOR THE SELECT

Chris is the associate director of customer service for a publishing concern, and oversees 150 employees. She has found another way that pay inequities come into play. It is a combination of the "old boys' network" and a hint of the glass ceiling. She was initially hired as the associate director of customer service. There were several other people doing similar jobs, but they carried the title of director.

At first, her salary wasn't a problem. She says she was able to negotiate herself up to where she thought she should have been. But becoming a part of the profit-sharing plan wasn't a given. There were strings attached—it was only for the chosen few.

> Participation in our profit-sharing plan was very political. I believe it was based more on the value, or perceived value, that upper management gave toward a specific group—i.e., customer satisfac-

tion versus marketing, circulation, or editorial within the company as a whole.

The company has a 401(k) plan, and I participate in that. But the extra that comes from the profit sharing is directed toward those the company favors. There are a few women in it, and they get in it by participating in the middle- to higher-level management areas. Most are men. At the lower levels of management like mine, where we are associate directors, by definition we are not included in the extras that the profit-sharing plan offers. Later, I found out that several associate directors were in fact granted participation. They were all men.

When I first joined the firm 5 years ago, I had asked for $50,000. They whittled me down to $40,000 and I negotiated, with certain parameters, that it would be at the $50,000 level in so many months. I met my parameters, and they did make good on their promises to increase my salary. The problem is, though, you hate to start fighting from day one on for what you feel you are owed and are qualified for.

BEING ASSERTIVE PAYS OFF

Chris showed an assertive approach to dealing with the pay situation. She felt she should be earning $50,000. When she compromised with a 20 percent discount—to $40,000—she put a strings-attached qualification on it. If she met her goals and deadlines, her income would be increased immediately. She did, and it was.

Naomi is not as assertive as Chris. She displays a more typical female response. Naomi has been in the same position for the past 19 years and makes under $30,000. As coordinator for a Head Start program in the West, she believes that she should make substantially more with the experience she has. She stays because she believes in the program, and she enjoys her work. She also notes that there is a high degree of personnel turnover within the program.

We have a lot of problems keeping people, which is historical for Head Start programs. Our program has become known as "The Training Program." We get individuals who are competent, they do well, and then they leave. The reason: they get paid only $5 to $6 an hour. The program does provide medical coverage, but most young people don't use it.

Naomi is correct. Most young adults, especially those without children, don't view health insurance as a key benefit. They still consider themselves invincible. Only the sickly need insurance, or those who have accidents. And, most people, especially young adults, believe they won't be in an accident requiring expensive medical procedures.

Naomi is caught in a common GenderTrap for women. She loves her job, but does the job love her? No, and management has manipulated women for decades by stroking them with verbiage of how wonderful, fabulous, and critical they are for the children. In other words, because they have the privilege of working, shaping, and caring for "our most important asset," pay concerns should be minimized. Secondary.

Needed personnel require training. Training costs money, at least for most enterprises. When women are directors, managers, or supervisors of businesses that hire predominantly women, owners often assume they will "donate" their time to bring the new employees on track. Salary earners rarely get overtime pay. The extra work they get is for the "cause." The cycle continues.

MORE THAN PEANUT BUTTER AND JELLY

When Marilyn Jancsy and Sally Bartolo spoke out about the just-above-minimum-wage jobs they had held for 19 years, their employers turned a stone-deaf ear. Both were cafeteria workers who earned $5.35 an hour. They, along with 29 other cafeteria workers, finally found their voice.

> We made 5000 to 7000 meatballs a day plus 32 cases of chicken—washing it, cleaning it, traying it, and baking it. And the school committee said all we did was make a few peanut butter and jelly sandwiches.

Jancsy and Bartolo lost their jobs; they did, though, win a precedent-setting pay equity lawsuit. At the same time that Jancsy and Bartolo were earning $5.35 an hour, the male custodians at the school were paid twice as much. In the view of the city, they (the custodians) worked harder and were more skilled.

Obviously, there is a discrepancy between the perceived value of the cook/food server and the custodian. Both occupations are dominated by their respective genders of female and male. Nineteen years is a lot of meatballs and chicken and minimum wages.

The cafeteria workers probably felt they were doing a good thing for all those kids. Serving nutritious meals was more likely part of their pay—providing food for the kids was virtuous. The good news is that they spoke up; the bad news is that it took 19 years.

REENTERING THE WORKPLACE

Cathleen is the project director for a program for single parents and homemakers—in particular, homemakers who are reentering the workplace or entering it for the first time. She ranks salary inequities and child care as the top two workplace traps that women routinely encounter today. Salary inequities come from a lack of value given to work traditionally done by women. That includes child care, homemaking, secretarial work, catering, housekeeping, and clerical tasks. Cathleen works with women who have to work, and women who usually believe that they will be working for a very long period of time.

> Right now, I have a résumé sitting in front of me of a woman who organized local parents and raised over $20,000 to create a playground at a local school. Now, when this woman goes out into the workplace, she is not going to be viewed as someone who can organize and raise money. She is going to be viewed as someone who has not been out in the workplace. She may be applying for a position that routinely pays between $10 and $15 per hour. They will offer her $7, because she has not been earning a regular paycheck.

One of the activities that Cathleen does in her program is to start homemakers on the road to acquiring self-esteem—even empowerment. Over the 6-week course, they spend a minimum of 20 hours with her each week. On the first day, she works each person through an activity whose purpose is to clarify the value of homemaker services. She has the women figure out how many hours per week they spend cooking, cleaning, taxiing kids, shopping, budgeting, hostessing, and so on.

Their next assignment is to visit the library to check the Department of Labor's data on what people with that set of skills can expect to earn as a wage, if they did it as a profession. The end result is the realization that it is a lot of money. The women energize themselves when they begin to see what their value is, and how it's translated monetarily. Cathleen says it is not surprising when her students say they are going home to tape their value to the refrigerator door for all to view.

What about the woman who organized the parents and raised $20,000 for the children's playground center? Well, she should put down that she was a project manager. She conceived, developed, and implemented a strategy, as well as raised the necessary funds to complete a successful project. Potential employers understand that process.

ENOUGH IS ENOUGH

Contrary to what many people (mostly men) say and believe, there is a wage gap between the genders. The only positive thing that I can say is that it has shrunk somewhat. In 1979, women between the ages of 25 and 64 made 62 percent of what men did. In 1992, for the same age group, women earned 74 percent of what men were making.

Back in the 1970s, when women were asked if they expected to work after the age of 35, the majority said no. In reality, the majority continued to work after they had children. In 1995, the Families and Work Institute released a study entitled *Women: The New Providers*. Over half of the respondents (1502 women) stated that they provided over 50 percent of household income. In other words, women's pay is critical to the lifestyle of their families.[2]

Pay inequities are the result of widespread, severe, and ongoing discrimination by employers and coworkers. As technology continues to evolve, the need for physical strength on most jobs will continue to diminish. The past decade has witnessed a great expansion in the service sector, which provides jobs that require mental acuity and social skills, both of which are areas of strength for women.

The downsizing and the layoffs of the 1990s scared many. Anxious, even desperate voices wondered where the jobs were. They gave up on the idea of training, as if to ask, "For what?" There will be a demand for workers—women and men—who are skilled in problem solving. Credentials will be redefined—education should be directed toward enhancing skills used at work. By not keeping up to date in your job, your paycheck will be reduced.

How much has changed? Consider that in 1990, 18 percent of the functions in a typical Ford automobile were computer-controlled. In 1994, the figure had increased to 82 percent. Technology will continue to alter the face of the workplace. That is a guarantee.

Applying technology requires a working brain—rarely physical strength. This is good news for women. Skills for the new jobs—jobs being invented daily—can be learned in apprenticeship programs, on the job, even through the local community college.

There are always going to be those who say that all is fair. Or that the disparity is so small, that a few cents don't matter. This is nonsense and representative of Neanderthal thinking. When women (and men) fail to speak up and act, their silence and inaction condone the continuation of nonparity.

To equalize pay inequities, women must take three major steps.

1. Determine if there is a disparity in pay for equal work that requires the same education and skills.
2. Approach management—the decision makers—and request an adjustment. Don't waste time grumbling about minor issues; present facts and data that support work done, value received, and impact on a project or the company's profits.
3. The art of negotiation requires finessing—facts and no emotion. If your request falls on deaf ears, know what your next step will be. It could include going over your boss's head or reducing your work to match what others are doing at your income range. It should include networking with other divisions (which is wise to do anyway) and determining if there are positions that you can transfer to. It also includes leaving.

Business believes that women will work for less money than men will. History has proved that assumption to be correct. Pay inequities should be addressed early on—not months or years later, as the cafeteria workers did.

You may think—believe—that you can't leave your job, you can't walk out. You need the money. Today. I believe you do need the money, and you also need it today. As long as women allow pay inequities to continue, the problem will only compound. Women have allowed businesses—men—to get away with offering them mediocre pay. Almost as if they were in a codependent relationship.

Time out is called for. Imagine the women power that would be demonstrated if *all* the women who were not paid on a par with the men in their workplace stopped working. And the women who were paid equitably in the same workplace also stopped to support those who weren't. And then the men—men who supported pay and salary equity—also stopped work.

The result? Business would stop. At this point, too much time has passed to level the field. There should be no disparity in anyone's workplace if equal work with equal skills are in place. Sometimes radical things have to be done to create change.

Imagine the power if all women took off their shoes and threw them into the workplace machinery. Our own version of sabotage—intentionally done to create mayhem. The result would be damage to an employer's reputation (discrimination toward women) and probable loss to profits (business responds to bottom-line assaults).

It's time to hit the streets together. No women operators, librarians, flight attendants, clerks, secretaries, bankers, editors, account executives, nurses, dental hygienists, and others will work on a set day. Businesses, the media, men, and women must understand the real value of all work by women. It's not second-rate and should not be paid as a percentage of men's.

The only thing that consistently gets the attention of business is the bottom line. If business proclaims that it can't afford to pay women equally, then how can it afford to pay men unequally?

Balancing: Any action that brings personal life, family, and work into harmony.

TRAP 6:
THE BALANCING ACT
Family Versus
Work

- Do your hours run out toward the end of the day?
- If you have children, and your company offered a child-care program, would you use it?
- Have you ever felt guilty about working when you have children at home?
- If you are a mother, are your children your primary concern?
- At times, do you feel you are overwhelmed with both work and home responsibilities?

Women are pooped. Many feel their workdays are too long, too hard, and definitely not fair. Most women are simply overloaded. They have extra pressures from balancing their family and workplace responsibilities as well as their own personal lives. Because women are overloaded, they experience stress, anger, resentment, worry, illness, and most of all exhaustion. Sometimes separately; sometimes in combinations; sometimes even all of the above.

Tiffany is one of those overloaded moms. She has three kids; two are in elementary school and her youngest is in preschool. She feels pressure from all sides.

There is pressure from her coworkers, who she feels resent her incoming calls from sitters and schools as well as her outgoing calls in checking up on the kids each day prior to leaving work; she feels pressure from her kids' school for her inability to commit more time as an assistant or room mother; she feels pressure from her kids when she is not able to attend all their activities during and after the school day; she feels pressure from her spouse, since she's often just too tired to make an intelligent sentence after she finally gets the kids down for the evening; she feels pressure from her friends, who keep wondering how she manages to do it all; finally, she feels pressure from society and the media, being bombarded almost daily on what and how she needs to do "it" to be a better mom, wife, friend, person. Not to mention the pressure from herself when she admits how tired, how stretched, and how worn-out she is trying to be all things to everyone.

> I am afraid to admit to others just how tired I am. With the downsizing at work, I have had to take on more tasks and put in more hours. As my kids get older, more and more demands are made on my time to participate in both school-day and extracurricular activities. My 4-year-old will be entering kindergarten next year, and the hassle that comes with the half-day program and then getting him to the day-care provider seems overwhelming to me.

> Then there are my friends. Although they are sympathetic, with all the demands on my time, they are also irritated that I don't have time for them. I miss going shopping; I miss being able to spend an hour on the phone, just doing girl-talk. But that is impossible at work, much less when you have kids in the background making demands on your time. My husband complains that I am not as much fun as I used to be, and too preoccupied with kids and work. What I think he really thinks is that I should be preoccupied with sex. Who's got time?

There is always good news and bad news in every situation. The good news is that Tiffany is not alone. There are megathousands of women who feel just as she does. And that is also the bad news. There are too many women who feel stretched to their outer limits. What most working women need is a wife.

THE SECOND SHIFT DOESN'T PAY OVERTIME

In the summer of 1994, Patricia Ulbrich at the University of Akron (Ohio) analyzed data from a study of 1246 couples nationwide. Her study revealed that women differed widely on how much time they spent on household chores, chores that never seem to go away. Some women do little; others actually have another full-time job. Among Ulbrich's findings:

- Women who work outside the home 35 or more hours a week spend an average of 26 hours on housework.

- Women who are employed outside the home less than 35 hours a week spend 33.8 hours on housework.

- At home, women spend an average of 38.5 hours a week on housework.[1]

In other words, whether you work inside or outside the home, the time that is dedicated to keeping the house up is fairly comparable. No wonder a woman's work is never done.

Between the two groups, the ones who get a paycheck and the ones who don't, they *average 32.3 hours of housework per week*. And that doesn't include child care. Men devote an average of 8.7 hours per week for the same chores. In some cases, men do nothing, and in others, they contribute greatly to the running of the household.

In *Second Shift*, Arlie Hochschild reports that when a woman ends the day at her paying job, she comes home to another shift. If she is married or living with a partner, the partner usually comes home to a more R&R status. Meanwhile, the woman proceeds with her domestic shift—kids, cooking, cleaning, and errands. Ulbrich's study supports Hochschild's previous work.

Women experience the pressure of trying to maintain a social life and a home life. When men begin their career advancement, they commonly find support from their wives or partners. A study released in the fall of 1994 showed that men make more money when their wives don't work for pay. Domestic chores are tended to. And wives are more willing to be patient with the professional male when he travels on business or puts in extra hours at the office.

The working woman who is married, whether she is in a non-managerial, managerial, or executive position, often does not have that luxury or support. Most of the time, she does the majority of the domestic work, as Hochschild reports. If she is single, a woman usually discovers that potential mates resent her time commitments. She may have trouble establishing a relationship, or she may even decide not to enter into a relationship because she doesn't have time to develop it. Relationships take work.

SUPERWOMAN IS EXHAUSTED

So what is a woman to do? Can she have it all? Most women who have some maturity—women over 45—will tell you it is possible to have it all. It is, though, impossible to have it all at once. In 1984, Marjorie Hansen Shaevitz penned her classic, *The Superwoman Syndrome*. Shaevitz wrote that in the 1980s women were unaware of what was going on—the Superwoman Syndrome. We were trying to be everything to everybody, without realizing that there were consequences. Now, women realize it's not healthy, it's not fair, and it's not realistic. But we still continued to do "it."

Doing "it" literally means women do too much. One button pusher for me was an ad for Enjoli perfume that gloated, "You can bring home the bacon, fry it up in the pan, and never, ever let you forget you're a woman." How many women do you know who come through the door, change their clothes, look like they stepped off the cover of *Vogue* magazine with perfect makeup, and then go out for the evening with their man?

Media advertising needs to get real. Most women would probably rather soak in the tub when they get home, without little ones demanding their time and attention, or at the minimum be able to sit or lie down and put their feet up. The reality is, it rarely happens. If a woman averages 32.3 hours of housework a week, she needs to hit the floor running when she walks through that door (or gets out of bed).

Sabrina is single and works for the marketing department of a technology-based company located in North Carolina. Presently, it has 100 employees. Management projects that the company will double, possibly triple, its number within the next 2 years. On the one side, Sabrina is invigorated by all the activity and promise that her present employment offers. On the other side, she feels that she doesn't have much of a life.

> When you work in a technology-based company, you find that what's new today becomes old tomorrow. I'm the marketing manager for a group of products that our company is basing its future growth on.
>
> It's a heady experience. I'm 31 years old. I feel quite complimented that the company has put so much faith into my abilities. It's what fuels me, and it scares me. Presently, I work 70 to 80 hours a week. When I am awake, all I think about is my work, and when I

go to sleep, I doze off thinking about what needs to be done the next day. One side of me says this isn't healthy, but the other side says to hang in there. It will last only a few more years, until the company makes it big. That's the voice I listen to.

I know that I am out of balance. I have few friends; those who are, are all from work. With my hours, who has time to develop friendships in other areas? I don't belong to any association or women's group; again, that would take time, and I just don't have it. Last month, I dropped out of the health club; it seemed like a waste of money to pay out every month when I made it there only a couple of times.

I know that I'm under stress and I worry about that at times. I also worry about meeting the right person, getting married, and having kids someday. But it's just not in the cards, at least not in the current hand. I'm grateful that I have a lot of energy, and that my health is good.

THE SATISFIED MOTHER

Anyone who has children knows there are going to be problems, and those problems will overflow and be acted out in a variety of ways. In such a case, does it make sense for a woman to work outside the home if she or her family doesn't need the money? According to a Gallup poll in April 1994, as reported in *Working Mother* magazine, the answer is yes. Over 1000 working moms with children under 18 were polled. Contrary to the rattled, stretched-out, and exhausted image portrayed by the media, the poll found that over 80 percent were satisfied with how well their children were doing and with the job they were doing as mothers.

Over 71 percent of the respondents reported that working made them feel good about themselves, regardless of what their job was or how much they earned. Seventy-five percent said they either liked or loved their jobs, and 82 percent said the reason they worked was to provide for their family. Over 90 percent of those polled said their kids were happy.

It is probably fair to say that if a mother believes her kids are happy, a positive side effect will result. The kids see that their mothers are excited about their jobs, using their education and skills, and may even be motivated to continue in school. One of the lowest responses in the poll reflected the barrage of demands on a working woman's life. Only 54 percent of the respondents said they were satisfied with the way they managed multiple demands.[2]

SOUNDS BAD...MAYBE

As in most aspects of life, there's a positive and a negative. Statistics and reporting are sometimes manipulated. In a September 1993 poll, Gallup analyzed the data for USA Today's and CNN's nationwide study of 1065 adults. The survey didn't reveal how many working mothers participated.

An article in USA Today summarized the findings. Forty-five percent of the female respondents said it was better if the man was the achiever outside the home and the woman took care of the family; 40 percent of the men concurred. Surprisingly, more men (59 percent) than women (53 percent) disagreed that husbands should work and wives should stay home. Forty-eight percent of the women thought that the women's movement had made life harder than it was 20 years ago; 41 percent of the men agreed.

Differences showed up more between age groups than between sexes. Older men and women tended to be more conservative, and younger women were more supportive of the goals of the women's movement. As a side note, 44 percent of the women and 33 percent of the men preferred a male boss. Almost half (49 percent) of the men said that the boss's gender didn't matter, where only 25 percent of the women had no preference.[3]

The article in USA Today created a series of responses from women. Many wrote that it was sexist. They sought more detail and wanted the responses broken down into gender and age.

A few days later USA Today reported the breakdown of how women responded to the statement "It is generally better for society if the man is the achiever outside the home, and the woman takes care of the home and family." Fifty-three percent of the women respondents disagreed with that statement, 2 percent had no opinion, and 45 percent agreed. When age groups were segmented, 75 percent of women in the 18 to 29 range disagreed, 67 percent in the 30 to 49 range disagreed, and only 30 percent of women 50 or over disagreed.[4]

In other words, statistics can be manipulated, deleted, and moved around to come in and support just about anyone's theory or prejudice. In many cases, it's the undisclosed data that are the most telling. In this case, in the initial article referred to above was titled "Many Say Their Place Is In The Home." Only women age 50 and over agreed with that statement.

So where does this all lead us? It means that flexibility and health—good health—are in order. Unfortunately, neither the workplace nor outside society has really created a fantastic day-care and support system for working moms and dads. Politicians—presidents, senators, and representatives—talk big about being family-oriented and supporting family values. Few put their money and votes in support for policies that are pro-working family—which is the majority of the American population.

NOT ALL WOMEN HAVE CHILDREN

Child care, or the lack of it, trickles down and affects single and childless women in the workplace. There is an assumption, almost a stereotypical factor, that all women will be supporting, caring, nurturing, and understanding of other women's situations and plights. What baloney.

Many women in the GenderTraps survey who were single and childless reported that they were irritated and felt put-upon by the need to help out women who had children. Whether these women were married or not, or had supportive partners or not, wasn't the issue. Several wrote that they had to arrange their working schedule around others' child-care needs in the workplace.

Melissa is single and has no children. She is an accountant with a medium-size firm on the West Coast. Too often, she feels that there are times when her days, and others', are affected by the needs and demands of employees' children.

> There are three of us who are full-time, single and have no children. I wouldn't mind it so much if doctor and dental appointments, meetings, conversations with schools, and check-ins with care providers were done at lunch time or at breaks.
>
> Maybe some of it is done during "time out" periods. But my experience is that many times, my day is scheduled around the day-care and doctor appointment needs of the women who work for me. It is almost as if our work gets scheduled around outside and social lives versus the outside and social life being scheduled around the work time.

A reality check is in order. What Melissa brings up is that even if employees designate their check-in call times, follow-up calls, or appointment makings during legitimate break or lunch hours, or even before work officially starts and ends, there is spillover. Spillover, meaning that it rarely stops with a call-in for an appointment or when a check-in is made; it doesn't end when the phone is hung up. Rather, there is a residual factor.

GATHERING CLOUDS

Some of the spillover affects others who work in the vicinity of the person making the call. If there is a sick child, most mothers check in. Those who work with her will know the child is sick and, most likely, will have some concern or empathy.

Depending upon the degree of the illness, a quasi-cloud can encompass the workplace. If it is a light illness, there is no darkness in it. But if it is more than a cold or the flu, it could feel like a downpour could occur at any time. When women are concerned about something, especially family, their emotions are more transparent than men's are. That's part of the trickle-down/spillover effect that Melissa refers to.

THE TYLENOL SYNDROME

Erica knows all too well the problems that working moms have with children, especially when the kids are ill. She is the director of a large child-care facility in the South. Within the system, there are five hospitals that offer day care. Of course, it's not for free. Erica describes the Tylenol syndrome:

> Many companies don't allow employees to use their sick time to care for sick kids. The result is that parents are forced to lie. If their little girl has a temperature early in the morning, they load her up on Tylenol and drop her off at our day-care center. After 4 hours, the effect wears off. Even if the child has that glazed look that goes along with a fever, if she doesn't register a fever, we can't turn her away.
>
> When the Tylenol wears off, and the temp begins to spike, we call the parents to come and pick up the child and take her home. For

us, Tylenol is a Band-Aid; for parents, it gives them approximately 4 hours of working time.

THE PERSONAL BANK

Lying to take care of a sick child doesn't seem to fit into the ethics and values of the workplace. Nor does the burden falling on one parent, to leave work to pick up a child or tend to an emergency, seem quite fair. In fact, it could jeopardize one's job. Is there a solution? Yes, but it's not common.

After employment for a few months or a year, most employees begin to earn—accrue—sick time as well as vacation time. In most organizations, sick time has to be used for illness, and the only person who gets to be sick to use it is the employee. If you need to take off time to take care of someone else who is ill, you end up using vacation time or personal days that you may not get paid for.

There is another way. On the West Coast, I've come across organizations that actually have a form of "bank account." Employees earn so many days off. Whether they use them for sick time—theirs, or that of people they are responsible for—personal days off, or vacation is up to them. The "bank account" is good only for one year. If you don't use up your accumulated hours or days, the employer cashes you out. Accrual is usually done on a monthly or quarterly basis.

An employee doesn't have to account to anyone for how that time is spent. She only has to notify the person who will be responsible when she is gone, as well as the personnel department. This approach is definitely more sane and more mature than the way that most organizations handle their employees' sick and vacation times. It is absurd to force employees to lie about sick time. And it's juvenile to require employees to bring "notes" from their doctors, even when they are home with the flu!

COMBINING FORCES CREATES A SOLUTION

Some businesses have taken it a step further; they are creating family benefits. Many companies may balk, saying they are too small and don't have monies to invest in capital equipment for, say, a day-care center.

A solution may be to form a partnership or joint partnership, in which groups of employers work together to establish and fund cooperative projects. By joining forces, they can provide for a center and contract with an outside professional group to manage it. They can contribute money, staff time, equipment, or services such as printing.

The American Business Collaboration is a coalition of 146 business and private sector organizations nationwide. It was funded in 1992 and, to date, has spent $20 million of its $26 million commitment as a group to establish 285 of 300 prospective dependent-care initiatives. More than 40,000 people have been served in the various programs that are offered.[5]

UNFREEZING DOING IT ALL

Years ago, I was interviewed by a national women's magazine. Somewhere along the line its editors had read that I worked more than 40 hours a week, had three children, was married, got involved in the community, and sat on several boards. In other words, they wanted to know how I did it all. When they called me for the interview, I told them that one of the factors that allowed me to do as much as I did was that I got help.

That was the wrong answer; it was not what they wanted to hear. In fact, it's the first interview that I felt I really flunked. As we pursued the conservation further, I learned what the interviewer wanted me to say—that I cooked and baked on weekends, late in the evening when I got home, and/or when I got up early in the morning. The product of my late-night endeavors would be frozen so my family would have casseroles, goodies, and snacks when the need arose. I remember telling the interviewer that I loved to cook and bake, but doing so for the mere sake of stocking up the freezer wasn't the objective, ever.

When she told me what the demographics were for the magazine, my response was, "It sounds like the average woman. Why don't you do this average woman a favor and map out a strategy and plan to show her how and why she should get some help if she is putting in the 40-hour week working outside the home." Her response was, "No! The magazine couldn't do that." She really wanted to write about women doing it all.

Well, women can't do it all at the same time, or have it all at once. We can do it all over a period of time by taking bits and pieces.

Women's magazines and TV shows do such an incredible disservice to their readers, viewers, and listeners with such poppycock. What women do not need is to have more responsibilities and obligations piled on them. They need some help in prioritizing so that there can be some balance in the day, including time for themselves.

According to the Bureau of Labor Statistics and the National Commission of Children, over 60 percent of married mothers work outside the home and have children under the age of 6. Over 6 million single mothers are in the workplace. For most women today, homemaking and working are not either/or lifestyles. Women's lives are more highly individualized, with roles changing from week to week and from month to month.

It is meaningless to label some women as homemakers and others as workers—every woman works. It's also important to delete outdated and unrealistic terms that throw us back into the "nostalgic" times of *Ozzie and Harriet, Donna Reed,* and *Leave It to Beaver.* Then, of course, there was the 1980s version of the most perfect family—the Huxtables, à la *The Cosby Show.* Few women really want to go backward versus forward.

Sure, life in the 1950s, for families at least, had a slower pace. There was a greater sense of community and a greater opportunity to evolve and move into a middle-class lifestyle with just one employed partner in a marriage. But there was a cost: men and women had to follow the rules. Those rules were that women stayed home, men went to work, women cared for the men and the family, and men financially supported the family. That was it—no variables.

Instead of bemoaning how things used to be, it's far more logical and reasonable to look at how things are and how we want to shape them as we go forward into the future.

PART TIME CAN BE FULL TIME

Marilyn has found the ideal job. It wasn't easy, and it didn't happen overnight. She is a PR consultant, and works part time. She remembers that when she graduated from college in 1975, the placement officer told her that if she wasn't mobile and willing to move, she'd better learn how to type. After 5 years of employment, she began her family. That's when her problems started. She found that there were all types of people against women who wanted to work part time.

Part-time employees were not considered serious. Now, that could apply to both men and women. I found that people assumed that if you wanted to work part time, you weren't interested in a professional position. There is a general assumption that if you take a part-time job, it is because it's all you can get, and you will be here only temporarily. You're going to be out looking for a full-time position to move to.

I was fortunate. I found a nonprofit organization which did not have the funds for a full-time staff. Many of us were hired part time. At all times, my boss treated us as professionals. She also gave us autonomy. We were allowed to manage our areas with our own vision and ideas.

One of the things that Marilyn brought up was the need to develop strong measurements for work performance, especially in the case of the part-time worker, and the worker who works out of the home instead of in an office space. It's probable that jobs in the future will be broken into a series of projects, and each project will be assigned a value. Piecework. The value will be translated into actual dollars.

A specific amount of money is generated and paid to the person or people who complete the project. The amount of time is not measured by an around-the-common-workweek clock. A project could be equivalent to a full-time position for a few weeks or months. Or a part-time one. The real measurement would be based on what is accomplished, rather than how much time is spent.

What most women desire are challenging, responsible jobs within clean workplaces, with reasonable hours. Is this a new oxymoron? Workplaces that offer responsible, challenging jobs in an attractive environment and that pay well rarely feature reasonable hours. Few companies offer any types of benefits to part-time workers. Health-care coverage, 401(k) plans, and pensions go out the door. So part-time work is actually delegated to the women in lower-paying, non-challenging positions.

In the old days, part-time work was assumed to be supplemental, as in working to pay for the fence, the doctor's bills, the pool, and so on. Few men work part time by choice. The pay scales, and the benefits, aren't good. In reality, many senior managers in companies work part time. They'd never admit so.

A great many senior management jobs are segmented. The segments can include personnel, management of a specific project or department, involvement in strategic planning, and positioning. All these areas can take a few hours here, a few hours there or lump hours of time—pieces to the workplace puzzle. It's never called part-time work, nor is it paid as a part-time job would be.

One of the results of the inflexibility of the workplace is that women are leaving in droves. And it's not so much a result of the glass-ceiling issue that has been mistrumpeted in the media. Women are leaving to start up their own businesses. The new cottage industries often work around their families' needs and demands or, in many cases, the needs of their owners. Women are also leaving for better workplace conditions over money. What an incredible loss for today's businesses, those dinosaurs that so badly need new ideas, new talent, and new energy.

WORKING WOMEN NEED WIVES

Unfortunately, most women don't have wives. Even some men may question whether they have wives, at least of the traditional *Ozzie and Harriet* style. Research in the early 1990s has shown that men would actually begin to work fewer hours if they had their "druthers." They don't mind the 40-hour-a-week job; it's the 50- and 60-plus week that gets to them. Yet employers demand it, and to a great extent society has come to expect it.

As enlightened as many people feel they are, most jobs are still designed for men as the primary breadwinner and for women as the primary domestic laborer in the home (which they are). Many believe that if there were adequate child-care facilities, there would be minimal problems for women at work. Maybe. But it's not that simple and it's not the final solution to the problem that women face in being overloaded, overworked, and at times overstressed.

When sociologist Arlie Hochschild identified the "second shift" on the home front, she did not discount the fact that some husbands do help out with domestic obligations. But few contributed in a 50:50 sharing. She found that women's ideas of domestic collaboration didn't pan out in most cases. And when husbands didn't participate to the degree which women felt they should, the women protected themselves from their disappointment and frustration by covering up for the men.

Typically, they would give their husbands more credit for what they contributed to household work and child-care tasks than what they actually did. In some cases, women became enablers and codependents—supporting their spouses' domestic laziness and shortcomings. Internal reactions, or reactions shared with those on the outside, would often be filled with anger.

I "failed" the interview with the national magazine—the one that wanted to hear that I worked extra hours baking, cooking, and freezing. Its editors refused to hear that I got help, and when I told them that one of the best things they could advise was to get help, they rejected me. Women do many tasks that are unnecessary or that could be deferred, done in a lesser quality, or done by hiring someone to help—if they would only give themselves permission.

From the years 1972 to 1986, I worked with clients on financial matters. Routinely, women would tell me that their money ran out before the end of the month. When checkbooks were opened up, it was easy to determine what they spent along with their ATM withdrawal cards in the form of cash. Usually, I found monies that I identified as "kiss-off."

You need to identify and learn what your priorities are. If it is to have more time for yourself, or to make more time for things you care about, you need to take some of those kiss-off dollars for yourselves. Whether it is for movies (you can pool funds with other friends and rent one), books (don't forget, libraries are free, and they usually have the latest best-sellers), or shoes and clothing (few of us have to pay top dollar for anything today; almost every city has some form of discount shopping), these kiss-off funds can be used to buy help. There are also kiss-off hours. Just 10 minutes here and 10 minutes there add up.

As more and more women find themselves in the workplace, their lives at home don't change a great deal. They still continue to shoulder most of the housework and child-raising responsibilities. In *Working Women Don't Have Wives*, Terri Apter points out that the reason women have failed to achieve equality is not that men are conspiring to keep them barefoot and pregnant, or that women secretly yearn to be taken care of by men. The disparity is really rooted in conflicts between work and family life—and in the fact that working women, unlike most working men, don't have wives.

In today's workplace, men are expected to labor longer hours, while their wives or partners watch the kids. Most workplaces are not set up to meet the demands and needs of working mothers. Most women find that if they opt to have children, and elect to take time off, they'll face some form of economic dependence or banishment to the "Mommy Track." If a woman does not take off, guaranteed she is going to be exhausted, not to mention guilty about not being with the family's latest addition.[6]

THE ENLIGHTENED WORKPLACE

No matter how enlightened the workplace feigns to be, for the most part it is still rooted in the traditional sense about where men and women belong. By the turn of the century, it is estimated that two-thirds of all workers will be women. Home-related types of problems will not disappear; they will just increase and compound.

Part of the flexibility needed is to further expand the option of job sharing. The idea of doing home-based work or sharing office sites and home sites for work appeals to many. The copout that if women work at home they'll start watching television is as absurd as saying that if men work at home they'll be practicing putting. With the broad usage of faxes, modems, computers, and telephones, a growing number of professionals work out of the home.

SUPERWOMAN DOESN'T LIVE HERE ANY MORE

When women juggle it all, something has got to give. The first thing to go is *time for yourself*. Feeding the goldfish and the hamster have priority over taking time for you. Technology has been wonderful in creating conveniences. Women, and men, have more gizmos to aid them in their work and household chores. But there is a dark side to the wizardry of the 1990s.

There is no question that our ancestors worked hard—from sunup to sundown. Their equipment is found in our museums. When they came home, the fire was stoked and they often did their bookkeeping after dinner. What they didn't have were faxes, E-mail, voice mail, beepers, or overnight deliveries demanding a response now—or at least within an hour. And the phones—there is no escaping them. Yesteryear, it was a car in every garage. Now, it is two and sometimes three cars, and within each is a phone, not to mention the cellular phone that is carried in a purse, briefcase, or pocket.

Today's technology has created a "no brain" downtime environment. It doesn't matter if it is at work or at home. Too many are working 24 hours a day, 7 days a week. There is little time out. Juliet Schor, Harvard economist and author of *The Overworked American*, hit the nail on the head when she wrote that Americans are working far more with much less leisure time. In the 1970s, it was expected that the average American would be working barely 30 hours per week at a "for pay" job as the 1990s unfolded. It just did not happen, and it never will with the business practices of today.

Many work 50-hour weeks, and that doesn't take into consideration commute time (yes, you too can have a fax, laser printer, and copy machine in your car to take advantage of the nonproductive commute time!). Where will the average for-pay working American be in the next decade? That's easy—exhausted and highly stressed.

With corporate America's cutbacks of thousands of personnel, more work has been piled on those left behind (forget the concept that doing more work creates more pay). A threat of "you too could be out the door" lingers in the air; management has removed most thoughts of leisure from the working person's vocabulary. The fear of losing a job propels you to hang in there one more day, week, month, even year at a time. You are afraid even to take earned vacation days.

In the end, business will lose big. Everyone is capable of working with bursts of creativity and production. The operative word is *bursts*. Bursts do not mean around the clock, 7 days a week. Bursts allow for downtime, brainstorming, and sorting out.

One of the challenges business and management must address is: How much profit is enough? Does it make economic, political, and ethical sense to *eliminate productive workers,* shifting their work onto others without additional compensation to the surviving worker for the added work to increase profitability? For that matter, if a business is profitable, why eliminate people and positions because it is "in the air" or in the "every business is cutting back" scenario?

When I do workshops and talk about the need to prioritize and get life in balance, I have my audience do a simple exercise. It involves taking a piece of paper and tearing it into four parts. On each part, a word or phrase is written that identifies one of the top four issues that are currently important to the participant. It could be going back to school, changing jobs, getting married, getting unmarried, starting an exercise program, or spending an extra hour each day with the children. You name it. We all have lists of wishes we'd like to do.

What are your top four? Take a few minutes and write them down. After you have identified the four most important items in your life that you'd like to concentrate on at the present time, look them over. Remove the least important of the four. Again, scan the remaining three. Remove the one that is the least important. Of the two remaining, put aside the one that is the less important. You have one left. The question becomes: Do you spend time each day focusing, concentrating, supporting, and encouraging whatever it is you have on your single piece of paper?

Now, many members of my audiences will nod their heads and say yes, indeed they do. But many don't. If you are one of the ones who doesn't—or maybe you're not sure, or you tell yourself that you would like to spend more time—then it's time for "time out." If you try to be all things to all people, you can be described in one word: *exhausted.* And not so smart.

Remember, the average woman does 32-plus hours of housework a week—whether she is married or not, whether she works for pay or is a homemaker. If you work full time *and* do your average of 32-plus hours of housework a week, when will you find time to dedicate to the top four items that are important to you?

Women need to practice the art of saying no. If you don't say no, your yeses become worthless.

If you are not dedicating some time each day to your number-one priority, and then bringing in numbers two, three, and four, then you need to become myopic and say no—no to this, no to that. Yes, you're going to disappoint some people. Too bad. You need to recenter and come back in and dedicate and support yourself. When you support yourself, you can reach out to others.

In 1971, my infant son died. I learned something very important. The dust will be here tomorrow, the next day, next week, next month, next year—it never goes away. I used to want to have my house perfect. Can you imagine that, with four kids under the age of 8? The reason Superwoman is dead is that she died from superexhaustion. Women must learn to delegate, to get help, and to ask for help. As Marjorie Hansen Shaevitz says:

> Ten years ago, none of us knew what was going on—the Superwoman Syndrome. We were trying to be everything to everyone, and not realizing that there were consequences. Now, women realize it's not healthy, it's not fair, and it's not realistic, but we still continue to do it.

Shaevitz recommends posting these rules for all household members:

- If you sleep on it, make it up.
- If you wear it, hang it up.
- If you drop it, pick it up.
- If you lay it down, put it away.
- If you eat out of it, wash it (or put it in the dishwasher).
- If you make a mess, clean it up now.
- If you open it, close it.
- If you turn it on, turn it off.
- If you empty it, fill it up.
- If you lose it, find it yourself.
- If you borrow it, put it back where it belongs.
- If you move it, return it to where you found it.
- If you break it, replace it.
- If it rings, answer it.
- If it howls or meows, feed or let it out.
- If it cries, love it.

Thank you,
The Management[7]

Women have babies and women work. No one has it all, there are going to be "give-ups" for men and women. A goal or mentality of having it all, doing it all, being it all propels women into a frenetic, almost insatiable quest for even more. For many, it becomes impossible to celebrate the victories along the way. Many men will admit today that they don't have it all. They just don't talk about it as openly as women do.

There are several factors that will assist in bringing some balance into your life. The first is to say no. All of us have taken on commitments and projects that we wished we had never heard of. In fact, there are times when we agree to do something just because we've been worn down by the proponent, and then we swear that will be the last committee we will work on—until the next one comes along. Say no! Without practicing no, your yeses do lose their value.

If you haven't already, begin now to educate—bring pressure on—your workplace. It needs more flexibility. Part-time work, shared work, and definitely a pooling of sick time, vacation, and personal days off into a bank-type of account—to be used at the discretion of you, the account holder—makes sense.

Get help. If you have to buy it, trade it, or enlist your kids and/or spouse, do it now. Don't make excuses or rationalize when other members in the household don't help. Professor Higgins' line from *My Fair Lady* "Why can't a woman be more like a man?" needs a twist: "Why can't a man be more like a woman?"

In the end, you will be less overwhelmed, more responsive, happier, and healthier. A win-win for everybody.

Confrontophobia: The fear of bringing face to face, especially boldly or defiantly; the fear of encountering or opposing another in a showdown or disagreement.

TRAP 7:
CONQUERING
CONFRONTOPHOBIA
Eliminating the
Roadblock to
Resolving Conflicts

- Do you feel that conflicts must be resolved immediately?
- If you had your "druthers," would you avoid confronting someone?
- If people take credit for your work, do you avoid speaking with them directly about their actions?
- If you become aware that rumors or gossip are being circulated about you, do you hope it will go away without your saying anything to stop or correct it?
- Has anyone ever verbally attacked you?

Confronting someone is not every woman's favorite pastime. When women are involved in a negative situation, they are more inclined to grumble about it to a friend, to a colleague at work, or to a spouse—rarely to the person who created it.

Little girls are taught not to make waves. A *momism*. It's one of the big lessons of early childhood that has been carried over into womanhood. One of the myths of the workplace is that nice girls do not confront. The reality is that nice girls can and do. Another myth is that people who work together and are friends won't have conflicts. In reality, that myth is about as absurd as a T-Rex walking through your neighborhood.

NICE GIRLS *SHOULD* COMPLAIN

Conflict and confrontation should go hand in hand. Unfortunately, they do not. Because of their upbringing, men are more inclined to handle conflict in a direct manner. As a result, they are able to stay more focused and objective. Women are less inclined to say that they are unhappy or not comfortable with a situation to the person who causes the discomfort or the person who has the capability of changing it. An old upbringing dictum is "Nice girls don't complain," another *momism*.

As a teacher, Roxanne has observed that men tend to be more direct in confronting conflict.

> Men tend to stay more objective and handle conflict very directly. We women were raised to be good girls, so we would never say, "I'm unhappy with this," or get it all out. We always wonder what the motive was behind a comment that was made by another, but we never ask directly.
>
> My experience with women is that they can be very pleasant and nice to you, and then turn around and talk about and against you. It's probably why a lot of women prefer working with male bosses.

Many women internally know that they should confront a situation. Our heads tell us, our bodies tell us, our hearts tell us. Society does not. Because of societal upbringings that gave out the message that confrontation, a conflicting situation, or being unpleasant wasn't acceptable for girls/women, it's quite normal for a woman to respond in a nonconfrontational style. Unfortunately, when there is a problem without discussion or confrontation, nothing changes.

NOT THE SEASON FOR GIVING

As the nursing supervisor for a fast-paced and sometimes hectic practice, Harriette feels that she has to watch out for her flock. She recalls that over the holidays a problem surfaced involving the medical director.

> There are five offices in our practice. Our administration is trying to be precise, to put together an effective management style and direction that involves the team leader approach.
>
> Several of the physicians have hollered at the nurses. The verbal attacks are getting louder and louder and are done in front of patients, with many of the nurses on the point of tears. Not only did the doctors yell at the nurses, so did the medical director. When I set up an appointment to talk with the medical director about some of the doctors' behavior as well as his own, he blew me off.
>
> I had had enough, so I approached one of the physicians about the verbal abuse directed toward the nurses. He didn't want to get involved and told me that I would have to take it to administration. Basically, I was on my own. Either the CEO would support me or I would be out of a job.
>
> The CEO came to me and talked to me about some of the problems. I told him that I felt it was pretty gutsy of me to approach him directly, especially in dealing with a problem that affects my immediate boss. I identified all the issues, describing what happened and how each impacted my staff. I told him that I knew my job could be on the line, but felt that something had to be done. The physicians and the medical director had no right treating nurses the way they had been in our offices.
>
> The CEO approached them a few days later supporting my position and that of the nurses in the offices.

One important item in planning a confrontation is to ask the question, "What's the worst thing that could happen?" In Harriette's case, there were three things: (1) she could lose her job; (2) the situation would remain status quo; or (3) she could quit. Harriette had terminated a job previously, so it was not a new situation. She was not afraid of taking the third option.

Many women are afraid to confront an unpleasant situation because they feel they have no alternative. It is very similar to the battered-woman syndrome. Women will often stay in a miserable situation because they feel they have no alternative. They become so embedded in the happenings around them that they can't put themselves in the position, or attitude, to say, "Take this job and shove it."

FIND THE SOURCE

Melissa is an administrative manager. She believes that the failure to confront is one of the biggest problems that women have to deal with. Melissa is a proponent of the rule that you have to go to the source of the problem.

> Confronting is one of the greatest problems that I see. An example would be when staff members call and say the lab did this and the lab did that. When I ask if they have talked to the lab supervisor, their response is, "Well, no." I then tell them not to call me, call the lab supervisor. Then, if there is still a problem, call me back. I'm not here to fight your battles like your mother. Go to the source and see if you can work it out before you involve others.

THE WRONG TURF

Joanna was hired a year ago. Her boss told her that her position was new and it would evolve. By the time she formally started, she felt she was on track. Her coworkers didn't. They had not been informed about any of the changes or expectations of her new position.

> By the time I got there, the job responsibilities had already changed. My coworkers had not been informed of what I would be doing as I joined the team. It ended up that everyone was basically mad at me all the time.
>
> Because they hadn't been told what I would be doing, they felt I wasn't doing my job. Somehow, my boss wasn't aware of their growing anger and hostility toward me. When someone finally blew, my boss became aware that everyone was angry. Everything escalated and work became tense. We all decided we needed to cool off, so we planned a pot-luck get-together. I volunteered my house.
>
> Now, I knew we were going to discuss the changes and attempt to clarify everyone's position. I didn't know that I was going to be the target of the meeting. I don't think anyone knew the position or the degree of uncomfortableness I felt. Eventually they all left.

If the clock could be turned back and rewound, Joanna felt her boss, and the entire team, should have clarified what everybody's role was. When she approached others within her group to clear up a conflict, she found it was often brought down to a more personal level, rather than dealt with on a professional level.

It's often a good idea to move to neutral ground in dealing with a conflict. Choosing Joanna's home as the designated "dumping" ground was inappropriate and out of line. When her coworkers left, she felt her home had been invaded. It had.

TRAITS OF CONFLICT

There are several traits and characteristics of conflict. As a conflict escalates, concern for self increases in a parallel manner. When there is conflict, the desire to win increases with the rise in self-interest. Saving face takes on an increased importance.

Management techniques for conflict vary. What works at a low level of conflict can be ineffective and counterproductive at an intense or high level of conflict. People can use different styles of conflict within a conflict. When dealing with someone you are going to confront, personally or professionally, it makes sense to identify what her strengths and weaknesses are by understanding her preferred style of handling conflict. It means you have to step back, change hats, and put yourself in her place by anticipating her responses or reactions.

Make a copy of the Managing Conflict Styles Questionnaire in Fig. 9-1. To score the questionnaire, total the number of A's, B's, C's, D's, and E's from questions 1 through 10 at the bottom of the survey. Your score will determine what your conflict style is. The style that has the greatest total is your dominant style in dealing with conflict; the second-highest total is your backup, secondary style.

Figure 9-1. *Managing Conflict Styles Questionnaire.* (Copyright The Briles Group, 1995.)

---

1. When you feel strongly about a conflict, you would:

_____ A. Enjoy the excitement and feel a sense of accomplishment.

_____ B. View the conflict as a venture and a challenge.

_____ C. Be concerned about how others are impacted.

_____ D. Be dismayed because someone could be harmed.

_____ E. Become persuaded there is little to nothing you can do to resolve it.

(Continued)

2. Ideally, what's the best result you expect from a conflict?

   _____ A. It will encourage others to look at the issues and face facts.

   _____ B. It will eliminate extremes in positions and enable a middle ground to surface.

   _____ C. It will clear the air, increasing commitment and results.

   _____ D. It will clarify the absurdity of a situation and draw coworkers closer together.

   _____ E. It will reduce complacency and apathy and identify who is to blame.

3. When you have the final word in a conflict situation, you would:

   _____ A. Let everyone know what your view is.

   _____ B. Attempt to negotiate the best settlement for all concerned.

   _____ C. Encourage others to share their opinion and suggest that a position be found that both sides might try.

   _____ D. Provide support to whatever the group decides.

   _____ E. Remove yourself from the process, citing rules if they apply.

4. If anyone is irrational, illogical or unreasonable, you would:

   _____ A. Be blunt and say that you don't like it.

   _____ B. Drop hints that you're not pleased; but avoid direct confrontation.

   _____ C. Identify the conflict and suggest that you both probe possible solutions.

   _____ D. Not say anything.

   _____ E. Keep away from the person.

5. When you become angry with a peer, you:

   _____ A. Rant and rave with little thought or concern.

   _____ B. Try to gloss things over with a good story.

   _____ C. Tell her you are angry and ask her for a response.

   _____ D. Offset your anger by saying everything is OK, it wasn't a big deal.

   _____ E. Withdraw yourself from the situation.

6. If you disagree with coworkers about a project, you:

_____ A. Hang firm and justify your position.

_____ B. Appeal to the logic and goodwill of the group in the hope of persuading most that your way or idea is the best.

_____ C. Identify and review areas of agreement and disagreement, then look for options that reflect everyone's views.

_____ D. Give in and go with the group to keep the peace.

_____ E. Withdraw from discussing the project and don't commit to any decision reached.

7. When someone takes an opposite position to the rest of the team, you would:

_____ A. Tell the others in the group who the roadblock is and encourage them to move on without him or her if necessary.

_____ B. Encourage her to communicate her objections so that a trade-off can be reached.

_____ C. Learn why she views the issue differently so that the others can reevaluate their own positions.

_____ D. Recommend that the problem area be set aside and discuss other areas that are in agreement.

_____ E. Keep quiet because it is best to not get involved.

8. When conflict surfaces in your team, you:

_____ A. Press forward for a quick decision so that the task is completed.

_____ B. Attempt to shift the dispute toward a middle ground.

_____ C. Analyze the problem with the group so that it can be discussed.

_____ D. Relieve the tension with a good story.

_____ E. If the conflict doesn't involve you, steer clear of it.

9. In handling conflict between coworkers, you would:

_____ A. Anticipate areas of opposition and prepare replies to perceived objections prior to open conflicts.

_____ B. Encourage coworkers to identify possible areas that may meet objections.

(Continued)

_____ C. Recognize that conflict does not mean disaster and encourage them to identify shared concerns and/or goals.

_____ D. Promote unanimity on the basis that the conflict can lead to the demise of friendly relations and friendships.

_____ E. Find someone who is neutral to arbitrate the matter.

10. In your opinion, why would one group fail to work with another?

_____ A. Lack of a clearly stated position or structure, or failure to back up and support the group's position.

_____ B. Tendency to force leaders to abide by the group's decision, as opposed to promoting flexibility, which could facilitate compromise.

_____ C. Tendency of groups to be myopic and view negotiations with a win-lose perspective.

_____ D. Lack of motivation to work peacefully with the other group.

_____ E. Leaders place emphasis on maintaining their own power versus addressing the issues involved.

Scoring

Now, total the number of A's, B's, etc. and insert below:

A _____   B _____   C _____   D _____   E _____
  Competing   Compromising   Collaborating   Accommodating   Avoiding

Complete the survey in two ways. First, answer as you normally would; then do a shift. Where you see the personal pronouns relating to you, revise and substitute *she, her, he,* or *him.* For example: "When *she has* (you have) strong feelings in a conflict, *she* (you) would _____." Now answer as you think the person you need to confront would answer.

After you complete the exercise the second time around substituting *she* for *you,* you should have a strong indication of what "her" style of dealing with conflict is. The result is that you are now in the driver's seat. You have the opportunity to take the lead and adjust your style to match hers. When this happens, she will be better able to "hear" what you have to say. A compromise that allows for a win-win result, versus lose-lose or lose (you)–win (her), is more likely to be achieved.

Use the conflict-handling analysis grid in Fig. 9-2 to identify your or another's method of using conflict. There are five styles: competitive, collaborative, avoiding, accommodating, and compromising. Look at the dimension of the grid that is labeled unassertive–assertive. You know when you are unassertive; it means that you want to pull back from a conflict; you will do anything to avoid a confrontation, to make it go away. If you are assertive, you will be more aggressive and active in dealing with it.

I have never met a person who said she did not know whether she was assertive or unassertive. If you speak up for what you believe in or what you perceive as justified, you are on the assertive

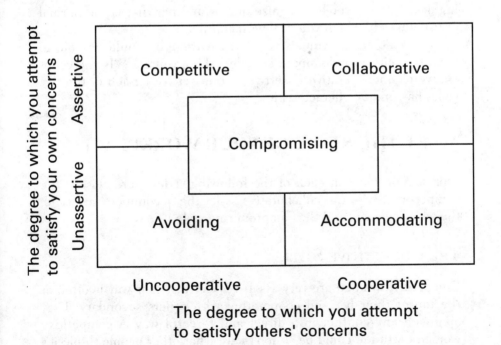

Figure 9-2. *The Five Conflict-Handling Modes.* (Adapted from the Thoman–Kilmann Conflict MODE Instrument, developed by Kenneth W. Thoman and Ralph H. Kilmann in 1972. (MODE is an acronym for "management of differences exercise."))

side. If you believe that others routinely take advantage of you and your voice isn't heard, you lean toward being nonassertive or unassertive.

Now look at the uncooperative–cooperative dimension—the degree to which you attempt to satisfy someone's concerns. If you are a cooperative person, you know that you will do what you can to work along with another, even when you don't agree with her. If you are the opposite, or uncooperative, your choice is either to avoid any dealings with her or to attempt to resolve the issue in your way.

Again, step back. If things don't go your way, have you ever felt or said, "I'm out of here"? Or do you say, "Hold on; let's continue to work and see if we can get a resolution"? The first is uncooperative; the second, cooperative.

By putting the two dimensions of the grid together, you will end up with a matrix of five different styles of dealing with conflict. The compromising style will be in the center. It represents the balance of being cooperative and uncooperative, assertive and unassertive. As you look more closely at the different styles and read the following descriptions, you'll recognize one or another that is the normal or usual way in which you deal with conflict.

Think about individuals you work with. You should be able to identify their more dominant style by asking yourself, "Is she cooperative or uncooperative, assertive or unassertive"? Each of the five styles has unique characteristics.

MEET THE STYLE OF YOUR WORKPLACE

This section looks at each of the following styles more closely: the competitive style, the collaborative style, the accommodating style, the avoiding style, and the compromising style.

THE COMPETITIVE STYLE

Competitive women are very assertive. Getting their way is often at the top of their list and cooperating with others secondary. They approach any conflict in a direct and forceful way. A competitive woman's attitude could be "I don't care what other people think; it's my way or none." Women whose dominant style is competitive are more interested in satisfying their own concerns, often at the expense of others, and they will do it by pulling rank, being forceful, and arguing.

The competitive style is a good one to have in your corner when you are in a position of power. It can, though, alienate people. If you are someone of little power (or you are wrong or you have no support) in a disagreement with a coworker, manager, or supervisor and you use a competitive style, you may find yourself without a job. A competitive style doesn't work without power contracts and/or support behind you. Competitive styles work when you:

- Create win-lose situations
- Use rivalry
- Use power plays to get what you want
- Force submission
- Feel the issue is very important and you have a big stake in getting your way
- Have the power to make the decision, and it appears that is the best way to act
- Must make a decision quickly, and you have the power to make it
- Feel you have no other options
- Feel you have nothing to lose
- Are in an emergency situation where immediate, decisive action is necessary
- Can't get a group to agree or feel you are at an impasse, and someone must make the group move ahead
- Have to make an unpopular decision, but action is required now, and you have the power to make that choice

Your primary objective when you enforce a competitive style is not popularity. You may pick up supporters and admirers along the way if your solutions work. A competitive style is used to get your way for something that is important to you. When you feel that you have to move quickly or act immediately, and you are confident that you will succeed, using a competitive style does not necessarily mean that you are a bully or pushy.

THE COLLABORATIVE STYLE

People who are collaborators are actively involved in working out any conflict. If your style is one of collaboration, you vocally assert what you want. At the same time, you also cooperate with others.

Being collaborative takes time. It is not an instant "my way," as someone with a competitive style would demonstrate. Collaboration takes longer because you have to first identify the issues and concerns. Then, each party must be willing to listen to the other's needs and concerns as well as other issues. If you have the time to process within the collaborative style, it's more probable that a win-win scenario will evolve.

A collaborative style may initially surface when parties say that their goals are the same. As the surface is probed, other issues emerge which can lead to confusion about the overall goal. The collaborative style works very well when the parties involved have different underlying needs.

When a collaborative approach is used, it often encourages each person coming to the table to identify her needs and wants. A key factor to a successful collaboration involves taking the necessary time to identify needs and interests of the parties involved. The issues are understood, and it is far easier to seek alternatives and compromises that will work for all.

The collaborative approach works when you:

- Are in a problem-solving position
- Confront differences in sharing ideas and information
- Search for integrated solutions
- Find situations where all can win
- See problems and conflicts as challenges
- Know that the issues are very important to both or all parties involved
- Have a close, continuing, or interdependent relationship with the other party
- Have time to deal with the problem
- Know that you and the other person are aware of the problem and are clear about what you want
- Are confident that the other party is willing to put some thought and work into finding a solution with you
- And the other party have the skills to articulate your concerns and listen to what others have to say
- And the other party have a similar amount of power in a conflict, or are willing to put aside any power differences in order to work together as equals in arriving at a solution

If the people involved in a conflict will not agree to any of these elements, a collaborative style won't work. Because collaboration involves more time and commitment, it's more complicated. Used successfully, it can be the most satisfying resolution for everyone involved, especially if there is a serious conflict.

THE ACCOMMODATING STYLE

The person who uses the accommodating style is one who likes to help or lend a hand, and often is someone who easily conforms. It's a style that works on a cooperative basis with another without asserting one's own claim for power. The accommodating style works well when the end result is not a key factor or concern for you. When you have assessed a situation and decide that it's a no-win for you, it makes sense to be accommodating. You might as well go along with whatever the other person wants. As an accommodator, you cede your own concern in order to satisfy another's, by sympathizing with another or otherwise giving in.

When you invoke an accommodating style, it means that you are willing to set aside your own concern; you feel that you do not have a lot invested in the situation or the outcome. But if you feel that in the end, you would be giving up something that is vital or key to you, or would not feel good about giving it up, then the accommodating style is not going to be an appropriate fit. It is a perfect style to use when you feel that you are not losing too much by your giving up or backing off. The accommodating style is also effective when your immediate strategy is to smooth things over and then bring the issue or subject up at a later time. This is viewed as a deferral, not an avoidance technique.

The accommodating style has some similarities to another style—avoidance. It may be used to delay a final resolution to a particular issue or problem. There is a difference. In avoidance, you back out or away from something; in accommodating, you are cooperative. You are willing to acknowledge the situation and agree to do whatever the other person wants to do. When avoidance is enforced, your position is that you do not do anything that will enhance the other's desires, and a decision is arrived at more or less by default.

Situations in which the accommodating style seems most appropriate include:

- Giving way
- Being submissive and compliant

- When you don't really care what happens in the end
- When you want to keep peace and maintain harmony
- When you feel like maintaining the relationship and don't want to get the other person angry
- When you recognize that the outcome is more important to the other person than it is to you
- When you recognize that you are wrong
- When you have minimal or no power
- When you have no chance of winning
- When you think the other person might learn from the situation if you go along with her, even though you do not agree or think she is making a mistake
- When you know you are wrong
- When you want a better position to be heard
- When you want to learn more
- When you want to show that you are a team player
- When you want to collect "chits" for later issues
- Minimizing a loss when you are outmatched and know that you are losing
- When issues are not as important to you as to others

When an environment is negative or hostile, harmony can often be restored by initiating an accommodating style in dealing with a conflict. By giving in, agreeing, or sacrificing your concerns and yielding to what the other person wants, you may be able to smooth over a bad situation. The resulting period of calm allows you to gain time. In the end, it enables you to work out a resolution that you would prefer.

THE AVOIDING STYLE

The fourth major style is avoidance. It occurs when you don't assert yourself, you don't cooperate, or you avoid the conflict entirely. The avoiding style is initiated when you feel that you are in a no-win situation, that you don't want to be a bother, or that the whole problem or issue is irrelevant. It is also used when you feel the other person has more power or is right or when, for whatever reason, you don't want to stick your neck out and take a position.

Your posture is more of sidestepping and ignoring the issue, delaying any input or decisions. It may also be that you don't have the time or choose not to deal with the issue now. Avoidance can work temporarily when you are dealing with someone who is difficult and you are not required to work together.

When you don't have to make a decision immediately or are unsure about what to do, the avoiding style may do the trick. Instead of getting stressed out trying to push for a resolution, you have extra time. In reality, you have made a choice *not* to make a decision. The Catch 22 is that if you don't come back at a later date to deal with the issue, others may view you as irresponsible or a procrastinator.

Avoidance also works when you have not been able to gather enough information to allow yourself to make a decision or recommendation. It gives you the ability to be late with your input. If deferral is your objective, be aware that eventually you may have to come back and deal with the issue. The avoiding style works well when:

- You want to ignore a conflict or hope it will go away
- You prefer to put the problems under consideration on hold
- Slow procedures can help stifle a conflict
- Secrecy is desired to avoid confrontation
- You feel an appeal to bureaucratic rules can aid in conflict resolution
- Tensions are too high and you feel the need to cool down or back off
- The issue is not very important or is trivial to you
- You are having a bad day and there is a high probability that you will get upset and not deal logically or rationally with the situation
- It's improbable that you will win, or you know that you can't
- You want or need more time, either to gather information or to get help
- The situation is complex and difficult to change
- You feel any time spent on the issue will be wasted
- You have little power to resolve the situation or get a resolution that is beneficial
- You feel that you aren't qualified to resolve the situation and others can do better

- The timing is bad; bringing the conflict out into the open might make it worse
- You want to let people cool down

Many think that when people use avoidance to deal with conflict, they are being evasive or running away from the issue. There are times when an evasive or delaying tactic is appropriate and can be constructive. And some conflicts do resolve themselves when given breathing room.

THE COMPROMISING STYLE

In the center of the conflict management matrix is the compromising or sharing approach. In other words, you end up giving up a little bit of what you want to get the rest of what you want. The other parties involved in the conflict do the same. A compromising solution is reached when exchanges, concessions, and bargaining are used to reach a conclusion that rarely satisfies everyone's concerns or objectives 100 percent. The solution will, though, meet the majority of each party's concerns and objectives.

One of the differences between collaboration and compromise is that in collaboration you search for underlying needs and interests. In compromise, both sides end up giving up part of their needs and/or interests before a resolution is reached.

A compromise approach is often used when each party wants the same thing but is not willing to give up certain things to get it. Let's say two of you have families and you both want to take the first two weeks of July off. You each have the same objective, yet only one can have vacation during that period. It's clear that one of you is going to have to work unless the company decides to close its doors for a very long Independence Day recognition.

The compromise will more likely be that one will take the long vacation this year and the other will take it next year. Who gets it first could be determined by the flip of a coin, seniority, work output, and so on. Whatever the solution, no one is going to be 100 percent satisfied, because neither of you got what you totally wanted.

In collaborating, you focus on resolving various issues and needs. In a compromise, the conflict situation is a given. What you are dealing with is a way to influence or alter the conflict to a give-and-take exchange. Often the goal in collaboration is a long-term win-win solution. In a compromise, the outcome may more likely be short-term and expedient.

At the end of a compromise, the normal response from the parties involved is, "I'm OK; I can live with the results." The emphasis is not on winning but on "We both can't get what we want, so let's see what we can work out to satisfy our most important needs." Ways in which a compromising style works best are:

- Negotiation
- Looking for deals and trade-offs
- Finding satisfactory or acceptable solutions
- When you have power equal to that of your opponent, and you are committed to mutually exclusive goals
- When you want to achieve a resolution quickly
- Saving money
- When you are willing to settle for a temporary resolution to a complex issue
- When you will benefit from a short-term gain
- As a backup when collaboration or competition is unsuccessful
- When the goals are not important to you and you are willing to modify your own
- When it makes the relationship or agreement work, and it's better than nothing

The compromising style can be valuable at the beginning, when you know you don't have the power to get what you want. This way, you get part of what you want, and the other party gets part of what she wants. You may come back to the table at a later date if the issue resurfaces.

In order to be successful in compromising, you need to clarify your needs and wants, as well as those of the other parties involved. Then, determine what areas you agree on. Once there is some agreement, a compromise settlement can be worked out. Listening is a critical part of the art of compromise.

Be willing to make suggestions and listen to what the other party says; she in turn should be willing to do the same. Be prepared to give some things up—make offers and exchanges. It is imperative that you identify areas that are uncompromisable—those that you are not willing to budge on. The end result is that both of you should have some satisfaction with the outcome.

WHICH STYLE IS YOU?

Remember, no one style works best in every situation. You need to be able to recognize what styles are surfacing when you are dealing with another party, as well as the styles with which you are responding. As you become more skilled in dealing with conflicts, you will be able to consciously choose the most appropriate style to use at a given time.

Look at the extremes. If you prefer working only within the competitive or avoiding style, you place yourself in a win-lose or lose-lose situation. Strict style preferences limit you. It's natural to prefer certain styles over others. One of the first steps is to assess your dominant style preference in approaching conflict (by completing the Managing Conflict Styles Questionnaire in Fig. 9-1). Usually, you have a dominant style followed by a secondary or backup style. It's also possible that you have two equally characteristic styles, such as avoidance and accommodation. A combination of these types indicates that your preference is to prevent any type of conflict. When you have two equally characteristic styles, you are *bimodal*. If you have three, you're *trimodal*. In most conflicts, it is normal to use your backup style first. If that doesn't work, then call up all your power or strength—and transition to your dominant style.

Stop now and think for a moment. Which of the five best describes you? Does one stand out, or do you feel that you are equally spread in your conflict styles? When you tallied your responses to Fig. 9-1 and identified whether you were competitive, collaborative, compromising, avoiding, or accommodating, did the conflict style identified match the way you perceived yourself?

When you have completed the *Questionnaire* and look at your results, your "hunch" about your style will probably be on target.

TURN THE TABLES

Now, switch. You need to confront someone. You have already identified what you believe the problem to be. The next step is to identify the dominant and backup conflict styles of the person you are confronting (again, by completing the questionnaire in Fig. 9-1). You now know how you and the other party normally operate in a conflict. There are times where it may make sense to use one style over another. Table 9-1 represents sample scenarios that work and don't work with each style.

TABLE 9-1   Sample Scenarios of Conflict Management Styles

STYLE	WHEN IT WORKS	WHEN IT DOESN'T WORK
Competitive	When you have the power	When others don't respect your abilities or power
Collaborative	When you have time; when you have a good relationship	When there is a lack of trust; when time is short
Accommodating	When the other person needs status	When you need a real solution
Avoiding	When you must have the other person's participation	When you have a lot to lose; when the other person is right
Compromising	When both parties are right; when you want to keep the relationship going	When only one party is right; when you have little to give

From Briles, Judith, *"The Briles Report on Women in Healthcare,"* *Healthcare*, San Francisco, CA: Jossey Bass, 1994.

The bottom line is that most conflicts need to be confronted for a resolution. Very few resolve themselves or go away with no action. Conflicts are similar to aging. Both are inescapable.

THE FACE-OFF

In addition to determining your conflict management style and that of the person you will confront, there are a few other techniques to use. The first is to identify a neutral area in which you can talk. Your office or "her" office is the wrong turf; neither can be considered neutral. So are any public areas in which anyone can watch and listen. Get a cup of coffee or tea and take a walk or find a quiet, isolated place where you can sit down one on one.

Before any confrontation, you need to set some rules for yourself—for your own behavior. First, calm down. If you don't step back and take a moment to compose yourself, you'll make the best speech you will ever regret. Second, take the time to assess what's happened. View it from two sides: your perspective—what the impact has been on you and possibly on others—and hers—what do you think her perspective is? Last, take a deep breath. You need fresh oxygen in your system.

A key skill is your ability to listen. Too many times, the mouth is put in gear before the brain has a chance to warm up. She who listens usually ends up in control. And don't wait for the other person to come to you. Ideally, you initiate the confrontation. As you listen, you will need to formulate the feedback you will give. Be willing to acknowledge that a behavior or action of yours may have been a factor in whatever the problem is.

> *Changes rarely happen overnight. It will probably take a few confrontations for an individual to stop doing whatever she is doing to you or to others. Confronting is not easy—it is painful and very uncomfortable. But each time you do it, it becomes less stressful.*

Many times, people hold back waiting for someone else to deal with the problem; they wait for someone who finally has the courage to speak up and say something. Talking with another person face to face is usually the best way to confront a problem. That way, she can see your body language and you can see hers. You can observe whether she is listening. Some face-to-face confrontations require nerves of steel. You must be composed and have your facts together. Otherwise, emotions can erupt, and you end up either attacking or retreating. At this point, the conflict only grows.

If meeting face to face is impossible, writing becomes your second-best choice. But it has drawbacks. You can't be sure that she will read your letter. Writing does, though, give you the opportunity to set out the facts as you understand them and to let the other party know how they have affected you.

Before you send any letters, have a confidante read over your words to eliminate undue sharpness or overemotional responses. This is a time to explain, rationally, how you perceive the facts. If you wait too long to confront, it also can be a disadvantage. The other party may be clueless as to what she did, or why you are upset about it.

A less preferred way to confront is over the phone. This has several disadvantages. First of all, less than 10 percent of communication comes through words that are spoken. The majority comes through seeing, feeling, and interpreting—through gestures, body language, and voice tone. Most is unspoken. You visually see and react to what the other person is saying. Phone calls eliminate this aspect of communication.

Second, if you attempt to confront the other party on the phone, you can't be sure that she is listening to what you say. In fact, she can put you on hold, walk away, or even hang up before you are aware the line has been disconnected. Even if you both remain on the line, you are unable to see her face, her eyes, and her body expressions. Nor can she see yours. She is unable to visibly see your anger or your hurt. She may hear it through your tone. By seeing you, she is able to visibly confirm it.

In summing up, the conflict management styles can be identified as competitive when you seek to get your own way; collaborative when you seek to work out a mutually satisfying solution; accommodating when you seek to work out an agreeable and satisfying solution with others; avoiding when you seek to avoid the conflict situation; and compromising when you seek to work out a solution in which each party gives up a little in order to get something in return.

When you anticipate a confrontation coming and you step back to look at what you perceive are the dominant and backup styles of the opposing party, your effectiveness in negotiating a successful resolution is substantially enhanced.

THE BOSS TAKES YOUR CREDIT

Many women do actively confront other women when they find themselves in a situation that is not acceptable. Unfortunately, the confrontation is never vocalized. It's a fabulous dialogue that goes on internally. I suspect that some great screenplays could evolve from the confrontations we create in our minds.

Sabotage is quite common when someone, especially a supervisor, is threatened by an employee. Because the employee is in the subordinate relationship, she feels helpless or severely constrained in confronting the supervisor. After all, the supervisor is the boss, and the link to the paycheck.

When Barbara first joined a publishing house, she worked as an editorial assistant. She soon learned that her supervisor did not have the educational background that she had. Over time, her supervisor would routinely take credit for the work that Barbara had produced.

> My supervisor was extremely threatened when I got there. My credentials were greater than hers. In the end, a lot of the procedures that I had created for processing and reworking manuscripts as well as for working with our authors were written up. Most turned up with her name on them, not mine. I didn't feel it was worth confronting her on the issue; you have to pick your battles to take on. I knew who wrote them and so did everyone else in editorial.

By not doing anything, Barbara gave her boss permission to continue to take credit for the work that she created as well as for the work that other members of the staff prepared. Until someone finally says, "Enough is enough," the plagiarizer is given permission to continue her act. Barbara viewed her time with the publishing house as "short-term"—she left a year later. Today, after several years, she is settled in as senior editor with another house. She is not the toxic boss to her assistants that her supervisor was.

WITHOUT CONFRONTATION, GENDERTRAPS FLOURISH

Most of the women interviewed for the GenderTraps survey felt strongly that dealing with conflict and confrontation is the key to solving several of the traps.

There are a number of myths about anger and conflict: that the development of conflict is the sign of a poor manager; that a conflict situation signals lower concern or support for management; that anger is destructive; that if you leave a conflict situation alone (avoidance technique!), it will go away; and, finally, that all conflicts must be resolved, no matter what—as in smile, shake hands, and let bygones be bygones!

All of the above are untrue. Conflict will arise in the workplace because people have different goals and objectives. People's perceptions vary; they hear differently; culture, race, and gender play a part. Also, general "noise"—news, events, happenings, fear, and concern—creates conflict. Most call it life.

There are several predictable factors that will move in and escalate the tension surrounding conflict and confrontation. Normally, the people involved in a conflict believe that they know the cause. But their analysis of the situation is usually in error. Most conflicts are thought to be rooted in some type of action and content.

The belief is that a deliberate action—whether it is negativism, a derogatory remark, or undermining behavior—was meant to be purposely harmful, to destroy another's career or position. In actuality, that is rarely the case. Conflicts are usually caused by a communications failure or breakdown, specifically in the listening area.

When you can identify a situation in which you strongly believe that another person is purposely trying to harm you physically, psychologically, or professionally, my advice is to get out. If you want to practice confronting, go ahead. It is improbable that you will have the time to go through a series of processes that might enlighten the other party. You are better off gathering up your marbles and finding another field to play in. Don't expect to change her—or her ways.

Most human beings have a strong need to be liked. This drive turns out to be a primary contributor to any type of conflict. After all, most of us think that if we don't win a situation, a point, or a cause, we lose. Who says? There are many people who are perceived as winners. When the cards are finally laid out, they don't have a winning hand; it's full of jokers.

Because women are more inclined toward confrontophobia than men, and because they will do just about anything to avoid a final confrontation, time can elapse. When time escapes, and a situation finally comes to a head, either by choice or because of another situation, the original conflict may actually be an accumulation of half-remembered and minor items. With the passage of time, nonresolution of a conflict is internalized. Women are more inclined to say to themselves, "What if I had done this?" Or "What if I did that?" Or "If only I hadn't let her get away with it." Instead of a problem of gnat size, they are now dealing with a gigantic one.

The best way to create a pleasurable work environment, for yourself as well as your colleagues, is to learn how to handle conflict in a reasonable and timely manner. When you know yourself, understand your conflict management styles, are willing to take responsibility for your actions, and can identify the style of the person you need to confront, everyone wins.

Bear in mind that almost all conflicts and confrontations involve a tap dance—a series of moves and countermoves by each person. Some dances end shortly, while others add new movements. As you learn more about the people you work with, and yourself, you will be able to move into a more powerful and confident style. Conquering confrontophobia will enable you to deal with conflict, miscommunication, power plays, sabotage, and discrimination.

With the subsiding and elimination of confrontophobia, you will add a powerful skill to your tool kit for the workplace. Confronting someone takes responsibility. It also holds the other person accountable for whatever her actions are. If you do not confront someone, your silence condones the offending behavior. It says that it is OK to continue to do whatever that person has done—not only to you, but to others.

Apathy: A numbing, disinterested attitude toward a job that guarantees your extinction in the workplace.

Complacency: A belief that all is well and that you are immune to any type of upheaval in your personal and professional life.

Changeophobia: The fear of pursuing personal or professional opportunity that can come from upheaval, flip-flops and workplace shifts.

TRAP 8: APATHY, COMPLACENCY, AND CHANGEOPHOBIA
Land Mines to Oblivion

- When you hear about business closings or downsizings, do you feel you are isolated and protected?
- Have you ever felt it's too late to change jobs or careers?
- Have you ever felt you don't have the skills or education to obtain a new job or a promotion?
- Has fear or uncertainty ever held you back from applying for a new position?
- Are you willing to "rock the boat," or do you want things to remain as they are?

Andrea's story is about a split personality. It belongs in the discussion of management chaos in Chap. 6; it also belongs here. Andrea has worked hard as a regional manager for a pharmaceuticals company—one of the Fortune 100. Over the last 8 years, she has exceeded every goal set and been one of the national stars. Nationally, there are 20 managers with 200 sales representatives reporting to them.

Her company's objective was to reduce expenses by $30 million over the next year. Its purge started with the sales force. On a Friday all managers were informed, via voice mail, that their positions had been eliminated. They were told to stay by their phones on Monday and a company representative would call and offer them another position.

Andrea's call came late Monday afternoon. She reports:

> All of us managers were told that we were eliminated. As the topper, each of us was offered a "new" position—as a sales rep, replacing one in our present region. *All* 200 sales reps would be terminated. We were told that our base salary would remain the same for a year and then at that time, if we were still wanted, it would be cut in half.
>
> I was furious. I had been with the company for 8 years. To be told by message, not even by a live phone call, that my job was gone and then to dangle over the weekend about my fate was cruel.

The company gave her 72 hours to decide if she was staying or leaving. So much for 8 years of excellent results and loyalty.

Were there signs of trouble? Absolutely. But Andrea felt protected, as so many managers do. After all, under her direction her group had performed beyond any corporate-directed expectations. So what happened? Simple. Change. New European shareholders, sales light in some areas, and reorganization. Downsizing. Rightsizing. The 1990s. Andrea and the entire sales division were invaded by change and caught off guard by their complacent "I'm OK" attitude.

FROM NONBELIEVER TO BELIEVER

In 1981 I published my first book, *The Woman's Guide to Financial Savvy.* At that time, I thought it would be the only book that I would ever produce and really didn't pay much attention to the process. After all, why bother when it's a one-time shot? Well, the one-time shot turned into many books with no end in sight. *GenderTraps* is number 13. Much has changed. What was normal to publishing in 1981 is dinosaurish in the 1990s.

I did not really tune into the changes that were going on in the book business until I began work on my second book, *Money Phases,* in 1983. New technology was rapidly coming on the scene. I was aware that there were some new gimmicks and gadgets out there. But I resisted jumping in and trying those new gadgets—computers. They weren't cheap either. Contrary to popular belief, most authors don't make a lot of money—the average income from their work is less than $10,000 a year.

My typewriter was good enough. And mine was impressive for its time. It had the capability of remembering 50 pages of material. In the early 1980s, it was IBM's state of the art for small businesses. Granted, I didn't use the machine for writing books at that time. I used it primarily for storing letters that would be sent to my clients, reused or slightly modified. In the old days—from 1979 to 1986—I wrote my articles and books on a typewriter, with each page retyped as changes were made. As I look back, I was in the Stone Age.

When people fear change, there are usually five stages; *resistance, skepticism, adaptation, shifting,* and *cohesiveness.* With my second book, I experienced both resistance and great skepticism. I knew there was another way to do it, but the old way—the typewriter—was good enough. And I wasn't convinced of the validity of the new equipment available that would supposedly speed up a writer's work.

It takes an author only a couple of retypes to realize there has got to be a better way—something better than rewriting an entire manuscript every time a paragraph moves or a few more typos are uncovered. In fact, back in the Stone Age of the 1980s, it was quite common to turn in manuscripts with typos and crossed-out sentences and paragraphs. We authors knew that the publisher's typesetter would "clean it up." Today, clean manuscripts from authors to publishers are the rule!

Within a year, I rented a computer for a month, just to give it a trial run. As Louie, my secretary, embraced the genius of it, I still *resisted.* I was *skeptical,* viewing the computer as a newfangled device. Since Louie was obviously taking my dictation, the vocal word, and transferring it to paper, I let her have her way. It soon became obvious to me that her speed and efficiency levels were enhanced.

I then moved into the third stage of change—*adaptation.* My attitude became, "Well, we'll keep it, but we won't get rid of the typewriters"—we had three. After all, we would always need a typewriter if we wanted to do something in a hurry. Personally, I had resisted diving into learning even to turn on the computer, much less how to operate it. To me, booting up was what a woman did with her fall or winter footwear. I didn't have a clue that it meant turning on the computer and opening a file.

In 1986, Louie went on a well-earned holiday, leaving me with written and detailed instructions on how to turn on the computer and access certain files that I might need during her absence. At that time, I had begun my research for the book that was published the following year, *Woman to Woman,* and was working on my doctorate.

My agent had asked me to make a few changes in the book proposal and return a clean copy to him in New York. The changes seemed simple: converting some single-spaced items to double spacing. With the magic of technology, I booted up the computer, opened the appropriate file, and proceeded to give it the commands to change from single to double spacing, as Louie had left instructions on how to do. In the process, I deleted 51 pages of manuscript!

Over the next 3 days, I brought in experts to help retrieve the lost material. To no avail. We were unsuccessful. My emotions ran the gamut—from disbelief, to denial, to anger and, finally, to let's get going. Because of Louie's absence, I would have to do it over. I was propelled to sit down and re-create what had been lost. Only then did I truly begin to marvel at the new gadget—the computer's ability to erase, delete, and edit, to move phrases, sentences, and paragraphs around with the tap of a finger. This computer was unbelievable to me. My "gadget" was a writer's dream.

By the end of the day, I went from *adaptation* to the fourth stage—*shifting*. I began to wonder what else could I do with the computer and the word processing programs. What kinds of overheads for workshops could be produced? What about cartoons to be used within lectures? How about pasting graphs into articles? I was sold. In a nanosecond, I moved to the fifth stage—*cohesiveness*. Within the year, three Apple Macintoshes found new homes in my office.

Today, I would openly and loudly say that I can't *imagine* not having a computer. There is no way that I could produce what I do without having computers as an integral part of my office team. Those original three have been replaced, upgraded, and added to. From one typewriter to five computers. What happened to our state-of-the-art, $3500 IBM memory typewriter? I gave it away!

THE VCR APPROACH

Everywhere you turn, there are tremendous changes. Usually, there are three reactions to it: *reactive, nonactive,* and *proactive.* People who are *reactive* jump out of the way. They'd rather not get involved. If they were a VCR, they would push the "pause" button. Human uncertainty and lack of confidence tell you to step aside and see what evolves. Unfortunately, what evolves may be exactly what you wanted and you are too late to get on the bandwagon. You pause too long.

Those who are *nonactive* stand still. They are paralyzed. Their VCR is set, not at pause, but at "stop," and in some cases at "rewind." Nonactive posturing means you are stuck. It is easy to end up being run over, ignored, or viewed as invisible.

If you take a *proactive* position, the odds are that you will win the race. Your inclination is not to get out of the way or stand still. Your

VCR is set at "play." You get involved, ask questions, and create your own future rather than have someone else make it happen for you.

THE WORKPLACE IS LIKE WALKING ON EGGSHELLS

Women interviewed for this book said that change was everywhere. Change, coupled with fear. Those who were apathetic felt they were surrounded by doomsday, that they had no choice and were unable to determine or make any change to ensure their continuing employment. Those who were complacent became fearful when downsizing got too close to them or they saw friends become unemployed overnight.

Dawn feels that, in some ways, big corporations seduce their employees and enhance the atmosphere of complacency. When salaries were reduced or positions were eliminated, the survivors in Dawn's workplace did nothing. She thought her coworkers were in suspended animation. Instead of grouping together and supporting a "maintenance level" of income when there were cutbacks, they withdrew. Many rationalized that part of their pay was the attractive, multimillion-dollar facilities that they enjoyed.

> Many of us have been humbled over the past year. We thought that we were lucky to have jobs and that there were worse ones. Some felt that the state-of-the-art facilities that we have were a benefit.

As a program manager, Jane finds that it's not uncommon for employees to dig in their heels in the belief that, because they have been with their company for a long time, it will take care of them. That belief is a myth. Today is not like the old days, when you went to work and basically stayed there until you retired. Jane has found that the West is far more progressive in accepting the wake-up call than are the South and the Northeast, where the corporate headquarters of her employer is located.

> The people in the West are more accepting of change. I don't know if that is due to the environment out here in California, where a lot of companies have laid off so many people that they are used to it.

> One of the problems that I have found is that when change is not acknowledged or accepted, too many become complacent. The belief is, "Nothing will happen to me and I will be taken care of." The true belief should be, "I'm here; what can I do to make a difference?" The normal response for most employees is to wait and hear what's going to happen versus being part of making it happen.

My company has routinely offered training allowances for every employee. Financially, it adds to approximately $2000 at the lowest level per year up into many thousands of dollars for those in management. If you wanted to go back to school, the company would reimburse tuition if your grades were at a B level or above. You had a blank check to use your training allocation for just about anything that you felt would make you better at your job. Some took advantage of it. A great majority did not. Those are the ones who have slid along for years. The sad thing is that they still believe that they can continue to be employed and slide—it's not going to happen. Many of our employees will be losing their jobs with their heads still in the sand.

THE BATTERED EMPLOYEE

Some of the women interviewed for *GenderTraps* talked about their inability to move on. The fear factor surfaced. As I listened to them, the comments they shared sounded too familiar. They felt they did not have choices; whatever they got was better than nothing. Some said that their employers took away little bits here and there until most of their benefits package has disappeared. One woman said her group should have gotten the clue when management removed the coffee service and installed a coin-operated coffee machine.

I would routinely ask women why they hadn't looked or didn't look for another job if their workplace environment or management was deteriorating or just plain rotten. The common response would be, "Where am I going to make the money I make?" That kind of attitude—"Where would I go?" or "How could I make what I do here?"—is comparable in many ways to behavior attributed to battered women.

In 1979 Lenore Walker published her ground-breaking book, *The Battered Woman*. In it she said the typical battered woman gains a sense of self-worth by being a good wife and homemaker. If she has a successful career outside the home, it is secondary. If you take Walker's description of a battered woman and change just a few words (in *italics* below), it fits the feeling of many women who work in places that they should have left long ago:

The typical *oppressed employee* (battered woman) has a poor self-image and low self-esteem, basing her feeling of self-worth on her perceived capacity to be a *good employee* (wife and homemaker) whether or not she has a *successful career/job* (life) within her *workplace* (home).1

YOU GET WHAT YOU ALWAYS GOT

As a director of customer service at a publishing press, Chris deals with change every day—change within the industry and change within her staff. Her company is privately owned and has plenty of the old systems in place. She routinely has to deal with the complacency of the workplace—"Everything is fine; I do my job therefore I am protected"—"along with the apathy of many who appear disinterested and show up primarily to get a paycheck every week. Since her company has grown in some areas and downsized in others, she's found resistance along the way.

> Over the past year, we've introduced seminars on time management and workplace efficiency. Any type of change that we attempted to introduce was an uphill battle. Some people looked at me as if I was an ogre when I tried to get them to do things a little faster or a little bit more efficiently. The objective, I explained, was to allow us to lower our costs and maintain our jobs.
>
> Every director prior to me was a man. Sometimes I feel that if there was man here telling them what to do, they wouldn't buck the system. I want my people to try things differently. If it doesn't work, or we need to go back to the old way, we will. If it works, it's great; if we need to try a different way, we will.
>
> I believe the resistance factor comes from them—the staff—not being encouraged to think on their own or be creative, or even encouraged to suggest something. Most likely if they suggested anything in the past, they were told no. The whole culture seems to be, "Well, we do it this way, because that's the way we've always done it."

What happens when you always do it the way you've done it? The answer is fairly simple. You'll get what you've always got. Today, the roadway of apathy and complacency leads in only two directions: either you get what you always got or one day you go into work and find out that your job is no longer there. Several of the women within this survey stated that they were returning to school to expand and enhance their skills. That's good news.

YOUR TURF OR MINE

As part-time and work-from-home scenarios are created and supported, management will most likely have to develop a system in which work is viewed as a project—piecemeal. An employee, independent contractor, consultant, and so on would be paid for the product delivered. As long as it was delivered in a specified time frame, management shouldn't care about the methodology.

For many companies, the piecemeal approach will be difficult, if not impossible. Management and employees have set up their respective turfdoms, and it is extraordinarily difficult to see beyond them. The area and the perimeter are inspected and protected, just as a dog goes about marking its spots each time it lifts its leg. The workers' position is not to integrate for the benefit of the whole, but to isolate and sometimes separate themselves.

Lynn is a vice president at a New England university. She sees turfdom actively engaged on her campus.

> People become so involved in their own turf. It's like a piece of pie: "It's my piece of pie, and don't touch it." If they thought of the whole pie, everyone would benefit. It becomes, "Don't cross over into my territory; it's mine and mine alone." The reality is that if there were crossovers, everyone would benefit, because the whole is only as good as its various parts.
>
> Turfdom is a major problem, both in the profit and the nonprofit world. You see it all the time in academia, where the faculty doesn't want to cooperate with the administration. My experience is that the faculty, more than the administration, resists any kind of change.
>
> In the past, it was actually healthy when we had turnover among faculty members, because new people with new ideas were brought in. Now, we've noticed that the faculty becomes cemented, viewing that this job is the first and the last stop. We now have a lot of older professors and teachers who are still teaching the same way they did 20 and in some cases 30 years ago.
>
> Their styles and attitudes are a relic from the past, but they are afraid. When people are afraid, they fear everything. The fear of change, of the unknown, is one of the biggest traps that people face today. It is the fear of something new, the fear of getting out of something you hate, because maybe you won't make it in the area where you'd be happier.
>
> So you stay put. All of a sudden, you wake up one day and you are 50 years old and you are miserable.

PASS THE SCALPEL

Tamar was one of those who did not want to stay put. Originally trained as a general surgeon, today she is a vascular surgeon and does a great deal of her work in the form of emergency care. She feels fortunate that, as a physician, she is forced and willing to make changes. It is part of her training. When doctors begin their medical training, they know from the outset that change will be an ongoing part of their professional lives. Tamar was told in medical school that the information she was learning would be outdated in 10 years, if it lasted that long.

In the health-care field, she sees three groups of people with differing responses to change.

> The first group is made up of people who are totally panicked. They don't know what to think, and they run around like chickens with their heads cut off. They're very nervous. The second group is composed of those who are trying to stay one jump ahead of whatever is coming down the pike, trying to outguess the future, and trying to create it. The third group is saying, "Hold on, some changes are needed. This is an opportunity to get more efficient, to look at what we are doing and see how we can improve it to become the very best we know how."

> Unfortunately, for the most part, I'm seeing people with their heads in the sand, just going along and doing their own thing.

Tamar pursued her specialty, vascular surgery, in response to change. It was generated from a challenge by a new surgeon in her community who wanted to raise the level of vascular procedures. Prior to his arrival, her hospital had granted her privileges to do vascular surgery on the basis of what she had done in her general surgery training. When the new surgeon arrived, he let her know that he was not happy about any privileges being granted. He wanted doctors who were fully trained and not just "occasional."

> He assumed that I wasn't the real thing. I'd already done some very good cases, and was furious at his response. When I stopped being furious along with crying, kicking, and chewing on my pillow, I realized he was talking about the kind of vascular surgery I wanted to do. He'd given me a challenge.

> So I took the challenge and I went and obtained a vascular fellowship. The moment I told him, he stood up to his full 6'4" height and said, "I'm absolutely delighted that you are going, and if there is anything I can do to help you at any time, please let me know." And he was as good as his word.

> If I needed a wise person in the middle of the night, if I had a difficult case, he was willing to be called. I knew I had made it when he asked me to cover for his office—it was the ultimate trust.

THE ENTITLEMENT TRAP

How do you evolve from "Woe is me, I have no control over anything that is happening" to the attitude of "I want it, and I'll go for
it" that Tamar displayed? How do you get past the sense of apathy
when you are numb and disinterested and have a distant and
unemotional attitude toward your work? Or how is a wake-up call
created for those who are complacent and feel they are protected
and will not be impacted by any changes within their workplace?

Judith Bardwick, Ph.D. is the author of *The Plateauing Trap*
and *Danger in the Comfort Zone.* She believes complacency comes
from a sense of *entitlement,* which she describes as an attitude and
a way of looking at life. People with the *entitlement* attitude believe
they don't have to earn what they get. Whatever they have, they
feel that they are owed it—entitled. When it comes to getting what
they want, they get it because of who they are, not because of what
they do.   •

> Entitlement is what I have been seeing in American corporations:
> people not really contributing, but still expecting to get their regu-
> lar raise, their scheduled promotion. When this rich nation
> stopped requiring performance as a condition for keeping a job or
> getting a raise, it created a widespread attitude of Entitlement.
> Entitlement destroys motivation, it lowers productivity, [and] in
> the long run, it crushes self-esteem. In spite of the layoffs of
> recent years, it is epidemic in this country. It's our legacy of the
> boom times that followed World War II.[2]

APATHY AND COMPLACENCY BREED MEDIOCRITY

Unfortunately, what Bardwick is referring to in today's workplace is
too commonplace. People are too complacent. They continue to get
raises, bonuses, and benefits as if they are on a regularly scheduled
calendar. "Every March 1, we deliver a bonus, and every September
2, we give a raise." It doesn't matter how hard any one person works,
because benefits are believed to be a *right* of the workplace. The
result is that there is no incentive to work hard, and people get lazy.

Many of the stories throughout this book have one common
theme, and the theme is fear. When it comes to traps, and

GenderTraps in particular, you can become unfocused, scattered, and paralyzed in the process. Because of the downsizing, rightsizing, outsizing—the layoffs of business—employees focus their energies on protecting their jobs. Whether they actually do the work is not the primary issue.

Hence, because of fear, *changeophobia* is seeded. Most people will do almost anything to avoid that step into the unknown. The journey in a personal and professional life is created because of the upheavals—the flip-flops and the shifts that are usually not a matter of choice.

Apathy is bred from unresponsiveness. When a business—your workplace—does not require high-quality work, outstanding performers are rarely if ever rewarded for their accomplishments and achievements. And when those who coattail and underperform are not punished, the attitude becomes, "Why bother?" When workers are rewarded as much for showing up or walking through the door as they are for bringing in a project ahead of time and under budget, a company's best and brightest people say, "Screw it." The motivation to excel is diminished and mediocrity, at best, becomes the common denominator. Bardwick adds:

> Historically, rich organizations in a rich nation were willing to be "nice" and carry even those who didn't add value. In large bureaucracies, it was also easy to hide, which made it even more likely that people would not be held accountable for real work. Over time, everyone who is not held accountable has all the time in the world.

Bardwick's solution to the entitlements stage is the *earnings* stage. In this stage, people are energized by challenge. They know that their work will be judged and that rewards will be based solely on accomplishment. It's called accountability, and earning your pay the old-fashioned way.

Does it work? Consider the scenario of General Motors just a few years ago. Faced with billions in losses, the company slashed dividends to shareholders, laid off megathousands, and shut down plants. Next to the federal government, General Motors is the world's largest corporate bureaucracy. It began to change its traditional adversarial relations with some of its workers and to emphasize cooperation instead. This is almost unheard of in union-entrenched environments such as the automotive industry.

In General Motors' case, workers once were required to "shut up and follow orders." Now, they were being asked to think. A team of hourly and salaried employees managed to cut the number of parts in the rear doors of Cadillacs and Oldsmobiles from 52 to 30. That reduced the number of stamping dies from 93 to 38 and the number of presses from 93 to 10. From those reductions, the company is saving $52 million a year.[3]

If General Motors had not laid off thousands, slashed dividends, and lost billions, the probability is extremely remote that their employees would have jumped up and said, "Let's reduce the number of procedures so we can save millions of dollars for the betterment of the company." What propelled them? Plain, old-fashioned fear. The 300,000 workers who came up with reductions knew that 40,000 GM workers had been laid off. They could be next.

THE THEORY OF 21

Studies have shown that any new behavior or activity needs to be reinforced approximately 21 times before it is learned. One of my favorite cartoon strips is *Cathy*. In one of them, she has embarked upon a new exercise program. She gleefully proclaims to the reader that it will take only 21 days of repetition to break in the new habit. After 21 days, she will be a changed woman. By the end of the strip, Cathy is asking herself, "What is 21 days?" Her answer becomes, "It is 20 days, 23 hours, and 59 minutes to get uncomfortable with a bad habit."

Few enthusiastically jump in and wallow in change. The norm is to avoid it. At the extreme, people practice the art of changeophobia. Any time business, management, your friends, or your family members make demands that require you to be accountable, it is normal to react with some form or variation of fear. When there is fear, there is usually slippage and regression. Morale can plummet. Common remarks heard among coworkers are "This place isn't the way it used to be" and, in some cases, "Management stinks."

Eliminating changeophobia, and embracing change, requires courage and confidence. Probably the only constant in today's workplace is exponentially increasing change. Will you get the help you need from management to embark on a path of change within your workplace? Most likely not. A good 95 percent of American managers say the right thing and use the right words—from *quality*, to *excellence,* to *empowerment,* to *transformation.* The reality is that only 5 percent actually practice what they preach.

THE NEW AMERICAN HERO

Are you ready for a job change? Any type of career change in the 1990s will be dramatically different from the routine processes used in the 1980s. This is a result not only of economic, technological, and political changes but also of the numbers of men and women looking for positions.

If you are fed up with the workplace as it's been known—primarily working for someone else—and are willing to stick your neck out and encounter risk in your quest for change, consider becoming an entrepreneur. According to *The Wall Street Journal,* more than half of the 3 million businesses formed in the United States in each of the past 5 years have been started by women.

U.S. Department of Labor statistics show that the net new job creation in the United States is primarily from small entrepreneurial companies, not from the Fortune 500. The small entrepreneurial company is usually headed by a woman, who in turn hires a work force that is two-thirds female. It's not difficult to come to the conclusion that women are being recruited by the growth companies more frequently than are men.[4]

In a study completed for *Enterprising Women: Lessons From 100 of the Greatest Women Entrepreneurs of Our Day,* author David Silver found that women were creating employment opportunities by tackling problems that women encounter. The sectors most often cited are health, education, child care, information networks, and beauty.

"What values," Silver asked, "could men possibly add to Jogbra, Inc., a manufacturer of a bra for women runners, or to Pleasant Co., a manufacturer of historical dolls and accompanying books that describe the role of American women in history?" Lucy McKall, founder and CEO of Have a Heart, Inc., a Boston manufacturer of shoelaces and other products adorned with hearts, reports that she does have a few men working at her company, but they are mostly in the mailroom.

Elisabeth Coker is the founder and CEO of Minco Technology Labs, based in Austin, Texas. Annual revenues exceed $15 million.

She believes in family and work. Coker opened a K–6 school at her company when she started it. All employees are encouraged to bring their young children to work, leave them at the school, and share their lunch breaks with them. After school, the children go to the company provided day-care center.

Women tend to create companies in certain types of fields: caring and curing, 36 percent of the time; dressing, beautifying, and feeding people, 32 percent; computers, electronics, and manufacturing, 19 percent; and entertainment and novelties, the balance of 13 percent. Very few female entrepreneurs choose asset-based businesses or capital equipment manufacturing, because these undertakings require a heavy infusion of capital, a feature frequently not available to women starting a new business.

Most women don't have a great deal of money when they start their own companies. The Body Shop, begun in 1976 in England for $7000, was worth approximately $624 million by 1994. Copely Pharmaceuticals, started in 1974 with $500, was valued at $445 million by 1994.[5]

Small businesses employ more individuals than the Fortune 500 companies combined. Female entrepreneurs may well be the heroes of the economic recovery of the early 1990s. Over 100 of the best and most expansive ventures grew from an average initial capital of $38,000 to an average evaluation of $90 million in 15 years. The other good news is the fact that women CEOs are providing training grounds for their employees—mostly women—to leave and launch their own businesses, continuing the cycle. This creates an ever-widening circle of women hiring women to solve the problems that affect women.

The bottom line is that change is everywhere. The only thing that being apathetic, complacent, or changeophobic will do for you is nothing. And that nothing can lead to a loss of job, a loss of self-esteem, and more fear. To overcome these detrimental attitudes, read Chap. 11, on self-sabotage, not once, but twice. Pay particular attention to confidence and failure. Anyone can eliminate changeophobia and find a new world. What you discover within that world will make a difference for others, and yourself.

CONQUERING CHANGEOPHOBIA

To survive and grow through a changing environment—whether it's professional or personal—takes a commitment from you. For most people, the old saying "One for the money, two for the show, three to get ready..." is never completed with the final phase, "...go." Most people get stuck on getting ready; no one gets stuck on going. Change doesn't wait until you are ready to deal with it. It just happens, moving quickly. The sooner you acknowledge it and get on board, the sooner you become a player.

As change evolves, it's important to position yourself. Begin by making a commitment for ongoing improvement. Learn new things. Start a program that either enhances the current skills you have or expands them and lets them take you into another field.

There is no question that positions have been and are being eliminated as you read this. Windows close, but new doors open. Thousands, yes even millions, of new products, jobs, and/or companies are created because of change.

Dramatic shifts in attitudes have emerged in the 1990s. New professions will open, expanding opportunities and creating businesses that are unheard of today. From that mere fact, gadgets and, yes, gimmicks will be produced—items that you can conceive, manufacture, and sell. The workplace must continue to reinvent itself. And so must you.

Embracing change enables you to take advantage of any opportunity that comes your way, including opportunities that you had not envisioned or contemplated. In other words, you won't be left behind.

Years ago, Helen Keller wrote:

> Security is mostly superstition. It does not exist in nature, nor do children of men (and women) as a whole, experience it. Avoiding danger is no safer in the long run than outright exposure. Life is either a daring adventure or nothing.[6]

Change is inevitable. Apathy and complacency are not.

In order to exist and grow in today's world, you need to accept the fact that change surrounds you. With your permission, or without it, change can deliver phenomenal opportunities. The elimination of old habits and comfort zones will be celebrated. And that's exciting. Tomorrow, truly, will be another day.

Self-Sabotage: The undermining and destruction of personal integrity, malicious supervision, and damage to personal and professional credibility, *caused by one's self*, any of which can lead to erosion and destruction of self-esteem and confidence.

TRAP 9:
SELF-SABOTAGE
Being Your Own
Worst Enemy

- Have you ever told yourself you can't do something (not knowing if you could or could not)?

- Do you maintain friendships with people, even when they insulted, abused, or were mean to you?

- When you are complimented, do you discount it or not feel you deserve it?

- Have you ever had an important project to complete and gotten sidetracked and missed your deadline?

- Have you ever avoided asking questions because you feared someone would think you were stupid?

Today, Shirley Davalos is a successful entrepreneur and partner with her husband in their company Orient Express. She acts as a consultant to individuals, personally or professionally, in putting together a package profile to help them get into radio and television or complete a national publicity tour. Based in Sausalito, California, Orient Express is known as one of the premier video reproduction companies in the San Francisco Bay area. Prior to forming her company, Davalos was a television producer with one of the top-rated morning shows in San Francisco. With her background, she can make up composite tapes to show the range of an individual's work, whether the client is an actor, a spokesperson, or a professional speaker.

In addition, the company strings together guest appearances from various shows that will enable other producers to check on a potential guest's style and versatility. Today, Shirley Davalos is very successful but she wasn't always so. Years ago, Davalos practiced the art of self-sabotage, which cost her 5 years of her professional life.

Prior to becoming the producer for *AM San Francisco,* she would have identified herself as a shy person. She wanted to go into television when she graduated from college. Everyone she knew told her to start in a small town. Instead, Shirley went straight to San Francisco. She obtained an interview with a local radio show, which offered her a job as its producer. When she asked what the job entailed, she was told she would be responsible for contacting individuals and asking them to appear on the show.

When I interviewed her for *The Confidence Factor,* she told me how it all began.

> As an example, the man interviewing me told me that if the mayor was involved in a breaking news story, I would be responsible for calling the mayor and asking him to be on the show the next day. I told him that I couldn't do that. I'd never done it before and I did not know how. I asked if I could start lower, not as a producer yet. My about-to-be employer quickly said, "Adios." It would be 5 years before I ever got another job in television.
>
> During those years, I worked for several banks, and I continued to go out for interviews. I finally landed a job as the receptionist at a local station. Once in the door, I went to every department and offered my services. I'd say, "I'm just sitting here most of the time. Is there anything I can do to help you?" Gradually, I was given more work. I became a production assistant and made the same kinds of phone calls I had panicked about years earlier. I also began to write movie vignettes for the newspaper.
>
> As I got to know people in the business, I learned of an opening up at the ABC television affiliate as the production secretary. It was only for a few months as a replacement for a woman on maternity leave. I decided to go for it. I survived, stayed on, and eventually became the production secretary on *AM San Francisco.* As the program grew in importance, so did I. A few years later, I became its producer.

Shirley Davalos says there are two keys to success in her life. One is to be in love with your work, and the other is to persevere. Before she discovered passion and perseverance, it was not uncommon for her to sabotage herself. The fear of failure, the fear of criticism, the fear of negotiation, the fear of confronting, even the fear of taking credit for accomplishments haunted many of the GenderTraps survey respondents.

Self-sabotage involves doing things that are against your own best interests. Common phrases such as "being your own worst enemy" and "shooting yourself in the foot" are often bandied about when self-sabotage is at work. Most of us practice some form of self-sabotage at some time in our lives. Some of us become quite proficient at it, knowing it's destructive, yet feeling helpless in stopping it. The result is self-defeat, and sometimes self-destruction.

IT'S NOT A BIG DEAL

One of the top movies in 1994 was producer and director Robert Redford's *Quiz Show*. In it the bright, articulate, and attractive Columbia University professor, Charles Van Doren, succumbs to the glitter of fame and money. By the time he finally loses to the new *Twenty-One* winner, he has been on the cover of *Time* magazine, has amassed over $100,000 (a lot of money in the 1950s) along with a $50,000 per year contract as cultural affairs advocate for NBC's *Today* show, has gained the adoration of his female students at Columbia University, and has created an awe and respect from the general public for anyone with brains—quite a feat for a young bachelor.

The only problem was that Charles Van Doren and other contestants on the program had been fed answers to the questions. It didn't start out that way, at least for Van Doren. He told the executive producer that he wanted to answer the questions on his own. He didn't want the "help." Eventually, he too took the answers to the questions.

When a congressional probe was initiated, Van Doren received intense pressure from the president of NBC to deny that he had ever received any answers to show questions. Van Doren had been seduced enough so that he didn't view it as a "big deal." He made a public statement that he had never been given any answers.

But the "deal" was growing to monstrous proportions. His conscience finally got the better of him, and at a hearing before Congress, he read a prepared statement. He had lied to the American public, and he regretted it. After his testimony, Van Doren learned that, not only had he been removed from his position at the university, he also lost the contract with *Today*.

The public felt betrayed. Its hero had fallen. The shame that Van Doren had brought upon himself and his family was more than he could take. In a sense, he has been in a form of self-imposed exile since those hearings of the 1950s, working for the Encyclopedia Brittanica and living quietly out of the limelight with his family.

When did Van Doren begin to practice the art of self-sabotage? Was it in the beginning, when he signed on and knew he would be fed answers to the weekly questions? Not necessarily so. In many ways, Van Doren was quite naive. He didn't have the "moxie" to realize that all the contestants had knowledge of the questions and answers that would be presented on air dates.

Van Doren got caught up in the glamour and recognition—fame. Who wouldn't, when your picture was on the cover of *Time* magazine? He believed he was doing something good for academia and intelligentsia. Most likely, the act of self-sabotage occurred when he made the public statement prior to the congressional hearings that he had never received any answers.

From that day on his days were marked, with the lie haunting him, trailing him wherever he went. His shadow. In the end, the loss of his credibility and reputation, not to mention two jobs, became the outcome.

IS THERE A SABOTEUR IN YOU?

Self-sabotage exists in varying degrees. At one end of the spectrum are individuals who are so destructive that nothing ever goes right for them and the people around them. Their careers and personal lives are a mess. These people are never happy about anything. In fact, they can be called negaholics, intense procrastinators—they moan and groan about everything and wallow in self-pity. Remember the song when you were a kid—

Nobody likes me

Everybody hates me,

Think I'll eat some worms.

It fits this group to a T. In the middle are those who act out self-sabotaging behavior on a periodic basis. It is not an everyday, or weekly occurrence. But once in a while they really blow it, and they know it. At the other end of the spectrum are those who have displayed some form of self-sabotage, recognize it, and make a concentrated effort to not repeat whatever the behavior is. Land mines in the workplace are inevitable. Your destruction is not.

Acknowledging that you are a self-saboteur is a major step on your road to recovery. Be willing to get outside help. You won't be the first person to enlist a psychotherapist to help you remove the barriers you have erected throughout your life.

If you have ever gone through a difficult time, you know that it is normal to experience self-doubt, paranoia, blame, loss of confidence, feeling of failure, or feelings that you have been victimized. All these may emerge at some time or another. The feeling "If only I had done this" or "Why is this happening to me?" gets internalized and vocalized. Everyone has voices. These inner, self-effacing voices are so subtle that you barely hear them, yet it's as if someone were shouting in your ear at close range.

THE INNER TRAPS

Within the self-sabotage trap are inner traps. All are situations and conditions that you manifest or encounter at some time. Feeling that your world may be caving in distorts your normal, everyday range of perceptions.

It does not mean you are going over the deep end, all is lost, and you are a total failure. Land mines don't always explode. By recognizing that inner traps exist and that there are solutions to them, you will be able to cope with and escape self-sabotage.

THE MOST COMMON INNER TRAPS

Here are the 12 most common inner traps associated with self-sabotage.

1. *Victimization.* You have an exaggerated sense that nothing is your fault and that someone else is the cause of your problems.
2. *Low self-esteem and self-confidence.* The lack of self-esteem and self-confidence disempowers you from stretching, reaching, and seeking new competencies and challenges.
3. *Negotiation avoidance.* Not understanding and using negotiation techniques can lead to both personal and professional disaster.

4. *Fear of failure.* Failure is a judgment about events, either yours or someone else's. When failure occurs, the results are often the loss of self-esteem, money, and social status. Anticipating or expecting too much too soon in any endeavor can lead to failure; and anticipating or believing that you will fail can enhance its occurrence.

5. *Fear of confronting.* Being unwilling to confront or even acknowledge issues sets you up for negative self-talk, failure, even paranoia.

6. *Paranoia.* Being suspicious of others takes a lot of energy. It also reduces and, in some cases, eliminates the ability to trust. Without trust, you will find it difficult if not impossible to tap into your creative talents.

7. *Egomania.* When egos get out of control, a bloated sense of value and importance, coupled with immaturity and the need to get attention, can lead to trouble.

8. *Revenge.* Plotting and planning a get-even strategy dilutes your energy and unfocuses your work and personal life.

9. *Blaming.* Seeking someone else to blame for your mistakes, inadequacies, or failures tells others that you are irresponsible and immature—both career busters.

10. *Negative self-talk.* Negative self-talk sets you up for failure through an erosion of self-esteem and self-confidence.

11. *Being too personal.* Divulging too much personal information to others can lead to gossip and the belief that you are a blabbermouth who is unable to maintain confidences. It can also set you up for being sabotaged by others.

12. *Procrastination.* Putting off anything and rationalizing that it's the wrong time or that you're not ready usually means you are afraid to fail. It's guaranteed to be a major roadblock to your success.

VICTIMIZATION AND BLAMISM

Being a victim has become the politically correct thing to do in the 1990s. It is also a great way to lose your job, decrease or destroy your self-esteem, and have friends and coworkers put you on their "Don't call me, I'll call you" list. Are there people who are victims? Of course! And there are many who are victims of their own self-talk and self-attitude—in other words, it's their choice.

VICTIMS, OR "IT'S NOT MY FAULT"

Shucking off responsibility, blaming others for your actions, or claiming to be a victim has become the battle cry for too many in the 1990s. When tennis star Jennifer Capriati was arrested for marijuana possession, her father stepped forward and took responsibility for her actions—"I pushed her too hard to compete when she was young." It is as if victims with privileged backgrounds are not responsible for their actions.

As a manager, Phyllis routinely sees employees blame things on others for their actions. She also believes that the "addiction" claim has been stretched beyond its limits.

> We have gotten too righteous and nonresponsible for our own good. Everywhere I turn, people are saying it's not their fault.
>
> I smoke. No one forced cigarettes into my mouth. I chose to do it in the first place and I choose to continue to do it.

If victims of poverty are not responsible for their actions, and if victims of various addictions are blameless and not responsible for their addiction, and if people who come from broken homes or dysfunctional families are not responsible or accountable for their behavior, who is? The psychobabble of the 1990s has allowed the general population to redefine bad behavior as a disease. The seven deadly sins have been reinterpreted as behavioral complexes that are somebody else's fault.

In the old days, 10 years ago, if you had squandered your money on shoes, clothing, and jewelry for yourself, or even on drugs, and not bought appropriate food for your children, society would have labeled you irresponsible, a misfit, and unsuitable as a parent. Today, you're excused—there must be some other reason for your action and neglect. It's someone else's fault.

FROM LEGITIMATE TO ILLEGITIMATE

Carolyn Zeiger, Ph.D., believes that, on the whole, the victimization notion started legitimately; that there is validity in recognizing that when people are politically and physically less powerful, they do get taken advantage of.

> It is important to recognize that people are taken advantage of, and hurt and victimized. Nonetheless, victimization has grown to be a state of mind and a way of being in the world. This really dis-

turbs me. It seems that anyone who is convinced that they are a victim, should sue somebody to get what they see as their rightful due. It has become a kind of way to be in the world. In the end, victimization turns into a cop-out.

It also puts you in a more powerless position to take the victim's posture. It says there is nothing I can do about it. The surest way to be unable to participate in solving the problem, is to fail to recognize your part in creating it. There is an old cliché, "If you're not part of the solution, then you're part of the problem." To be part of the solution, you need to recognize in what way you are part of the problem.

Women are also players in this problem. They play at little girl, they play helpless, as if daddy and the troops will take care of me. A common attitude is that if I wait long enough for Prince Charming to come along, my life will work.

Women are usually more identified as victims than men are. They must say, "Wait a minute, if we want real equality and freedom, there are things we have to give up—like sugar daddies."

Women have fantasies. Even the most independent professional women have dreams of playing the little girl and being helpless. And it backfires. Many judges (usually white males) view women as helpless, even paralyzed, victims who can't manage on a daily basis. Or, if a woman seems too capable, too self-confident, and too in charge of her life, judges don't believe she's a victim. Rather like "Damned if you do and damned if you don't."

According to Nan Hunter, a Brooklyn Law School professor in New York:

> Woman-as-victim is a cultural script that evokes sympathy without challenging the hierarchical structure. It's kind of a melodrama that doesn't lead to any change in the conditions that cause the victimization.[1]

HEAR THEM WHINE

What about the whiners in your workplace? These are the people who routinely say: "Do I have to do it?" "Martha is late from lunch, ask her!" "This is a crummy computer, it's always crashing." The whiners of the workplace grumble about everything—they are the first to complain and the first to blame someone or something.

Whiners are like kids. They do it to get attention: "Look, hear, see me." If you are the boss, determine if the complaint is legitimate or not. Put out the clear message that whining is not allowed. When it starts up, ignore the whiners. When it stops, acknowledge and reward them. In Chap. 6, on management chaos, the technique is referred to as *behavior shaping*.

For a coworker, the same advice stands. Remove yourself from the whining arena and *don't* join the gripe session. Whiners get the message when you remove yourself from earshot. Another method is to call for the solution, which whiners don't include in their diatribe.

Many people believe "Once a victim, always a victim," which is a statement in itself that is victimizing. Being aware that you have sidestepped issues or responsibility, even accountability, is the first step. The next step is to take little steps. Tell yourself, "I'm not going to get pulled back. I'm not going to blame someone else if something doesn't go right or it goes wrong." Get a trusted friend or coworker to develop a buddy and feedback system.

As a rule, no behavior is changed overnight. It takes time—in fact, it takes lots of times to be reminded and reinforced that reactions or responses may not be OK or are inappropriate. It's also important to develop realistic expectations with those you work with. They are not going to change overnight either, but it doesn't mean they can't change.

If you communicate directly about what you like and do not like, as well as what constitutes unacceptable behavior around you, you'll gradually feel that you are back in the driver's seat, taking control. Once you take control and recognize that the force behind your own destiny is you—not your parents, your spouse, your children, your coworkers, your boss, government, society, or the media—you are no longer a victim. And that is victorious.

Remove yourself from the age of victimism and stop blaming others. Over 100 years ago, Susan B. Anthony said, "Woman must not depend upon the protection of a man, but must be taught to protect herself." In the eighteenth century, Mary Wollstonecraft wrote, "I do not wish women to have power over men, but over themselves." If you allow yourself to get stuck in the victim and blaming trap, then you will sink. You then do not believe you are able, nor do you have the responsibility, to change yourself.

LOW SELF-ESTEEM AND LOW SELF-CONFIDENCE

Confidence, or the lack of it, is the single link in all the books I have written. Whether it is money—how to get it and how to make it grow; or divorce—how to strategize and plan it and survive it; or sabotage—

how to identify it and remove yourself from the target range; or adversity—recognizing that you can't rewind your life and that you have to move on—lack of confidence is the key ingredient. The recovery and growth of confidence is one of the foundations for living.

Confidence and self-esteem get used interchangeably. There is a slight difference. Self-esteem is the regard, appreciation, and caring you have for yourself. Confidence is the power to create the regard, appreciation, and caring that you have for yourself. In other words, you are in charge of building and, sometimes, of demolishing your own reputation with yourself as well as with others.

The popular belief is that confidence comes from your upbringing, especially if it's an ideal upbringing. The opposite is true. A study I conducted with 6000 men and women suggested that confidence came from disaster and crisis. The number-one professional crisis was being fired or laid off, and the number-one crisis on the personal side was a breakup of a long-term relationship or a marriage. This study was used as the genesis for my book *The Confidence Factor.* I found that the more successful people were, the more crises, mistakes, and failures they had experienced.

Liz is the elected county recorder in a small community in the East. As she learned the ropes and found her voice, she propelled her participation to the state level. Now, she routinely speaks out and states her opinion. She is the incoming president of her State Association of County Recorders. It wasn't always so.

> I'm in my second 4-year-term and will be our state association's president this year. The first 4 years were not easy. I felt totally without ease; it was difficult for me to stand in front of any group and talk, so I rarely spoke up on any issue. Finally it dawned on me that my vote counted as much as anyone else's within the group. And, if I didn't speak up, my opinion would never count.

Acquiring confidence and becoming empowered does not happen overnight. Supreme Court Justice Sandra Day O'Connor has said that her confidence comes from age and maturity, from life's experiences. On ABC's *Prime Time,* powerhouse Diane Sawyer said that she daily looks in the mirror and forgives herself for the mistakes of yesterday, any mistakes that would be made today, and for mistakes of the future.[2] In other words, both of these very accomplished, successful, and highly visible women say that, when it comes to confidence and empowerment, the workplace road always has land mines and potholes.

Eleanor Roosevelt's often quoted words, "No one makes you feel inferior without your permission," are an ideal reminder that confidence building begins with you.

NEGOTIATING

For many women, negotiation is equivalent to conflict and therefore should be avoided. Learning how to negotiate will resolve conflict, not create it. One of the most common areas that survey respondents referred to was not knowing how to negotiate when it came to pay. Not only did women respond that they were paid less for the same job than male coworkers; they also reported that they took on more tasks without any pay increases.

Prior to her present position as a recruiter, Gayle worked within the human resources department of a manufacturer of baby products. She was told that she had to train an employee for a position that was higher than the one she held and had been turned down for.

> I was turned down for the position I wanted because I was needed in another department. In addition, it fell upon me to implement a new computer system along with my regular work. I was told I was the only one who had the knowledge of the various departments to fully computerize them and, therefore, I couldn't be promoted into another position.
>
> Initially, it was nice for my ego to be told that I was needed and no one else had my knowledge. But then it dawned on me that I was doing two jobs and getting paid for one. My male counterpart does just one job. I didn't know how to ask for more.

THE 80/20 SOLUTION

Viewing negotiation as a matter of cooperating and resolving a problem versus creating a conflict is one of the first steps in creating a negotiating mentality. Negotiation plays a key role in your workplace and personal life. The most important step in any negotiation process is to be prepared. In any negotiation, 80 percent is planning and only 20 percent is action.

Being prepared means knowing what you want, and also knowing what the other side wants. You should be able to clarify—assuming you get what you want—exactly what's in it for the side that concedes to you. You must have a clear picture of what your goal is in any bargaining process. Without it, the outcome could be significantly different from what you desire. It is also important to have some type of ground rules. By developing common rules before beginning, you simplify the negotiating process and help to focus on the end results.

> *Savvy negotiators hope for the best but plan for the worst.*

Sometimes, an impasse is created. It becomes evident that your desires may not be fully satisfied. If that's the case, one of the strongest strategies that you can have is to be able to walk away.

KEEP IT CLEAR

The essence of any good negotiation is clear communication. Understanding that everyone has different communication styles and predetermining what each style is before a negotiation begins can put you ahead of the game. According to Nichole Schapiro, author of *Negotiating for Your Life,* negotiation is done on many levels, from simple bartering to problem solving and conflict resolution. Negotiation is the give-and-take, back-and-forth process of solving problems, large and small, that arise every day while you try to obtain or accomplish something.

Cooperative negotiation achieves a balance between two differing points of view—what Schapiro calls *partnership negotiation.* It's a mutual education process. Partnership negotiation eliminates *ego exchange negotiation,* a negotiation that is used only to put on a display of power and pretense and fear. She advises that many negotiations get off on the wrong foot because one or both sides are insensitive to differing cultural factors.

A partnership negotiation absolutely requires awareness of the personal and situational variables that are inherent in multicultural/global relationships—business, professional, and interpersonal dealings, along with the casual contacts in everyday living and travel. Implicit mutual respect and understanding for one another's value system is a basis for initial trust in any dialogue. Without them, making a deal is virtually impossible.

KNOW WHAT YOU WANT

Schapiro strongly believes that goals must be set. Knowing what you want and need to come away with is a strong card in your negotiating hand. If it is a materialistic goal, name it and quantify it; if it is something intangible, describe it sufficiently to give it some substance. People are often more willing to give you what you want if they know exactly what you want instead of being confronted with general dissatisfaction or feeling attacked or criticized.

She also advises you to set your aspirations high, because you'll never do better than what you aspire to. If you don't reach the highest level of your aspirations, you may be disappointed. But, in retrospect, you probably went further than you would have if you had set more modest goals, which is what most women do. Women rarely ask for enough when it comes to money or position.

According to Schapiro, claiming authority over your own life is a critical step in preparing to negotiate for your life—and that authority is a nonnegotiable requirement. Her wise words:

> First always negotiate with yourself. You should not trade off the right to make decisions about your life, for money, love, security, prestige, affection, or fame—not until you reclaim yourself, or understand what you are about, will you be able to go forward.
>
> Don't confuse "authority" with "control." The desire to have total control over your life is unrealistic, since you may depend upon others also. You cannot control the behavior of other people—in your own families or in the world—and you can't control the course of nature. Within that reality, it's foolish to think that you, who function much of your life in conversation with other people in the world around you, can be in total control.
>
> However, you can have authority over your life. You choose to be the final decision maker on important issues that concern your minds, your bodies, and your work.[3]

WHAT'S NOT NEGOTIABLE

Some areas are nonnegotiable. They include age, family background, and physical factors. You can't change your age, but you can do a number of things to minimize its influence, such as practicing preventive health measures, exercising, watching your diet, and getting regular checkups. It's impossible to change your parents—they are who they are—and you can't change any children you have given birth to, although you can alter your interactions with them.

If you have a physical handicap, you have a handicap. You can't negotiate for better eyesight or unslurred speech. You can, though, negotiate for better circumstances that allow you to perform effectively both at home and at work. At some point, disease can become a part of life. If cancer hits, it's nonnegotiable. It is the same with Alzheimer's, diabetes, AIDS, and a labyrinth of other diseases. You can, though, determine what type and course of treatment you will participate in, as well as who treats and cares for you.

THE DOS AND DON'TS

Nichole Schapiro offers one gem that has assisted me countless times: At the beginning of any negotiation, don't fuss over your first sentence. It's usually a throwaway and no one pays attention to it. Make it casual, humorous, and welcoming. But the next sentence is crucial. She advises you to address the person who has the power in the room, with the second sentence.

Where you sit should be strategic. If you want someone you don't like to agree to a solution you propose, sit next to him or her. You appear confident and brave in your ability to handle pressure in that close proximity. If it's someone you don't know well, it's more appropriate to sit across so you can establish eye contact and observe body language. Schapiro believes that this allows you to get a handle on the other person's personality and conflict management style as well as his or her intentions. Schapiro's dos and don'ts include:

- *Don't* go in cold. You can't wing it. *Do* bring in some facts that you prepared in advance.
- *Don't* pitch to the wrong person—someone who can't do anything for you. *Do* know and see the decision maker.
- *Don't* force your style on someone—for example, by giving reams of paper to a bottom liner or one piece of paper to someone who acts only on reams of information.
- *Do* be aware of your employer's personality and work style; try to match it to create safety and trust.

- *Don't* lead with emotion. *Do* stay calm and focused on your goal. Ask what is the goal, what are the obstacles.

- *Don't* assume anything. *Do* know what you *do* know, and what you *don't* know.

- *Don't* argue or attack. *Do* be prepared to make concessions without forfeiting your goal.

As you practice negotiating, you'll find that you can and do get more of what you want. At the same time, you'll build skills confidence, and exchange ideas by working with others—critical tools for survival, growth and advancement in today's workplace.

FAILURE

Successful men and women are separated from those who are not successful by their attitude about failure. People who are successful don't fear it. They don't like it either, but they recognize rebirthings can happen, and, for many, they may pronounce it's one of the best things that happened to them. At some point in your life, you will experience failure. Whether it's public or private, it happens.

Failure has stages similar to the ones identified by Elizabeth Kubler-Ross in her book *On Death and Dying:* denial, anger, bargaining, letting go, and acceptance. In their 1987 book *When Smart People Fail,* Carole Hyatt and Linda Gottlieb also identify stages of failure: shock, fear, anger, blame, shame, and despair.

According to Hyatt and Gottlieb, failure is a judgment about one or more events. Whether a failure is personal or professional, it impacts self-esteem, social status, and money. When their book was first published, failure was considered by most to be embarrassing and a secret that shouldn't be discussed publicly. Hyatt and Gottlieb described it as the "last taboo."

Since then, a lot has happened in the world. Big businesses have collapsed and solid employees with impeccable reputations have lost their jobs. Failure has become a fact of life for many, which means it's normal. The good news is that it is no longer a taboo and it can be openly discussed.

The bad news—it doesn't hurt any less. When failure hits, it's common to feel you are alone; only you are experiencing the pain, the humility, the financial disaster, the status as a social outcast (whether perceived or real). If you are going through failure of some sort, you are inclined to believe it is a unique, once-in-the-universe's-lifetime experience.

The downsizing mania of the 1990s has been the door opener in acknowledging and talking about failure. Thousands of women and men who have done terrific jobs within their workplaces, and for their companies, got pink slips. What moved from the back page of the newspapers was on the front page, and routinely spoken about on radio and television news broadcasts. Still, when failure does occur, it is absolutely normal to feel the shock that Hyatt and Gottlieb referred to.

Some failures can actually take years to be birthed; others spring forth in a very short period of time. When failure is at your doorstep, it is common to feel isolated and numb. But the full range of pain—for some emotional, and for others physical as well—hasn't really hit. There are a variety of reasons that failure happens. Yet, when people are asked in the midst of failure or shortly after it has hit, most aren't able to step back to interpret how, why, and at times even when it all began.

According to Hyatt and Gottlieb, it's normal to blame other people and cite economic factors for failure. Only later can you step back honestly and determine what part you actually played. This scrutiny is critical.

Poor interpersonal skills are the primary cause of career failure. But few realize it. Most people blame "office politics" for failure. Yet, according to Hyatt and Gottlieb, "office politics are really nothing more than office interactions among people." They liken interpersonal skills to "social intelligence," which consists of five components:

- Being sensitive to others
- Being able to listen
- Giving and taking criticism
- Being emotionally steady
- Being able to build team support

Developing social intelligence provides a tremendous backdrop when disaster hits. Because of your ability to listen, to give and receive criticism, and to be sensitive to others when bad times or bad news hits you, you'll find that you have a support network in place. Whether your failure is caused by outside forces (you lost your job because your position was eliminated along with a lot of others) or you simply blew it, people will be there to support you.

In *When Smart People Fail,* Hyatt and Gottlieb identify eight other common reasons for failure.

- The wrong fit
- The halfhearted effort: lack of commitment
- The wild card: bad luck
- Self-destructive behavior
- Too scattered to focus
- Sexism, racism, and ageism
- Poor management: over- or underdelegation
- Hanging on[4]

When you feel that you are paralyzed, you can't move on, and you are no longer in control, the result is negative self-talk. You end up being totally disappointed in yourself. The solution is to tell yourself that this is only temporary, and that there are options out there. When you can step back and explore what those options are, you will add to your self-esteem and build up a belief system that you can move on—out or up.

> *Failure happens, and it happens to the best of people. Rarely once, but many times. The key to growing out of failure is to learn from it.*

CONFRONTING

Not being able or willing to confront guarantees a nonresolution of your conflict. In not being able to confront the negative situation, you, in effect, allow it to continue. Your silence says it's all right. (This issue is dealt with in Chap. 9, on conquering confrontophobia.)

There are several key factors to keep in mind in confronting. First, just because a conflict exists that leads to confrontation does not mean that you are in an abnormal environment. Conflicts arise daily from living and working with others. It is how you manage the conflict and the confrontation that makes the difference.

Second, in any confrontation the person who is the better listener usually wins. Listening is a skill that is not learned overnight. An expert listener listens with her eyes and her ears, and pays close attention to the words, tone, gestures, and body language of the other party.

Third, understanding personality styles and communicating the issues of your concern by using the other party's personality style puts you ahead of the game. This takes practice and is not an easy task.

Finally, it is important to document the facts of what you want to confront about. Documentation does not mean that you will give an item-by-item agenda of your complaints. It means that you get your thoughts in order: circumstances, dates, and outcomes. If the other party is a master in derailing—getting you off track onto other topics—your documentation and mindset will give you the support to get her refocused and back on track.

You will address a series of conflicts throughout your life. Self-sabotage multiplies when you avoid them, when you fail to confront. You move yourself into a victim mode, blaming problems on others, reducing your confidence, avoiding any type of negotiation, enhancing negative self-talk, and procrastinating about any type of commitment because of the fear of a future confrontation. It becomes an insidious chain of events.

BEING TOO PERSONAL

The *momism* message of "Be nice, be friends" leads women onto the path to being too personal, or overpersonalizing situations. There is no question that women talk about a greater range of topics, horizontally and vertically, than men do. On the vertical axis, it could be about hopes, dreams, aspirations, and blunders. On the horizontal side, it could be relations—who you are connected to as well who you are disconnected from.

Gwen is a credit analyst for a wholesale book distributor. She deals with the big boys—those who owe over $1 million to the company. At times, Gwen feels she lets her personal feelings guide her actions.

> I have a hard time because I let personal feelings get involved in work. I'm one of those who wears my heart on my sleeve. If anyone gets too mad at me, or doesn't like the way I do things, I feel I'm being personally attacked. I don't have problems on the phones when I'm telling customers to get their money in. It is here, in person. I can't handle it. When I'm collecting money, it's just a business; but when it comes to personal information about others, or revealing personal information about myself, I don't handle it well.

Gwen has already identified areas where she has problems—personal issues. With business related issues—i.e., send the check in, or we won't ship you any more books—she doesn't have a problem. There's distance involved, first, because of the phone communication—no one is in her face—and, second, because no direct personal issues are involved.

If the customer were in the next office and she knew him, his family, and problems his company might be having, she would have far greater difficulty asking him to send the check in. If someone says anything negative to Gwen that could possibly be interpreted as a personal attack, she turns into Jell-o.

Part of Gwen's solution is to keep things separate; business is business. Coworkers are also part of business. By not overly personalizing, or at least not including the entire workplace as a close friend, she should be able to begin to depersonalize comments or actions that can be construed as negative. They are directed, not toward her as a person, but more to the business or the nature of the business.

In female-dominated professions—teachers, bank tellers, secretaries, clerical workers, flight attendants, nurses, and so on—women tend to be too open and sharing before they have had the opportunity to evaluate or determine whether coworkers are entitled to their trust and confidences. Until you know for sure what someone's style and pattern is, you should think about how and what you share with another. Ask yourself: How would this look on the front page of the company newsletter? If you wouldn't like it, keep quiet.

EGOMANIA

Valuing your worth and your importance is critical in building self-esteem and confidence. But some people overvalue it, or they devalue others around them. It is not uncommon for an overinflated ego to always seek the spotlight, grabbing it from others. Egomaniacs find it very difficult to allow someone else to shine, or be given accolades and awards, without attempting to crowd in. Crowding includes taking credit for some of the work that has been done, or even claiming to be the initial genius behind whatever is being applauded.

Egomania is much more than being confident or overconfident. Confidence is the power to create and support the value, caring, and sense of worth that you have about yourself. Egomania is much more. Those with bloated egos view themselves as the *key and only central figure* in their circle of friends (if they have them), in their workplaces, and within their families.

Those with inflated egos want to be admired, even worshipped, by others. They believe they can do no wrong and can fail at nothing. And when they do—and they will fail and fall—any acknowledgment and acceptance of being part of the failure will be out of their realm. Overinflated egos are proficient at blaming others or events for any problems that they might have.

Overstated egos believe—truly believe—that they are indispensable. That their workplaces, their friendships, and their families could not survive without their presence. The reality is that their personae and talents would be missed, at least in some cases, but most can be replaced. No one is indispensable. Everyone, including you and I, can be replaced. It may be bumpy and create a few land mines for those who worked, played, or lived with you, but in the end life goes on.

If you are someone who leans toward egomania, it's time to change circuits. Consider developing a buddy system with someone in your workplace, someone who you trust and is willing to give you feedback when you seem to be pushing the line, from taking credit for work that you have actually done to grabbing credit for the work that someone else has done. Having a healthy ego is very important but so are eating, sleeping, laughing, and playing.

REVENGE

"Hell hath no fury like a woman scorned" and "Don't get mad, get even" are common phrases we've heard for years. Planning, plotting, and acting out revengeful action is usually a direct result of anger—yours. Being angry does not mean that you are unhealthy. Everyone at some time is going to feel anger. It is how that anger is directed that determines whether it's healthy or unhealthy.

Acts that are rooted in anger can be delivered in a variety of ways. Consider the most common piece of equipment outside of the telephone—the computer in the office. Incredible degrees of destruction can be generated from deleting files, inputting erroneous information, introducing viruses, or sending libelous and slanderous messages throughout a network. You name it, it's been done.

Recall that in Chap. 5, on the sabotage trap, workers in Lucille's salon introduced a virus into her computer when she was ill. With her weakened energy level, she ended up closing the doors of an award-winning business of 10-plus years.

GOSSIP AND THE GRAPEVINE

Believe it or not, office gossip is probably the most common form of revenge. Gossip can be likened to a pool, but not the kind of pool that you swim in and do laps in and feel refreshed when you get out. The gossip pool is like a cesspool: the more you use it, the smellier and the more unpleasant it becomes.

Not all office gossip is bad. If you are not tuned into the office grapevine, you could miss out on valuable information, including what positions are opening up and who's leaving the company. Gossip that is destructive and vicious is created from misdirected anger. It's a way to let off steam.

For women, gossip is also a way to connect with other women. In effect, it acts as a builder, most likely temporary, of self-esteem. If you know some tidbit about someone else, and believe that others would like to tap into your information, you get a momentary boost in self-esteem.

If you find yourself a target of ugly rumors, you must address and confront them immediately. If someone is slandering you, you'll need to sleuth and find out who the slanderer is. You can simply say to the person you suspect, "Do you have any idea who could have started such an outrageous rumor?" Your tone is not accusatory, merely questioning.

You must make it clear that you will not tolerate malicious and unfounded gossip about yourself. When others try to get even with you by starting gossip, their response to your query is usually one of denial—they don't have a clue who started the rumor. If you again respond that it is outrageous, and that you'll continue to ask others if they know who started it because it is important to clear your name, your slanderer knows that the jig is up. She knows that you know, and that you know that she knows that you know.

Don't be part of the link in spreading negative rumors about others. If you know something is untrue, speak up and say so. When you defend others from a smear or shark attack, your reputation for being fair and supportive will spread, fast.

The bottom line is that if you are angry, feeling revengeful, or stuck in a situation where your manager, coworkers, or just your job frustrates or drives you crazy, get some help. If you can identify what the problem is, sit back and strategize various ways to confront it. If you have a trusted colleague or friend, get some feedback. Maybe you haven't assessed the situation totally, and you are actually blinded to it.

Even if you aren't the primary factor in the identified problem, it may be distracting you from your work or causing you to act out and experience anger. If so, the best approach is to jump in and resolve it. By being revengeful and acting on your feelings, you set yourself up for failure. You may feel satisfaction, but it's only for a brief period of time. It is a tiny win that carries a losing coattail.

PARANOIA

Paranoid people believe the world is out to get them and suspect everyone around them of just about everything. Being paranoid distracts you from your work. Your energy and creativity are used up in a variety of manifestations. You honestly believe that others are out to get you, to destroy your work, or to discredit your capabilities.

Paranoid people enclose themselves in a glass box. They want to look out and see what is going on, and at the same time isolate themselves—because they are sure that everyone is going to get them or, at least, think the worst of them.

Paranoia is often a creature birthed from self-doubt. Don't be so harsh on yourself. It is time to step back and do a reality check. Stop treating yourself, or believing that you are treating yourself, unfairly. Granted, there are going to be people out there—family, coworkers, even "friends"—who wouldn't mind if you looked foolish once in a while. If you have concerns that coworkers or others are motivated to do you in, get some feedback from someone you trust.

If you believe you can't trust anyone in your immediate circle (coworkers, family, or friends), seek out professional help. Included in those professionals could be a manager, someone in the human resources department, or a professional career counselor. If you persistently lack a sense of trust, and feel that nobody likes you or cares for you, and that others want you to fail, you may require the help of a therapist.

NEGATIVE SELF-TALK

Any type of negative self-talk, from "I'm a jerk for blowing the presentation" to "I'm worthless and shouldn't be alive," is destructive and paralyzing. When your inner voice says that your idea, your concept, your work, your friendships (whatever it comes up with) are useless and have no value, you infect yourself with a virus. That virus sets up a progression of thoughts that literally says that your ideas are dumb and stupid and a waste of everybody's time.

Remember Shirley Davalos, owner of Orient Express? Early in her career she sabotaged the TV production job she aspired to by her negative self-talk. Davalos took it a step further. She localized her negativism to the person who wanted to hire her. She did not believe that she could fill the position and she said so—to the decision maker. That delayed her career for 5 years.

When you fill your mind with statements like "I am too young/I am too old/I don't have the talent/I didn't go to college/I can't use the computer/I can't type/I can't...," you lose. Your inner voices are taking you down with each variation of "I can't."

Procrastination is career suicide, just in slow motion.

If you are a procrastinator, your speech is probably littered with phrases such as these:

"If only..."

"I can't afford to."

"I'll get around to it one of these days."

"I don't have the time."

Procrastination occurs for a variety of reasons. Leading the list is the feeling "I don't want to succeed." There's an actual fear of success. If you put it off until tomorrow, someone else may come in and do the project. Or, if it doesn't work when someone else tries it, you can rationalize and say it was a mistake or shouldn't have been done in the first place. Procrastinators avoid doing things that they perceive are uncomfortable, or simply overwhelming.

A classic example of procrastination hits millions of Americans every year. It's called filing your income tax. Many routinely ask for extensions because they just don't want to deal with it—tomorrow is another day. Others are so busy, or at least perceive themselves to be, that they just don't have time—tomorrow is another day. The only time this attitude really works is when you really are busy and will have more time in one of your tomorrows—and you are not owed a refund.

On the work side, many people procrastinate when making a decision about participating in a project, or even putting their résumé in for promotion consideration. Their fear is that they may actually get it—the project or promotion—and if it doesn't work out or they don't work out, their problems will be compounded. They will look foolish or will be considered a failure in others' eyes. By procrastinating, they practice the art of avoidance and enforce their fear of failure.

The way to overcome procrastination includes being aware that you are doing it. When you come across a project that seems overwhelming, instead of doing the standard, "I'll do this tomorrow," try doing it in chunks.

PUTTING THE PUZZLE TOGETHER

Most projects, whether at work or at home, have stages. Some stages follow one another sequentially; others can be pulled out of turn. There may be one stage that is easier for you than others. If the project won't collapse, do it first. Why not? It's like taking steps. Once you take the first step, the second, third, and fourth steps come more easily.

The books I write have multiple stages. The first stage is research, in which I gather material from a study I conduct. Then there is the analysis of the research to identify key points that will be carried throughout the book. The next stage is follow-up, in which I explore the key points with individuals who said they would be willing to be interviewed when they returned the survey. After the interviews are transcribed, I determine where they will fit in which part of the book. Finally, there's the actual writing.

It's like a giant puzzle. When you read a book, you may read it from the preface or introduction straight through to the very end. Or you may select a chapter that fits a need you have. Guaranteed, few writers write from page 1 to page 300 in the exact order. Ideas get pulled out in bits and pieces, and as they are brought together, bridges are formed from chapter to chapter. It is not an overnight process. It takes many months, sometimes years.

REMOVING THE SELF-SABOTAGE TRAP

Self-sabotage is like erecting a barbed-wire enclosure around yourself. Moving on to other enterprises or personal pursuits is substantially inhibited. One of the first steps in getting out of the self-sabotage trap is to be aware of when you work against yourself. When figure skater Kristi Yamaguchi won the gold medal at the 1992 Winter Olympics, commentator and former gold medalist Scott Hamilton remarked, "Kristi's strength is her lack of weakness."

By knowing what your weaknesses are, and in what areas you sabotage yourself, you can initiate a concentrated effort to eliminate them from your life. When you deny that you self-sabotage, whether it is through negative self-talk, procrastination, or being too personal, you do yourself no favors. You need to acknowledge that it is a problem. Are you alone? Absolutely not—everyone has practiced the art of self-sabotage at some time.

Everyone needs appropriate feedback, whether it's accolades or caring criticism (that's not an oxymoron). You need to know how you are doing. Take advantage of your company's employee assistance program (EAP). Its primary purpose is to help employees overcome problems that interfere with their productivity: drugs, smoking, gambling, money, abuse, and other types of self-sabotaging behavior. If your company uses an EAP (ask personnel or human resources), you have two big advantages.

First, EAPs work regularly with individuals whose negativity and problems are impacting their performance; second, the company pays for it. Other resources, which you get to pay for, include psychologists and career counselors. Get references, and interview these professionals before you begin work with them.

Whenever I do a keynote speech on my book *The Confidence Factor*, I always highlight my "second commandment of confidence": *create positive thinking*. Many think it is a lot of nonsense. I don't. Many, many books have been written about the topic. Is the glass half empty, or is it half full? It depends upon how you look at it.

I'm also not shy in saying that you need to remove—delete—the energy suckers in your life: people who are negative; people who barely see the glass as half empty and never as half full; people who have nothing good to say about anyone or anything at any time; people who, when they walk through the door, will start the conversation with whatever horrible things are happening to them or in the news.

In 1993, Norman Vincent Peale, the father of positive thinking died. His book, **The Power of Positive Thinking**, has sold over 20 million copies. His vision was timeless and his success phenomenal. After all, how many people do you know who are successful, or have succeeded in overcoming tragedies and adversities go by the philosophy, *The Power of Negative Thinking*? There are times when optimists are right, and there are times when pessimists are right. You get to choose which one you'll be.

Power Play: An action directed at an individual who is perceived to have less influence and authority than the individual initiating the power play.

TRAP 10:
POWER PLAY BEES
Queens,
Princesses, and
Phantoms

- If you had your "druthers," would you rather work for a woman than a man? If you are a manager, would you rather manage other women or men?
- Have you ever been disappointed by the management styles of any women in your workplace?
- Do you feel that any women misuse their power on other women at work?
- Have you ever been told you are in charge, yet have no authority to change anything?
- Have you ever felt you were caught in the middle of a power play?

Women managers don't always support other women in their workplace; employees don't always support female managers in their workplace. Many feminists do not want to admit, acknowledge, or give any credence to the fact that women sometimes don't support other women and that the manipulations directed toward other women are power plays.

Are these feminists so isolated or so underground that they do not truly see, experience, or believe that women behave this way? There is tremendous support by women and for women, but there is also a dark side. For every macho male who has used or misused women, there's a chauvinist female counterpart, the woman who uses "feminine" manipulations to gain power over women and men. Many of the respondents to the GenderTraps survey stated that some of the women managers and bosses they encountered were actually tougher and harder on them than men were.

Ashley is a travel agent in a multimillion-dollar agency on the West Coast. She considers herself more of a humanist than a feminist. She encountered difficulties when she first joined the agency as a secretary and began to learn the business.

> In the travel business, the majority of the employees are women. I was treated as a lesser being, in a rude and demeaning manner, never with respect. The women managers' attitude was that I was here on a temporary basis, not looking for full-time employment. I never said that; just somehow that was how it was interpreted.
>
> My manager would repeatedly make a point of telling me dumb-blonde jokes—I'm blonde. What's ironic was that our company had recently completed several seminars on diversity. All the women who were selected to attend were in the upper-level positions, including my manager.
>
> I appreciate and tell jokes, but her nonstop, dumb-blonde routine got old fast. Not that she didn't know other jokes—she did, but she saved them for my coworkers. I just got the dumb-blonde ones.
>
> Recently the company started a leadership council and I was selected to participate from our division. There are 10 of us and I always come away feeling so disappointed and let down after we have meetings. I've always been supportive of women's issues, and it gets me to find out that "they"—the women—are the very ones who have doubts about other women.

WOMEN AS BOSSES

A survey on women bosses published in the June 1993 issue of *Working Woman* received 2250 responses from the magazine's million-plus readers. When queried about placement within their organizations, respondents stated that 49 percent of middle-management positions were held by males, 27 percent by females; 19 percent of all respondents stated that there was equal representation of the sexes in middle management. As would be expected, respondents said that 75 percent of their top management was male and 9 percent, female. The remaining 16 percent was split between both sexes.

When the respondents identified their own placement within the organization, only 12 percent were in top management, 32 percent in middle management, and 23 percent in lower management. The remaining respondents were spread between nonsupervisory professionals or specialists (18 percent), clerical workers and administrative assistants (11 percent), and service workers (4 percent).[1] The *Working Woman* study reveals that there are definitely more women in the upper echelons of management today.

Individuals in top management have little free time for off-the-job politics or the pursuit of personal goals. The bulk of the respondents in the *Working Woman* survey are not in top or senior management. They have more time to pursue their own personal goals as they build their career paths. Are women in senior management supportive of other women in general, and of women moving up? Not necessarily so.

THE BEES

The *Queen Bee* is well known in the workplace. She is the woman at the top who got there by hard work. She will claim that her position is a result of her efforts, and hers alone. Her attitude is one of nonmentoring and nonsupport of other women. She is extremely territorial and feels that any woman who wants to advance has to do it the hard way—just as she did—with no help.

In the 1980s, the queen was joined by the *Princess Bee*. The princess is supportive of other women within her own work environment—that is, as long as the other women do not invade her territory, her hive. If she is in marketing and another woman is in education in a hospital, she would actively support the other woman, as long as she showed no desire to transition into marketing. The Princess Bee openly supports women moving up. She is an active mentor of other women, as long as she believes that her job and future are nonclaimable.

The 1990s introduced the next generation of bees, the *Phantom Bee*. She is a woman who, when asked if she knows of any women who are suitable and qualified to fill a position that she is about to vacate, responds: "There is no one; there is not another woman who can do the job as well as I do. I will keep my eye out and let you know when I have identified a woman who is qualified." The end result is that a man often gets the promotion and the pipeline in bringing women to the top narrows.

What's disturbing about the bees is the shift in attitudes among younger managers. In the *Working Woman* survey, 61 percent of women 40 and over said that women had a responsibility to help other women climb the corporate ladder; only 45 percent of those under 30 supported that philosophy. This could mean that the newer, younger manager may have closed the pipeline before other competent and qualified women have had the opportunity to be identified.

In addition, 83 percent of the respondents said that the best way to help women was to mentor them and set a good example. Overall, 34 percent of the respondents stated that women bosses were tougher on female employees and 30 percent would rather work for a male boss. Respondents who earned under $15,000 reported a greater dissatisfaction with female bosses. Forty-seven percent of the $15,000-and-under wage earners felt that women bosses were harder on women in the workplace. This compares with only 20 percent of the women earning over $75,000 per year.

Fifty-four percent of the *Working Woman* respondents stated that female managers had a special responsibility to help other women rise through the ranks. Sixty-nine percent felt that women bosses should advocate family- and female-friendly personnel policies. Over half of the women earning over $75,000 stated that they mentor as many men as they do women, and 34 percent of them said that they do not view themselves as different from male managers.[2]

Mentors can be toxic. Some individuals use their connections with an advocate higher up to undercut a boss whose position ranks lower. As a strategy, a woman may act to ensure her own power base by making alliances with more than one mentor. If her sponsor falls in power, she won't go down with the ship. Men, more than women, experience mentoring at some time in their careers. A hedging strategy of having more than one mentor has become common among women. A woman's power may be more tenuous than a man's and her position is more at risk. If another woman chooses to turn on her, she usually can be undercut. It makes political sense to have more than one advocate.

POWER SQUEEZES

The woman manager is in much the same situation. She has fewer power links. Typically, her position is unprotected from power squeezes. She has to carry out the demands of higher-level managers while contending with employees who resent being stuck in their low-opportunity positions and who are bitter that she got ahead. Employees may engage in aggressive actions, such as slacking off and not being available. Their objective is to undermine the woman manager's credibility and show her that she's no better than they are.

Her response to these actions makes her appear as a stereotyped, demanding, critical, and pushy boss in order to stay in charge. These reactions help to perpetuate the cycle. Additional hostility and resentfulness lead to more efforts to criticize and dominate. The basis of this problem is that women have much less power than men—still. Until there are several generations of women in power and a norm is established, women will have more difficulty handling their power.

Rosalind works in the rapidly changing field of health care. She believes that a lot of the erratic behavior from nurse managers within her hospital is directly linked, not only to the current uncertainties of the health-care industry, but to the fact that the managers are relatively new to the power arena.

> Managers in our hospital have caught some type of disease. We have both men and women who work in our unit, but with the women staff members, it's a more volatile situation—they seem to get set up more easily than the men do. It is typical for nurse managers to instigate some type of action or demand and then sit back and see how everyone reacts. Their reactions to the responses of staff members seem inappropriate and out of proportion.

> In reality, what is happening is that the nurse managers' power bases are being eroded. They've withdrawn, closed in, become more secretive and less willing and less likely to share information with the rest of us. It is as though, by not giving information to us, they maintain power to keep us attached to their "apron strings."

> Because of all the confusion, a lot of the power and authority we individually had to do routine matters for patients, such as bringing them water, now has to be formally written up and requested. I feel at times that I have to hold up my hand and ask permission to go to the bathroom.

MISGUIDED POWER

Many women who move into management, or have authority/power over other women in the workplace, forget that women look for connectedness much more than men do. And many women fear that if they open up to that connectedness—reaching out, showing concern about personal issues as well as workplace issues—they may be construed as being too soft and nonmanagerial.

Today Jacqueline is the senior vice president of a bank with branches in several states. She is routinely written up in the press, quoted, admired, and regarded as a role model by many. Just a few years ago, she wouldn't have been considered a role model. In fact, she would have been identified as someone to avoid like the plague. Jacqueline's career path was dramatically altered when Marion, a fellow manager, pulled her aside and told her she'd better get her act together.

As Jacqueline progressed through various departments at the bank, she had developed a reputation for being a risk taker, intuitive and clever. She was able to put packages together—even match customers in various business deals that paid off handsomely for her bank. And she was rewarded—with more pay, bonuses, and titles. As she moved up, she did what many did: she stepped on the "little people." Jacqueline became all business and no play, and definitely, no connectedness.

> I felt that when meetings were scheduled, we should start on time. Any time people started personal chit-chat, I would become irritated or glare at them. I was very busy and had no time to waste. When I look back at my style a few years ago, I'm surprised they all didn't jump on me. I never asked how they were, how they were doing, or even what was going on in their lives. I would routinely say this doesn't work, or this is inconsistent, or this needs more documentation and background.

> Compliments rarely came out of my mouth. I would address people with negative remarks, never complimenting them about items that they did well. When I said that a meeting was going to be held from a certain time to a certain time, I meant it. When the meeting was over at the designated time, I left. People never seemed to complain; they would follow me and go to their respective work stations.

> Initially, I was invited to participate in their celebrations—birthdays, babies, even going on vacation. Of course, I always declined. Somewhere along the line, I got the idea that a good manager doesn't mingle with the staff. I didn't want to hear about their vacations, their babies, or anything else they did with their personal lives. I avoided all "girl talk."

> I was always in the office before my staff was, and I left after they all had gone home. If I found myself out in the lobby at any time

when one of them would be leaving, I would avoid going down the elevator. It seems crazy now, but I did everything I could to keep my distance.

Marion saved my career—at least the vision I had had for it. After about 4 months of observing my pattern, she asked me to lunch. That lunch changed my career. I looked forward to being with her, someone I had admired and viewed as a role model for myself. I felt horrible—sick—when it was over.

She told me my style of managing the other women in my department was horrendous. She listed a series of activities from avoiding any personal interaction to not admiring the secretary's new baby. To top it off, she told me that overall production and morale were down in the department—which was not normal, especially during that particular time of the year.

Marion did one other thing that was very important. She complimented me on areas that I was doing well on, such as organization, dedication, and thoroughness. She warned me that if I didn't find some balance within the department, my tenure would be short-term.

Well, that got my attention. I had viewed the women's socializing before meetings and at break time as idle chit-chat. Marion suggested that I lighten up. There was nothing wrong with admiring a new baby, or even sharing in a birthday or engagement celebration. Granted, she said, there must be some separation between management and staff. It was an overall mistake for a manager to cross the line and try to be a personal friend to everyone.

Did I change overnight? No. But I did change over time, and the change within my staff was dramatic. I mentally dedicated 10 to 15 minutes at the beginning of every meeting so that each of us could do a quick catch-up with what was going on. Sometimes the catch-up was as simple as what movie we saw over the weekend. I actually found out about what others were interested in.

Several of the women who worked under me had interests in gardening, cooking, and quilting. One collected first-edition books. Some loved sports: mountain biking, skiing, and tennis. As I learned more about them, I kept their hobbies in the back of my mind, and when I read magazines or newspapers and saw articles that pertained to them, I'd actually clip them out and give them to them. What a difference that made.

In the end, I found that I didn't have to compromise my personal or professional expectations. The work my group produced was better than ever and at the high level I expected. I am where I am today because someone I respected forewarned me to get my act together. And my former staff invited me to a celebration lunch when my new position as senior vice president was announced. I gladly accepted.

Jacqueline is powerful. When she was a vice president, somewhat misguided but still a vice president, she also had power. As a middle manager, she could have disappeared easily, either into oblivion into the corporation or out the door. Her staff would have probably said good riddance. Whether Marion recognized that Jacqueline had the talent she had (Jacqueline is now Marion's boss) is unknown.

What Marion did do, though, was exercise her power in speaking up and speaking out about a series of conditions that were impacting the bank. Those who were working under Jacqueline hadn't said anything to anyone in upper management, but it wasn't difficult to see what was going on. All one needed was eyes and ears to see that there was stress, tension, and not a lot of loyalty in Jacqueline's department.

POWERLESS TRAPS

When women feel that they cannot speak up or speak out about a situation, whether it's a working condition that's inappropriate or a manager who is a maniac, they experience a powerlessness. Powerlessness has three internal traps.

The first is the *victim trap*, as described in the preceding chapter. The power victim says that she can't do anything about it, that the system is set up and works against her. She feels she doesn't have any skills, is not worthy, and can't raise a fuss. In the end, she'd rather suffer and be a martyr than make waves. The flip side of this is that she has to figure out how to survive and make it work. And she does, contrary to the statement of not having any power. The power victim becomes more dysfunctional because she is at the mercy of everyone else. Her response is to manipulate—manipulate others and manipulate herself.

The second power trap, *denial*, is prevalent in a lot of women. A woman in denial will say, "I have no problems, and I don't understand what your problem is," "I've never been subject to prejudice," "I've never been paid inequitably," or "I've never had someone sabotage me."

Many women deny the pay inequities, sabotage, or other problems of the workplace because somehow they have figured out how to jump-start themselves or take the glass elevator and leap several floors ahead. The Queen Bee is classic in this area. Her attitude is, "If I can do it, so can everyone else, and you'll have to do it by yourself." This woman is usually very myopic, self-centered, and judgmental.

The third power trap is *mastering it like a man*. Women caught in this trap are very ambitious, egocentric, dictatorial, directive, and again much like the Queen Bee. Jacqueline viewed her power as growing if she'd model herself after the men whom she had observed and known in the banking profession.

Stephanie Allen (not to be confused with Stephanie West-Allen) is president of the Athena Group and coauthor (with Caroline Zeiger, Ph.D.) of *Having It All Isn't Everything*. She believes that when women get stuck in one of the three traps of power—victim, denial, and male cloning—they put themselves in an impossible situation.

> You can't truly become a master power as a woman, if you define power that either takes you out of the game or puts you in the game in the wrong suit of armor. What women have to do is to define power in a way that takes advantage of their own authentic self so that they can claim it as their own. When they take on the male image, it's all directed toward the bottom line. It doesn't have a lot of value sets within it. It also denies a variety of interests among other people within the community. One of the offshoots is burnout.

Women who practice denial put out false boundaries. They limit themselves, not allowing or granting permission to stretch or aspire higher. At the same time, boundaries are imposed on other women who don't fit the "mold." One of the best examples of the denial of power is politics, or political appointees.

In 1992, Hillary Rodham Clinton, Janet Reno, and Dianne Feinstein arrived in Washington, DC. Washingtonians (men and women) raised their cries: "Who voted for her?" (First Lady, Hillary Clinton). "She's more concerned about kids than crime!" (U.S. Attorney General Janet Reno). "What does she know about guns?" (California Senator Dianne Feinstein in her opposition to assault weapons).

These women and others like them are testing the image of the traditional woman. What they're saying is that there are other ways to succeed. The mold is not permanent.

Allen routinely consults and trains corporations on women and leadership. Many of her programs are structured around Janet

Hagberg's book *Real Power*. Allen describes Hagberg's six stages of power, with the first stage being total powerlessness and the sixth being power by gestalt.[3]

STAGE ONE: POWERLESS

In stage one, you feel trapped. All power is outside of you and the only power that you might have is manipulation. Powerlessness is expressed through whining, threatening, withholding favors, passive-aggressive behavior, sabotage, and the like.

> People in stage one are very hard to handle because, if they are helpless, then they are stuck. If you can rekindle the hope, then you can get people to move on by teaching them something—a feel that gives them self-worth.

The first stage is characterized by being insecure, dependent, low on self-esteem, uninformed, and helpless but not hopeless. Fear is the primary culprit that holds you back. What enables you to move to the next stage is confidence. Build up your self-esteem, forge networks, find allies—get support, expand your skills, appreciate yourself, confront the fears, take responsibility, talk with your boss, change jobs if you need to, get out of an abusive relationship if there is one, and, most of all, confront yourself.

STAGE TWO: POWER BY ASSOCIATION

In stage two, you've got enough skills to become part of a group, whether it is medicine, sales, clerical, or sports. You've mastered and fit into a culture and have become a player—you're one of the gang.

> People who are within the second stage of power don't like to see people break out. If you see Breanne raise her head and become a leader, you or the group become tough on her. You pull her down because it is a threat to the group if she leaves and rises above it.
>
> The power that gets played is, "Let's make a deal. You do this for me, I'll do that for you"—better known as a win-lose negotiation, not win-win, unless it's a win-win in the sense that we all hang in together and no one moves on and up or out. Anyone in stage two of power doesn't have a lot of vision for long-term growth.

In corporate America, more women are inclined to be in stage two than are men. Men move out of the second stage as fast as possible. The characteristics of this stage include learning the ropes and the culture, being dependent upon the supervisor and leader, and at the same time creating a new self-awareness.

Overall, there is a stay-put attitude with a slight nudge of wanting to move on. The need for security and lack of confidence are the two primary ingredients that hold someone back. Ways to move on include finding a mentor, getting feedback, being competent at the skills you have, expanding your credentials or getting new credentials, becoming more involved, taking risks, expanding your network, taking care of yourself, doing something on your own, using masculine tactics if necessary, and working out any negative or hold-back relationships.

STAGE THREE: POWER BY SYMBOLS

Men usually get stuck in the third stage. They like status toys more than women do. When women reach it, they usually pass through it very quickly. The third stage is what Hagberg calls the *dynamo stage,* or *control stage.* As Allen describes it:

> Power by symbols means, "I've got mine, I'm in control, and I want more." It is the accumulation of whatever counts in your particular group. It could be college degrees, credentials, even a make of car. You have position power, and feel you "cause things to happen."
>
> To move out of stage three, you become uncomfortable. The question drops in, "What is life about?" That question causes you to redefine power, and then you begin to start thinking more long-term. You move out of thinking "What's in it for me?" and "What will I lose?" into "What can I give?"

Characteristics of stage three include egocentricity as well as being realistic and competitive. Individuals in the third stage are experts, ambitious, and often charismatic. The area that is a hold-back is not knowing that you're stuck or there are greater things in a cosmic sense. The crisis that usually moves you forward is what I call "the cosmic goose." Allen calls it, "God drops you on your head."

Two movies of recent history are examples of the cosmic goose. In *The Doctor,* starring William Hurt, Hurt plays a fast-track egocentric surgeon who develops cancer of the throat—the cosmic goose. After a series of traumatic events, he eventually recovers and turns his personal and teaching style within the hospital around.

In *Regarding Henry,* Harrison Ford is the fast-track whiz lawyer who is shot—the cosmic goose. And through his slow recovery, he comes to realize that some of the cases that he successfully argued and represented were unethical. He sets out to sort out the wrong he has done via his legal skills; at the same time, as the good doctor did, he gets his family and life back in balance.

Ways to move beyond stage three include learning to be alone, reflecting on yourself, trying new things that make you think, doing things differently, continuing to expand networks, concentrating on the present, being reflective, and developing relationships with and obtaining support from individuals who have entered the next three stages.

Stage Four: Power by Reflection

Stage four can best be described as a sandwich stage and one of influence. This stage often drives men crazy because it is too passive—remember, they love the power of symbols. Moving from there into reflection means quiet time. If you don't feel a "purpose" in life, this stage is impossible to pass through. Allen adds:

> This stage is like an ulcer that causes so much pain. You finally stop and really ask questions and start looking for answers. Some people will cycle back and say, "I'm losing power, I'm losing a sense of myself." They just can't let go of their ego. They are stuck. That is, until God decides to drop you on your head.

> People in stage four have plenty of life experiences under their belt. Age and wisdom are assets. The key issue surfaces: How do you best use your experiences without compromising your values?

> If you are in stage four, this is the time to begin to test your skills as a mentor, reaching out, sharing wisdom and information with others. Your interest grows in issues that are far bigger than yourself or your family. This stage is a stage of tolerance and one in which egos are let go.

Stage Five: Power by Purpose

The fifth stage is supported by vision and passion. Common characteristics include calmness and humbleness, being a visionary, being self-accepting, feeling purposeful, being comfortable in allowing others to stretch and reach, making mistakes, being competent in life, and expanding spirituality. What holds people back in stage five is their lack of faith and the feeling that they have too much to lose if they follow their passion and vision, even if they believe that vision to be their true sense of purpose.

> You have some overriding areas that you wish to devote your life to and you have the skills to do it. Whatever it is, you have the technical expertise, the conceptual expertise, and the people expertise.

An example of a company which practices power by purpose is Ben & Jerry's Ice Cream. Ben and Jerry, the cofounders, put financial constraints on what they can make in relationship to their lowest-paid employees.

STAGE SIX: POWER BY GESTALT

The sixth or *the Great Saint* stage is like the wise old soul. Its characteristics include being unafraid of paradoxes or of death, being ethical, going beyond the need to exercise power—because of your very nature, you in effect have spiritual power—and being quiet in your overall service. Mother Theresa is a classic example. It is a stage that is not populated by many.

ABUSES OF POWER

There will always be abuses of power. Denial of abuse is ignorance. In a recent experience with a Fortune 100 pharmaceuticals company, Allen was hired to consult because of her expertise in sexual harassment.

> At a meeting that had presented the data we had gathered, a young woman in the management program said, "I don't think we have any problem with gender around here." The leader of the group said, "You've got to be deaf, dumb, and blind." Then he quoted the data that we had gathered.
>
> With his response, he basically gave her permission to open her eyes and see it, and to acknowledge the fact that she had denied what was going on. The result was that she started asking questions and came back at a later meeting and said, "You are right, it's ugly out there."

The young woman Allen refers to is in a glass elevator. She's one of those women, usually under 35, who is bright and attractive, and has been moved along almost as a type of token, rarely in sync with the other women or attempting to be connected with them. In fact, being connected is viewed as a weakness, as Jacqueline viewed it earlier in this chapter.

Women who are in denial of any types of inequities that other women experience don't want to recognize their own exempt status. If they do, they may begin to question whether they got where they got because of their merit, or because they were female, bright, and attractive.

Failing to identify and circulate the unwritten rules of your particular workplace is a zap for many women. Every workplace has written rules—as simple as "Go to work and do your job." It's the little, unwritten ones that can do you in, from not sitting in someone's special chair during a meeting, to not refilling the coffee pot after you have poured the last cup, to not putting your phone on voice mail when you are away from your desk, to not changing colored paper back to white paper in the copy machine, to not turning off certain equipment in the office. By identifying and passing on unwritten rules and networking with other women—and men—in the workplace, you can eliminate a great deal of stress and game playing.

Other areas of abuse include "poisoning the well" and misusing networks. Poisoning the well refers to actions by women who discount the fact that they are women. Women who poison the well view themselves as the exception, because they are like the men. If at any time feminine traits are exposed, revealed, or used, those traits are discounted. Remarks such as, "Well, I don't have my children, but she does," create zingers. It's a type of bitchiness that is directed toward women, and it's far more detrimental than if a male makes the same type of comment.

In addition, too many women keep the old boys' network to themselves. By sharing the labyrinthic multitude of contacts within the workplace, women can grow in their vocal presence and power.

One of the hit movies of the early 1990s starred Kathy Bates, Jessica Tandy, Mary Stuart Masterson, and Mary-Louise Parker. It was adapted from the Fanny Flag novel *Fried Green Tomatoes at the Whistle Stop Cafe*. In one of the most memorable scenes, Evelyn (Kathy Bates' character) is outraged when two bimbos in a Volkswagen cut in from of her and steal the parking space she has been waiting for. "Face it, we're younger and faster," they blithely tell her when she complains.

A transformation comes over the meek, compliant Evelyn. "Twanda!" she yells out, calling forth her version of a gutsy female warrior. She then backs up her car and rams it into the back of the now-empty Volkswagen. Not once, but six times. When they rush out to the scene of automotive mayhem, Evelyn says, "Face it, girls, I'm older, and I've got more insurance."

Although you may not approve of someone ramming someone else's car, the point that Evelyn made is critical. She called up her power and she took it. But only after her sense of fairness had been taken advantage of. Women should not have to wait for their sense of fairness to be violated before they vocalize their power—or lack of it.

When women misuse power, whether it's setting others up, sabotaging them, not giving them credit for appropriate work, or not respecting some of the unwritten rules such as *connectedness* in the workplace, they continue to poison the well.

AFTERWORD

It amazes me that intelligent women and men deny that there are disparities in the workplace.

I have never been in a room of women and not heard comments about pay inequities, work-balancing issues, bias, sexism, communication fiascoes, manipulative and undermining scenarios, fear of change, and variations of a number of the snares identified in *GenderTraps*.

Granted, they don't happen all to the same person; nor is each fully represented at any one time. Yet they are there. And, they are real.

My dream is that they will be eliminated in every workplace. It can happen, but it needs the support of you and everyone you work with. With a committed and energized effort, women can be paid equitably, prejudice can be controlled, and women and men can be humane to one another.

What a commonsense concept.

THE WORKPLACE TRAP SURVEY

SURVEY SCOPE

The Workplace Trap survey consisted of questionnaires distributed in an informal manner to 5000 attendees at my speaking engagements from the fall of 1993 to the spring of 1994 (See Fig. A-1). The respondents had the opportunity to complete the questionnaires during the day or to mail them in later. Of the 5000 surveys distributed, 1270 were returned by the cutoff date; 130 follow-up interviews were conducted by phone.

GEOGRAPHICAL DISTRIBUTION

The majority of the respondents came from the East, followed by the Midwest, West, and South (see Table A-1). The greatest responses from individual states came from California, Michigan, Wisconsin, Pennsylvania, Tennessee, North Carolina, and Oregon.

AGE RANGE

Ninety-eight percent of the respondents were female; 3 percent were under 26 years of age; 27 percent were over 26 years of age; 35 percent were over 36 years of age; 27 percent were over 46 years of age; and 7 percent were over 55 years of age (see Table A-2).

Figure A-1 *Workplace Trap Survey Questionnaire.* (Copyright © 1994 The Briles Group.)

Workplace problems, "traps," are encountered every day—traps like communication styles, sexism, discrimination, sexual harassment, salary inequities, the glass ceiling, and child care. There are dozens, even hundreds of different traps. What are yours?

Please identify the three biggest traps that you have encountered. Describe how they have impacted you and how you have dealt with them.

1. _____

2. _____

3. _____

My age is: ____ under 26; ____ 26–35; ____ 36–45; ____ 46–55;
            ____ over 55

I work: ____ full time ____ part time; I am ____ female ____ male

I am employed as _____ (specify title or position)

My income is ____ under $25,000; ____ $25,001–$45,000
              ____ over $45,000

I reside in (city, state) _____

I am ____ married; ____ single (never married); ____ widowed;
      ____ divorced; ____ cohabiting

I have ____ (number of) children; their ages are _____

My race/nationality is _____

Thank you!

If you would like a copy of the results of this survey, please complete the following:

Name _____

Address _____

_____

Phone _____ Fax _____

Would you be willing to discuss your responses to this survey in an interview? Is so, all conversations will be strictly confidential. No information obtained in any interview can be used by Judith Briles without your written consent.

The best time to reach you is _____

Please return your completed survey to:

Dr. Judith Briles

PO Box 22021

Denver, CO 80222-0021

TABLE A-1 Geographical Distribution of Respondents

GEOGRAPHICAL REGION	% (NUMBER) OF RESPONDENTS
East	30 (389)
Midwest	30 (381)
West	22 (276)
South	18 (224)
TOTAL	100

TABLE A-2   Age Range of Respondents

AGE RANGE	% OF RESPONDENTS
Under 26	3
26–35	27
36–45	35
46–55	27
Over 55	7
Not stated	1
TOTAL	100

RACE

Eighty-one percent of the respondents were Caucasian, 7 percent were African-American, and 1 percent each were Native American, Hispanic, and Asian (see Table A-3).

MARITAL STATUS

Sixty-six percent of the respondents were married; 12 percent were single (never married), 17 percent divorced, 2 percent widowed, and 1 percent cohabiting (see Table A-4).

TABLE A-3   Race of Respondents

RACE	% OF RESPONDENTS
Caucasian	81
African-American	7
Native American	1
Hispanic	1
Asian	1
Other or no answer	9
TOTAL	100

TABLE A-4   **Marital Status of Respondents**

MARITAL STATUS	% OF RESPONDENTS
Single	12
Married	66
Divorced	17
Widowed	2
Cohabiting	1
No answer	2
TOTAL	100

SIZE OF FAMILY

Sixty-six percent (835) of the respondents had children. Of the 66 percent, 45 percent had two; 22 percent, one; 20 percent, three; 8 percent four; and 5 percent, five or more children (see Table A-5).

EMPLOYMENT STATUS

Seventy-eight percent of the respondents worked full time and 11 percent, part time. The remaining 11 percent did not specify employment status (see Table A-6).

TABLE A-5   **Family Size of Married Respondents**

NUMBER OF CHILDREN	% OF MARRIED RESPONDENTS[*]
1	22
2	45
3	20
4	8
5 or more	5
TOTAL	100

TABLE A-6   Employment Status of
Respondents

STATUS	% OF RESPONDENTS
Full-time employee	78
Part-time employee	11
No answer	11
TOTAL	100

INCOME RANGE

Earning power in all areas was well presented. Twenty-seven percent of the respondents made under $25,000 per year, 44 percent
made between $25,001 and $45,000 a year, 20 percent earned over
$45,001 a year, and 9 percent did not state what they made (see
Table A-7). These salary ranges are consistent with ranges reported
in *Working Woman* magazine's annual survey and the study from the
Women's Bureau of the U.S. Department of Labor.

TABLE A-7   Income Range of Respondents

INCOME	% OF RESPONDENTS
Under $25,000	27
$25,001–$45,000	44
Over $45,001	20
Did not state	9
TOTAL	100

JOB TITLES AND OCCUPATIONS

Job titles and positions varied. Over 35 percent held administrative and managerial positions; 5 percent were in sales and marketing; 19 percent were in technical and nontechnical support occupations (administrative assistants, clerical workers, programmers, secretaries, cashiers); 2 percent were in child care; 2 percent were CEOs and business owners; 31 percent were professionals (analysts, accountants, stockbrokers, consultants, legal professionals, recruiters, fund raisers, teachers, professors, ministers, nurses, doctors, dentists, hygienists, nutritionists, psychologists, therapists, technicians, engineers, scientists).

Other occupations within the groups covered were spread among image and fashion, human resources, agriculture, public relations, advertising, design, and construction. Six percent identified themselves as homemakers who volunteered their outside time to community activities (PTA, church, politics) and classroom aides—nonpaid positions in every case.

For additional characterization, all occupations were grouped into four main categories: business (private enterprise), 60 percent; education (private and public), 5 percent; government (including military), 5 percent; and medical and health care (profit and not for profit), 24 percent. The remaining 6 percent of the respondents were homemakers (see Table A-8). Business, by far the largest category, included farming, image and fashion, the law, marketing and sales, and professional specialties (including science, engineering, and statistics), as well as nontechnical and technical support and service occupations outside of government, health care and educa-

TABLE A-8 **Respondents by Occupational Category**

OCCUPATIONAL CATEGORY	% OF RESPONDENTS
Business	60
Education	5
Government	5
Medical and health care	24
Homemaker	6
TOTAL	100

TABLE A-9   Respondent Occupation by Function

FUNCTION	% OF RESPONDENTS
Administrative/managerial	35
Administrative/managerial support	15
Craft labor/common labor	1
Executive/business owner	2
Homemaker	6
Marketing/sales	5
Professional	31
Service	1
Technical support	4
TOTAL	100

tion—from campaign assistant to Kelly temp to maintenance supervisor to jailhouse cook.

Respondent occupations were also classified under nine occupational groupings, resulting in the percentage distributions shown in Table A-9.

THE TRAPS

Of the 1270 respondents who returned the questionnaire by the cutoff date, 53 (4 percent) said that they had not felt or had not experienced any problems in their workplace or did not identify any traps. A majority of these respondents identified themselves as homemakers. The remaining 1217 (96 percent) responded by elaborating on the problems or traps that they felt were most significant in their workplaces. As surveys were returned, some of the traps were easily identified because of their early repetition. Other traps surfaced as more questionnaires came in. Respondents were asked to prioritize and elaborate on each trap that was identified.

The top 10 GenderTraps, and their order of importance, statistically, are presented in Table A-10.

TABLE A-10   The Top 10 GenderTraps

RANK	TRAP	PERCENTAGE*
1	Prejudice	63
2	Communication	36
3	Sabotage	33
4	Management	27
5	Pay inequities	19
6	Family	17
7	Confrontophobia	12
8	Apathy/complacency/changeophobia	11
9	Self-sabotage	10
10	Misuse of power	3

*Table exceeds 100 percent because of multiple answers.

NOTES

CHAPTER 2

1. A. Noir and David Jessel, *BrainSex* (New York: Delta, 1991).
2. E. Macoby and C. Jacklin, *The Psychology of Sex Differences* (Stanford, CA: Stanford University Press, 1974).
3. C. Tavris, *Mismeasure of Woman: Why Women Are Not the Better Sex, the Inferior Sex, or the Opposite Sex* (New York: Simon & Schuster, 1992).

CHAPTER 3

1. William F. Howell, *The Empathic Communicator* (Prospect Heights, IL: Wave One Press, 1982).
2. Wilma Mankiller, *The Denver Post*, March 3, 1994.
3. Mariah Burton Nelson, *The Stronger Women Get, The More Men Love Football: Sexism and the American Culture of Sports* (New York: Harcourt Brace Jovanovich, 1994).
4. Burton Nelson, ibid.
5. "9-Zip, I Love It," *Time*, November 22, 1993.
6. Deborah Flick, more to come.
7. "The Workplace," *The Wall Street Journal*, February 7, 1994.
8. Studs Terkel, *Race: How Blacks and Whites Think and Feel About the American Obsession,* (New York: New Press, 1992).
9. "Job Strategies," *Glamour*, September, 1993.

CHAPTER 4

1. Dianna Booher, *Communicate With Confidence*, New York: McGraw-Hill, 1994.
2. Deborah Tannen, *You Just Don't Understand*, New York: Morrow, 1990.

CHAPTER 6

1. "Brutal Firings Can Backfire and End in Court," *The Wall Street Journal*, October 24, 1994.
2. Paula Ancona, "The Workplace," *The Albuquerque News*, January 17, 1993.
3. Michael LeBoeuf, *The Greatest Management Principle* (New York: G. P. Putnam, 1988).

CHAPTER 7

1. Judy Rosener, *America's Competitive Secret: Women* (more to come)
2. *Women: The New Providers* (New York: Families and Work Institute, 1995).

CHAPTER 8

1. "'Superwomen' Find Themselves Grounded by Housework," *USA Today*, August 11, 1994.
2. Judson Culbreth, *Working Mother*, April 1994.
3. "Many Say Their Place Is in the Home," *USA Today*, September 20, 1993.
4. "Letters," *USA Today*, September 23, 1993.
5. Carol Kleinman, "Employers Band Together to Provide Benefits," *Denver Post*, June 3, 1994.
6. Terri Apter, *Working Women Don't Have Wives: Professional Success in the 1990s* (New York: St. Martin's Press, 1994).
7. Marjorie Hansen Shaevitz, *The Superwoman Syndrome* (New York: Warner Books, 1984).

CHAPTER 10

1. Lenore Walker, *The Battered Woman* (more to come).
2. Judith Bardwick, *Danger in the Comfort Zone* (New York: AMACOM, 1991).
3. Alex Taylor III, "The Task Facing General Motors," *Fortune*, March 13, 1989.
4. "The New American Hero," *The Wall Street Journal*, May 9, 1994.
5. David A. Silver, *Enterprising Women: Lessons From 100 of the Greatest Women Entrepreneurs of Our Day* (New York: AMACOM, 1994).
6. Helen Keller, more to come.

CHAPTER 11

1. Quoted in Tamar Lewin, "Ideas and Trends," *The New York Times*, May 10, 1992.
2. Judith Briles, *The Confidence Factor* (New York: Master Media, 1990).
3. Nichole Schapiro, *Negotiating for Your Life* (New York: Henry Holt, 1993).
4. Carol Hyatt and Linda Gottlieb, *When Smart People Fail* (New York: Penguin Books, 1993).

CHAPTER 12

1. Pam Krueger, "What Women Think of Women Bosses," *Working Woman*, June 1993, pp. 42–43.
2. Ibid.
3. Janet Hagberg, *Real Power* (San Francisco: Harper & Row, 1984).

INDEX

ABOUT THE AUTHOR

Judith Briles, Ph.D. is the best-selling author of 13 other books, including *The Confidence Factor, Woman to Woman, The Briles Report on Women in Health Care, Money Sense, The Dollars and Sense of Divorce,* and *When God Says NO.* She is the founder of The Briles Group, Inc., a research and consulting company that specializes in conflict management and women's issues in the workplace.

Dr. Briles speaks to 20,000 women and men each year. She is known as a motivational speaker who delivers programs of substance that apply both to professional careers and personal lives. Her clientele include hospitals and health-care facilities, professional and political associations, and businesses.

She holds both a master's degree and a doctorate in business administration. Her real degree, though, is in Life 101. Her opinions and voice are frequently heard on TV and radio, and in print.

For information on her keynote presentations, workshops, or her annual Confidence Cruise for women, or for a copy of *The Woman's Voice* newsletter, call 800-594-0800 or write The Briles Group, Inc. at PO Box 22021, Denver, CO 80222.

AN INVITATION FROM THE AUTHOR

I would love to hear from you, whether you want to share your GenderTraps—what they are and/or how you overcame them—find out more about my audio and video programs, or request information about my speaking availability.

You can contact me in three different ways:

1. Call me at 303-745-4590 or 800-594-0800.
2. Send me a fax. My number is 303-745-4595.
3. Write me at PO Box 22021, Denver, CO 80222.

Judith, please (check one or more):

___ Contact me about your availability to speak at my professional association, company, or health-care facility.

___ Send me information about audio and video programs based on *The Confidence Factor, Money Sense, Woman to Woman,* and *GenderTraps.*

___ Send me information about your other published materials.

Name _____

Title _____

Company _____

Phone _____ Fax _____

Address _____

City _____ State _____ Zip _____